Bicycling the Lewis & Clark Trail

Michael McCoy
Field Editor, Adventure Cycling Association

FALCON®

GUILFORD, CONNECTICUT
HELENA, MONTANA

AN IMPRINT OF THE GLOBE PEQUOT PRESS

Adventure Cycling photos by Dennis Coello
Maps: Carla Majernik, Jennifer Milyko, Tom Robertson
Text design by Mary Ballachino
Project Editor: David Singleton

Library of Congress Cataloging-in-Publication Data is available.

ISBN 0-7627-2545-1

Manufactured in the United States of America
First Edition/First Printing

Contents

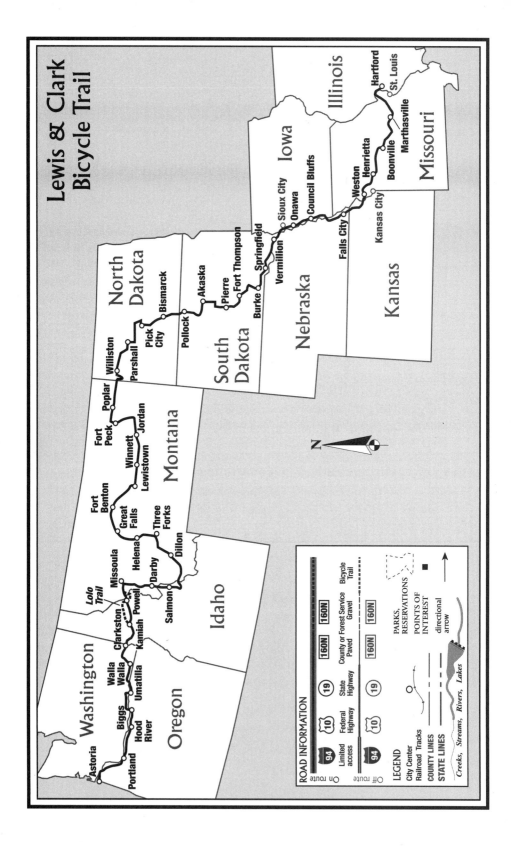

Acknowledgments

It never ceases to please and amaze us at the Adventure Cycling Association how the cycle-touring public is so ready and willing to open their hearts and pocketbooks when we announce a new project such the Lewis & Clark Bicycle Trail. The route, and this book, would not have been possible without the help, financial and otherwise, of hundreds of individuals and dozens of organizations. Recreational Equipment, Inc. (REI) of Seattle helped get the ball rolling in a big way with a $25,000 matching-funds contribution for route research and mapping. That was quickly matched, and then exceeded, by the Adventure Cycling membership.

As was so obviously the case with President Thomas Jefferson's Corps of Discovery, the Lewis & Clark Bicycle Trail was in good hands when it came to planning and laying out the route. In summer 2000 the veteran husband-and-wife field team of Ernie Franceschi and Gayl Teichert completed research from the route's beginning point in Hartford, Illinois, to tiny Bainville, in far eastern Montana. Subsequently, the research for the western half of the route was completed in 2001 by a number of other talented and dedicated field hands: Dallas and Joyce McKenzie, Adventure Cycling members from Lenexa, Kansas; Adventure Cycling's routes and mapping department director, Carla Majernik; department cartographer Tom Robertson and his partner, Ruth Anderson; and Brian Martindale, who oversees the organization's tours program. Cartographers Majernik, Robertson, and Jennifer Milyko performed a superhuman effort to ready not only the Adventure Cycling maps but also the maps for this book in time for the 2003–2006 Lewis & Clark Bicentennial.

A number of other individuals and organizations were helpful when it came to route planning, including the state bicycle coordinators of many of the states the route passes through. The Twin Rivers Cyclists in Lewiston, Idaho, helped tremendously with routing through their tricky area. And James Lamiell and Tom Walker sent notes to Adventure Cycling after riding their own rendition of the trail; these were particularly helpful when it came to determining which side of the Missouri River to take the route along.

The route really comes to life within these pages thanks to the photographs of Dennis Coello, America's foremost cycletouring shutter-snapper. Simple words could never do the Lewis & Clark Bicycle Trail justice, but Dennis's photos can—and do.

—Michael McCoy
Teton Valley, Idaho
February 2003

Introduction

On May 14, 1804, Capt. William Clark, accompanied by a contingent of nearly four dozen men, began traveling upstream along the swollen Missouri River from its mouth at Wood River, Illinois. (Capt. Meriwether Lewis, organizer of the expedition, was in St. Louis finishing up some business. He would meet the others in St. Charles on May 20.) The men traveled in a trio of boats, including a 55-foot keelboat and two smaller open boats known as *pirogues*. In their company were a pair of horses, which were walked along the riverbanks to aid in the hunting and hauling of game. (Read more about the expedition's beginnings in Chapter 1.)

The adventure they were setting out on was destined to become the most important, the most written about, the most *amazing* expedition in the history of the United States of America. While it is virtually impossible for a human to go forth on a journey of that scope and magnitude today—with the possible exception of astronauts—it is still possible to gain an inkling of what the members of the Corps of Discovery must have felt as they penetrated country known at the time only to a few Native American tribes.

The mode of choice for many explorers in the twenty-first century is the bicycle. That is why it was a natural for the Lewis & Clark Bicycle Trail to be conceived, planned, plotted, and mapped. The trail extends from Hartford, Illinois, to Astoria, Oregon—a distance of more than 3,200 miles. Where relatively low-traffic roads exist in close proximity to the rivers traveled by Lewis and Clark, cyclists can look down on portions of the actual route followed west by the expedition in 1804 and 1805—rivers, granted, that often have been dammed or otherwise diverted and therefore appear quite different from the way they did 200 years ago. Elsewhere, portions of the bicycle trail follow the exact route taken by the Corps of Discovery when they were traveling overland. On both river and lake sections of the trail, riders can camp where, or very near to where, the expedition camped.

There's no disputing it: The adventure remains for those willing and ready to take it.

A Brief Look Back

The Lewis & Clark Bicycle Trail was researched and mapped by the Adventure Cycling Association. The organization is based in Missoula, Montana, a city situated just 10 miles from Traveler's Rest (Lolo, Montana), one of the most important junctures on the Lewis and Clark National Historic Trail. The not-for-profit organization began in 1974, under the name Bikecentennial, when a group of idealistic young bicycle-touring enthusiasts came up with an ambitious plan: "Let's celebrate the 200th birthday of the United

States by staging a huge cross-country bicycle ride!" The resulting event, one of dozens held during the American Bicentennial summer of 1976, was a huge success. Some 4,000 individuals from around the world pedaled all or parts of the 4,500-mile TransAmerica Bicycle Trail, which had been mapped by Bikecentennial staff and volunteers over the previous two years.

Although the founders envisioned the Bikecentennial celebration as a one-summer event—they thought it would fade along with other Bicentennial celebrations into history—America's burgeoning hordes of adventure cyclists wouldn't let it rest. The Bikecentennial organization took on a life of its own as hundreds of avid and would-be bicycle tourists, inspired by stories in the media and by experiences shared by those lucky enough to ride in '76, clamored for their own shot at cycling across America.

More than twenty-five years have passed since summer 1976, and Bikecentennial, rechristened Adventure Cycling Association in 1993, is stronger than ever. It is the largest recreational bicycling organization in North America, claiming nearly 40,000 members. For more than a quarter century, the organization has been dispatching research teams into the field to track down the very best low-traffic cycling byways in North America, both paved and unpaved. This has helped ensure not only that bicyclists can continue claiming their rightful place on public roads but also that transportation departments keep cyclists in mind when building or reengineering highways and back roads.

During the last quarter century, Adventure Cycling's research sojourns into the rural outback of North America have resulted in the mapping of many new long-distance routes (as well as the revising of existing ones), including the heralded Great Divide Mountain Bike Route, which parallels the Continental Divide for 2,470 miles from the top of Montana to the bottom of New Mexico. In all, Adventure Cycling's National Bicycle Route Network now encompasses more than 30,000 miles of roads, primarily rural byways perfectly suited for bicycle travel. And the maps created by the organization to guide cyclists along those back roads are regarded as second to none.

Field research on the Lewis & Clark Bicycle Trail began in summer 2000. Early in the planning phase, some Adventure Cycling staff members were asked by certain curious individuals (although not one of them a savvy cyclist, as we recall!), "Why a bicycle trail? The Lewis and Clark expedition traveled primarily over water."

Our answer came easily: A bicycle trail is a perfect fit. One of the objectives of the Adventure Cycling Association is to encourage using the bicycle for exploration and discovery—the very concepts that were at the heart of President Jefferson's planned expedition through the Louisiana Purchase. As almost any serious cyclist might instinctively assert if asked the same question, the bicycle is ideally suited to exploring historic landscapes and mindscapes. A bicycle covers ground relatively quickly, yet it forces modern-day explorers to leave their cars behind to slow down and be exposed to the same elements that Lewis, Clark, and their fellow travelers faced day after day for more than two years.

Here, near Elk Point, South Dakota, in the first election involving American citizens held west of the Mississippi River, Patrick Gass was chosen to replace the recently deceased Charles Floyd as sergeant.

Bicycling the Lewis & Clark Bicycle Trail, which for the most part comprises existing paved roads, will permit riders to see many of the same sights, hear the sounds, and smell the smells that Lewis and Clark experienced 200 years ago. Moreover, just as the Lewis and Clark expedition opened America's eyes to the West two centuries ago, an adventure on the route today will open cycletourists' eyes to a vivid page of American history, as well as some of America's most stunning scenery.

For the Lewis & Clark Bicycle Trail, Adventure Cycling's newest project as of this February 2003 writing, the organization is, in a sense, returning to its roots. "Our first route was the TransAmerica Bicycle Trail," said routes and mapping director Carla Majernik. "The TransAm was created to help celebrate the 1976 American Bicentennial. Now, a quarter century later, we've mapped this new trail to honor the 2003–2006 bicentennial celebration of the Lewis and Clark expedition."

At the same time, the Lewis & Clark Bicycle Trail marks a bit of a departure for the organization. "Traditionally," Majernik said, "we've depended on geographical boundaries, barriers, or features to dictate route corridors. The Great Divide Mountain Bike Route, for instance, approximately parallels the Continental Divide. The Great Parks North Bicycle Route links together the national parks of Montana and the Canadian Rockies. Our coastal routes stay as close as possible to the Pacific and Atlantic Oceans. Even the extremely diverse TransAmerica Bicycle Trail was designed specifically to introduce cycletourists to as many geographic regions of the country as possible."

In contrast, Majernik said, the Lewis & Clark Bicycle Trail is based on the goal of tracing the route of an exploratory mission, the greatest in American history. "It has been a huge undertaking," she added, "but hugely rewarding, as well."

An immense undertaking, yes, and just one of hundreds of projects and events culminating in a three-year celebration of monumental proportions. In response to all the interest and activity in the years leading up to the bicentennial celebration, the National Council of the Lewis & Clark Bicentennial was formed. Working hand in hand with federal and state agencies, Native American tribes, and other groups and individuals, the council coordinated dozens of partners, programs, and events concerned with commemorating the bicentennial. The staff, board of directors, and members of Adventure Cycling are proud that their organization played a part in that greater effort by sending representatives to annual conferences hosted by the national council and through networking with many of the other entities involved. (You can learn about some of these groups and many upcoming events and festivities slated for the bicentennial at the council's Web site: www.lewisandclark200.org.)

Unlike many of the other events and festivities created to commemorate the Lewis and Clark bicentennial, the Lewis & Clark Bicycle Trail will persevere long after the official celebration is over, tempting and encouraging personal adventures on and near the Lewis and Clark Trail far into the future. Consider, for example, that more than 4,000 cyclists rode all or parts of the TransAmerica Bicycle Trail in 1976—and an estimated 15,000 have ridden it since the Bicentennial summer.

"We don't expect to have quite as large a concentration of riders on the Lewis & Clark Bicycle Trail during any one summer as we had on the TransAm Trail in 1976," said Adventure Cycling's executive director, Bill Sawyer. "However, it won't surprise us if during the three-year celebration we see at least 5,000 riders—and far, far more as the years continue."

Getting Ready and Gearing Up

Training
A fair number of individuals go into long-distance bicycle tours cold, without any specific training, and "ride themselves into shape" as they go. However, most of those individuals are miserable for at least the first couple of weeks of their trip, and a substantial portion wind up with overuse injuries—riding themselves *out* of shape and calling it quits altogether. The

more prudent bicycle tourist plots out a progressive training program that will deliver him or her to the trailhead in good riding condition. Different training programs work for different people, obviously, but the following program has worked successfully for hundreds of individuals joining Adventure Cycling tours.

No fewer than eight weeks before your trip is slated to begin, two or three times a week you should be doing rides of 10 to 20 miles on an unloaded bike. With six weeks to go, up the distance to 40 miles for at least one weekly ride, and add lightly weighted panniers to your bike for that outing (or a trailer, if that's how you'll be hauling equipment). Four weeks before your tour starts, continue doing two or three weekly 20- to 30-mile maintenance rides, while increasing the week's long ride to 50 or 60 miles, even longer if you plan to be putting in days of more than 70 miles on your tour. If possible, include hills in the route, and go with the full complement of gear so that you can get a feel for weight distribution and how that weight changes the handling characteristics of your bicycle.

With two weeks to go, head out for an overnight shakedown ride. Camp out if you'll be camping on tour: Now, not after you leave home for the open road, is the time to learn whether your equipment has problems or you need to obtain additional gear.

Bikes and Gear-hauling Techniques

After her first research outing on the Lewis & Clark Bicycle Trail, field researcher Gayl Teichert remarked, "This is not a route for narrow tires and fast bikes. There is more gravel than on most of our road routes. If I were doing it, I'd use the fattest tires possible on my road bike." Teichert said that fatter tires might prove useful, too, in case a defensive move needs to be made on one of the busier roads that lack paved shoulders. And "the Lewis & Clark Bicycle Trail has fewer bike shops available than almost any other route we offer," suggesting that the shock-absorbing qualities of fatter tires might also help minimize mechanical problems.

Many riders these days are choosing mountain bikes for touring, arguing that the comfort they afford is worth the trade-off of covering the miles a little more slowly; others prefer all-out touring bikes. Each style has its advantages and drawbacks. If you're shopping for a new bike, read Adventure Cycling's *Touring Bike Buyer's Guide* online at www.adventurecycling.org. The guide breaks touring bikes into several categories, including loaded touring, light touring, and off-road touring, while providing valuable information that will help you quickly narrow down the choices.

Assuming that you are bicycling the Lewis & Clark Bicycle Trail self-contained, in the spirit of those who blazed the trail 200 years ago, plan on keeping your panniers loaded with between thirty and forty-five pounds. Try to maintain a 40 to 60 percent distribution of weight in the rear and front panniers, respectively. Your sleeping bag, pad, tent, and body weight will add additional weight over the rear wheel, balancing things out. If you're

History lives along the Big Muddy, from its mouth in Missouri to its source in Montana.

hauling gear in a trailer, such as a BOB (Beast of Burden), you can get away with carrying more gear; this is one reason such trailers have become so popular for touring where services are few and far between and where the capacity to carry several days' worth of food and water is needed (such as on the Great Divide Mountain Bike Route). An advantage of panniers, however, is that they can be taken into your tent and loaded and unloaded there—a real advantage, say, during a rainstorm. Panniers also have lots of separated spaces, making it easy to compartmentalize your gear, while trailers tend to have just one big waterproof duffle to stuff. A lot of traditionalists also claim that bikes carrying panniers handle better on pavement than do those pulling trailers.

Before packing them, line your panniers with heavy-duty plastic garbage bags, which will do wonders to keep gear dry in the rain. Roll clothing and pack it vertically (in individual plastic bags, if you want to go that far). Begin your trip with spare room in the panniers for those odds and ends you're bound to acquire along the way. And keep your wallet, camera, and other often-used items in a detachable handlebar bag (don't let its weight exceed seven or eight pounds) or a fanny pack, and always take it with you when you leave the bike. Tools for fixing flats might go in your handlebar bag; other probably less-used tools and spare parts can be packed in your trailer or panniers.

Essential Items

Your basic warm-weather riding outfit should consist of cycling shorts with synthetic-chamois lining, a cycling jersey or other lightweight top, cycling shoes, a helmet that fits correctly, synthetic-material socks, cycling gloves, and high-quality sunglasses. When it turns chilly and/or wet, it's best to layer clothing for warmth (see suggested clothing list). Avoid cotton undergarments and long underwear when riding; rather, wear items made of synthetic fibers, which will wick moisture away from your skin. Your rain/wind jacket serves as the outer layer. It should be made of a breathable waterproof fabric, such as GoreTex, which will keep you drier and also serve as an effective windbreak. (Some of the best cycling clothes and accessories manufactured are available through Adventure Cycling's *Cyclosource* catalog; call 800–721–8719 to request a copy, or order online at www.adventure cycling. org.)

Add to or subtract from the following lists of suggested gear as your experience and/or preferences dictate:

Clothing

- Cycling helmet
- Cycling shorts, synthetic-chamois lining (2 pair)
- Synthetic cycling socks (2 or 3 pair)
- Leg warmers or tights for riding
- Short-sleeved shirt (2 or 3)
- Light, long-sleeved shirt for sun protection and off-bike wear
- Wool sweater or fleece jacket
- Rain/wind gear (jacket and pants of GoreTex or a similar waterproof, breathable fabric)
- Comfortable shorts and pants for off-bike wear
- Cotton underwear and socks for off-bike wear (2 or 3 pair)
- Touring shoes that are comfortable for both riding and walking
- Cycling gloves
- Polypropylene glove liners for cool/wet weather
- Wool or polypropylene hat, mittens, and socks for cold weather
- Waterproof shoe covers
- Bathing suit
- Sandals or other comfortable footwear for off-bike wear

Miscellaneous

- Toiletries
- Lightweight towel
- Multitool pocket knife
- Lightweight lock and cable (not a U-lock)
- Two or three water bottles; or, if you prefer, a CamelBak or similar product
- Basic first-aid kit

- Sunglasses
- Flashlight or headlamp
- Sewing kit
- Insect repellent
- Nylon cording
- Bungie cords
- High-quality water filter
- Items you might not think of include baby wipes (great for personal hygiene in the absence of showers), camera, binoculars, extra plastic bags, petroleum jelly (to prevent chafing), toilet paper, pencil and journal, foldable camp chair, and a good book for wet mornings when you don't want to get out of your tent.

Tools and Spare Parts
- Tire levers/patch kit
- Spare tubes
- Small pump
- Spare spokes and spoke wrench
- Allen wrenches to fit your bike
- Extra Allen bolts and other appropriate nuts and bolts (particularly for racks)
- Chain tool
- Electrical tape
- Loctite adhesive
- Screwdriver
- Chain lubricant
- Six-inch locking pliers
- Spare brake cable
- Spare derailleur cable

Camping Gear
- Sleeping bag. Down-filled bags are warmer, lighter, and more compressible, but they're worthless when wet. Synthetic-filled bags are less expensive for comparable warmth and will keep you warm even if they're wet; the disadvantage is that they're heavier and bulkier.
- Sleeping bag liner, easily removed for washing (a cotton sheet sewn in half works well)
- Sleeping pad (self-inflating style recommended)
- Tent (lightweight and freestanding, with a detached rainfly)
- Waterproof ground cloth
- Cook stove, cook set, and eating utensils

Heading Out

Safety Concerns

Motor traffic presents the greatest hazard to cyclists touring on shared-use roadways. When a vehicle passes you from behind, assume that there are more cars coming behind it—and that the drivers of those cars or trucks haven't seen you. RVs and pickups towing trailers are often equipped with mirror extensions that can clip unsuspecting cyclists. (Practice looking behind when you're hauling a load; you'll find that the bike tends to veer to one side as you turn your head.) A helmet- or handlebar-mounted rearview mirror can greatly enhance your awareness of what is approaching from behind. Be attentive and prepared to leave the road if necessary, and try to avoid riding directly into the rising or setting sun, as motorists coming from behind also will be facing the sun and may have problems seeing you.

Watch for things in the road and/or on the shoulder, such as oil, wet leaves, and loose gravel. If you can't avoid these hazards, ride a straight line through them (don't turn the handlebars). If you encounter railroad tracks that are diagonal to the road, swing out (if there is no traffic approaching from behind) and cross the tracks as close as possible to a 90-degree angle.

Brake before you must, particularly on downhills and before entering curves, and *never* slam on just the front brake! Before heading out, practice emergency braking, which entails shifting your weight toward the rear of the saddle while moving your hands onto the brake handles and applying firm, even pressure to both front and rear brakes.

Weather and Other Hazards

Hope for the best, and prepare for the worst. On the eastern stretches of the route—particularly in the midst of summer in Missouri, along the Iowa-Nebraska border, and in eastern South Dakota—you'll likely encounter high humidity with temperatures in the high 80s or 90s. In the West, where the relative humidity is lower, you may encounter temperatures in excess of 100 degrees at lower elevations; then, just days or hours later, you may hit cold rain or perhaps even snow in the high mountains. Always drink a lot of fluids; dehydration will drain your energy and can contribute significantly to heat-related health problems.

Hypothermia, a condition where the core body temperature plummets, is the most common killer in the outdoors. It is a particular threat at temperatures between 30 and 50 degrees. To avoid it, add or remove layers as the situation warrants. Your goal is to stay at the happy medium where you're neither cold nor sweating heavily, which can both dampen your clothes and bring on dehydration, compounding the problem. Wear a light layer of a wicking fabric against your skin, and drink lots of water—often.

Be aware of possible heat exhaustion and heat stroke during the hot days of summer. Cover up with lightweight clothing and, to avoid sunburn, apply a high-SPF sunscreen on any exposed skin. Depending on the temperature and the length of the day's ride, try to drink between one and two gallons of water each day. Also take frequent rest breaks in the shade to allow your body temperature to lower. (If you can't find shade, as will be the case in much of the rural Great Plains, create your own using your rain tarp, tent poles, and bicycle.)

Lightning can be a real danger. Try to get off the road if you get caught in a lightning storm, but avoid lone trees and open areas. Instead look for a heavily timbered area or a low spot between ridges.

Giardiasis, a debilitating intestinal illness caused by the one-celled organism *Giardia lamblia,* can be contracted by drinking surface water, even in the Rocky Mountains. The waterborne cysts end up in streams and other waters via animal droppings or human waste. Carry a water filter and use it whenever you're forced to drink surface water. The filters are commonly available at sporting goods stores.

Direction of Travel, When to Go

Because the Lewis and Clark expedition traveled from the relatively settled East toward the untamed West, it is assumed that the majority of cycle-tourists will also travel east to west. Therefore, the book's narrative logs are written to guide you in that direction of travel. For those who prefer to ride west to east, both west-to-east and east-to-west narratives can be found on the Adventure Cycling maps.

Doing It in Pieces

The average bicycle tourist will need about two months to ride the entire Lewis & Clark Bicycle Trail. Lacking that much vacation time, many riders will pedal the trail in pieces, eventually completing the route over the course of three or four summers. This could be particularly fitting for this route; since the bicentennial celebration spans three years, there will be no shortage of things to do, see, and take part in all along the trail from 2003 to 2006.

A good strategy for breaking the route up into three trips of approximately three weeks, with each leg ending within reasonable distance of an airport and other transportation facilities, would be to ride from Hartford, Illinois, to Pierre, South Dakota (1,041 miles), the first summer; Pierre to Great Falls, Montana (1,048 miles), the next; and wrap up the trail in summer number three by riding from Great Falls to Astoria, Oregon (1,165 miles).

A Few Riding Tips

• Try to relax while you ride, particularly in the neck and shoulders.
• Eat small quantities frequently rather than stuffing yourself with three big daily meals.
• Drink more water than you think it possible to hold.
• Help prevent knee problems by spinning the pedals at a lively cadence of 70 to 90 rpm; also, your saddle should be raised to the point where there

Hauling her bedroom and kitchen in her BOB, this cyclist is camped outside Chamberlain, South Dakota.

is only a slight bend in your knee when your foot is at the bottom of the pedal stroke.

• Ward off numb hands, a common problem among cycletourists, by wearing padded cycling gloves and frequently changing hand position.

• To prevent chafing, use talcum powder or petroleum jelly in chafe-prone areas, such as the crotch.

Camping Tips

While camping along the Lewis & Clark Bicycle Trail, in some instances you'll be using primitive campgrounds with only the barest of basic necessities: a pit toilet, picnic table, and possibly a water supply. At other times you'll probably stay at commercial campgrounds boasting showers, laundry, a store—perhaps even a kitchen sink! Between these two extremes are state park, national park, and national forest campgrounds. While these tend not to provide the degree of niceties that some commercial campgrounds do, in general they are the most aesthetically pleasing campgrounds and often have tent sites nestled in the trees, away from RV camping areas.

When choosing a campsite, look for level, dry ground with natural cover (grass, pine needles, or leaves) located at least 200 feet from open water. Avoid gullies and damp areas, which tend to be chillier and harbor more insects. On warm nights, a high, open site will permit the breeze to blow through, reducing the bug factor. If electrical storms threaten, don't sleep near a solitary tree, which could act as a lightning rod.

In some instances there will be no grocery store close to camp. That is when those extra bungie cords will really come in handy, whether you're carrying your gear in panniers or a trailer. Once you get the food to camp and prepare to cook it, never put a working stove on a table where you or others are sitting. Keep the fuel bottle capped and away from a lit stove. Also be aware that campstoves generate carbon monoxide, so never operate one inside a tent.

Carry water to your site for dishwashing (don't wash dishes under pumps, in bathrooms, or in surface water). Dispose of gray water in a service sink or toilet; if neither is available, empty it at least 100 feet away from your campsite. Food odors can attract animals such as rodents, raccoons, and even bears—not in Missouri or Iowa, perhaps, but in the mountains of Montana and Idaho. When departing a campsite, leave it at least as clean as you found it, preferably cleaner.

How to Use This Book

Each of the first seven chapters is designed to match its counterpart in the Adventure Cycling map series that covers the route in regard to beginning and ending points. Following a short introduction, which in general terms describes the terrain and riding conditions to expect as well as a synopsis of the Corps of Discovery's travels through the area, each chapter is broken down into several riding days. You'll first find a "minilesson" for the day, typically including some information related to the Lewis and Clark expedition—for instance, an explanation of what wildlife the expedition might have encountered in that area and how that has/hasn't changed—and information pertaining to something you'll encounter on that day's ride, or at least have the option of visiting on a side trip. Here and there you'll find included a not-to-miss restaurant or campground, particularly where careful planning of overnight stops is necessary. But for a comprehensive listing of services—including campgrounds, motels, bike shops, grocery stores, and post offices—you'll want to obtain the more-detailed Adventure Cycling maps.

Following each narrative is the day's mileage log, telling you where to turn left, where to turn right, and basically how stay on the route. In all, the route is divided into forty sections, each with a corresponding map and encompassing between 60 and 100 miles, for an average of 80 miles per map section.

This guidebook is a work in progress. It will be updated as time goes on, as the collection of trail lore grows. Please help us, and those who will ride the route in the future, by sending in corrections, suggestions, campground tips, your favorite ice cream stops, and other information to: The Globe Pequot Press, Reader Response/Editorial Department, P.O. Box 480, Guilford, CT 06437; or editorial@globe-pequot.com.

For More Information

Several excellent guidebooks to the Lewis and Clark National Historic Trail offer far more information than the cycling-specific scope of this book would permit. A couple of favorites include *Traveling the Lewis & Clark Trail* by Julie Fanselow and *National Geographic's Guide to the Lewis & Clark Trail* by Thomas Schmidt. It is highly recommended that you carry at least one of these along in addition to this book in order to have a more comprehensive understanding of the expedition and to learn about additional side trips you may want to consider. Other great books to read before and/or during your ride include *Undaunted Courage* by Stephen Ambrose and *The Journals of Lewis and Clark*, edited by Bernard DeVoto.

Have fun—and be safe—exploring the Lewis & Clark Bicycle Trail!

CHAPTER 1

Hartford, Illinois
to Council Bluffs, Iowa
(555 miles)

Your first pedal strokes on the Lewis & Clark Bicycle Trail will take you along the Confluence Bikeway, which you access at the impressive new Lewis and Clark State Memorial Park Visitor Center outside Hartford, Illinois. The center is near the mouth of the Wood River, on the opposite side of the Mississippi from where the Missouri feeds into it. It was at the mouth of the Wood where the members of the Lewis and Clark expedition spent the winter of late 1803 and 1804, making final preparations for a spring departure up the Missouri. Their encampment was known as Camp Dubois, stemming from the French name of the Wood River, *Rivière à Dubois*. (The Missouri's course has shifted eastward over the ensuing 200 years, and it is thought that the camp's precise location is now in Missouri.)

The expedition members included co-leaders Meriwether Lewis and William Clark, both of whom were officers in the U.S. Army; fourteen soldiers already serving in the Army; nine volunteers from Kentucky; an interpreter-hunter named George Drouillard; a pair of French watermen; and a black slave owned by Captain Clark. All except York, the slave, were enlisted in the Army for the expedition's duration—all of them as privates except Nathaniel Pryor, John Ordway, and Charles Floyd, who were appointed sergeants. In addition to these twenty-nine men, it is believed that a total of sixteen others—a corporal, six soldiers, and nine watermen—accompanied the expedition as far as the Mandan nation in future North Dakota. Also along for the ride was Captain Lewis's Newfoundland dog, Seaman.

It's noteworthy that officially, in the eyes of the Army, Lewis was a captain and Clark his lieutenant, but this didn't set well with Lewis. He chose Clark as his co-leader because Clark had been Lewis's own commanding officer in the Army. In practice, the men were equals in every sense of the word. Lewis always referred to Clark as captain, and they called themselves co-captains.

Come spring, they would set forth upstream in three boats: a 55-foot-long, 8-foot-wide keelboat outfitted with twenty-two oars and a mast, and two open boats known as *pirogues*, one of them 42 feet long with seven pairs of oars and the other 39 feet long with six sets of oars. Additionally, a pair of horses would be walked along the riverbanks to aid in the hunting and hauling of game.

The party departed on May 14, 1804, although without Captain Lewis, who was in St. Louis seeing to some final arrangements. He caught up with the rest in St. Charles on May 20. It was spring and the Missouri was running high and fast, so for the first few days the expedition covered only 10 to 14 miles per day.

As you set out on your own adventure two centuries later, you will find the riding conditions along the easternmost sections of the Lewis & Clark Bicycle Trail to range from traffic-free pathways, to low-traffic rural roads, to back roads in the greater Kansas City metro area that can carry substantial car and truck traffic. A real highlight in Missouri is the 150-mile stretch along the Katy Trail State Park, one of the longest and best-known rail-trail conversions in the country. With its smooth surface of crushed limestone, the Katy traverses the floodplain of the Missouri, often running immediately beside the river and just above the water level—unfortunately, *below* water level during flood periods, a situation that will necessitate finding higher, drier ground to ride on.

Much of the Missouri countryside that was wild frontier when Lewis and Clark passed through has been transformed into densely settled urban and suburban pockets. The Missouri River corridor can be considered a heavily used recreational and industrial strip linking the St. Louis and Kansas City metropolitan areas. Kansas's short contribution to the route, by comparison, is more rural, winding amidst rolling grain fields. Riding conditions in southeastern Nebraska and southwestern Iowa range from rural to urban, the latter particularly around Omaha–Council Bluffs.

1 Hartford, Illinois to Marthasville, Missouri
89.5 miles (89.5 miles cumulative)

"This Village Contns. about 100 houses, the most of them small and indefferent and about 450 inhabitents Chiefly French, those people appear Pore, polite & harmonious."

—CAPT. WILLIAM CLARK
Wednesday, May 16, 1804
At St. Charles

The route begins outside Hartford, Illinois, at **Lewis and Clark State Memorial Park** (Route 3 at Poag Road, Hartford, IL 62048; 618–251–5811). From there the new, smooth-surfaced Confluence Bikeway goes both northwest (that's the way you go) and southwest (into greater St. Louis). Newly opened for the Lewis and Clark bicentennial celebration, the park's visitor center sits on the east bank of the Mississippi, where you can look across at the Missouri feeding into the Father of Waters.

After leaving the bustle of Alton behind, watch for barges plying the Mississippi to your left as you ride between the river and high, white limestone bluffs, their tops embellished with pockets of stunted juniper trees. In April bursts of redbud lend wonderfully bright splashes of contrast to the otherwise rather uniform spring-green surroundings.

Soon you'll come to Elsah, a picturesque village set back in a hollow in the hills. The entire town, whose streets and structures keep alive the spirit of the nineteenth century, is listed on the National Register of Historic Places. A large share of the venerable settlement had to be patched and re-plastered after the devastating Great Flood of 1993. Not only were homes and other buildings badly damaged, but many old maple, cottonwood, and sycamore trees were killed, dramatically altering Elsah's character. Nearby Grafton, with its flood-prone location at the confluence of the Mississippi and Illinois Rivers, suffered even worse. Water covered most of the city for months, 15 feet and deeper in places. More than one hundred homes were severely damaged; a few floated away altogether.

The explorers Louis Joliet and Father Jacques Marquette traveled through here while exploring the Mississippi in 1673. Although they preceded Lewis and Clark by 131 years, they were inspired by one of the same goals that drove the Corps of Discovery: The French government wanted to find a northwest passage to the Pacific Ocean and suspected that the Mississippi might provide that route. Marquette and Joliet got as far south as

Riding in Calhoun County, Illinois, between the Brussels and Golden Eagle ferries.

the mouth of the Arkansas River before turning around, convinced by then that the Mississippi flowed not to the Pacific but to the Gulf of Mexico. Father Marquette returned to the confluence of the Illinois and Mississippi Rivers in spring 1675, intending to convert the local Kaskaskia Indians to Catholicism; failing health, however, forced him to retreat not long after arriving. Marquette's namesake park, **Père Marquette State Park** (Route 100, P.O. Box 158, Grafton, IL 62037; 618–786–3323), is located just north of the Brussels Ferry landing and makes a great place to pitch your tent.

You may not even notice the subtle change, but just north of Grafton you'll leave the Mississippi and begin riding alongside the Illinois River. Four miles later, the first of two ferry crossings takes you across that river into Calhoun County, Illinois, a.k.a. "the Kingdom." Surely one of the longest and skinniest counties in the nation, Calhoun is made up of a peninsula of land lying between the Mississippi and Illinois Rivers, which grow ever closer to each other as they flow south, finally merging at the southeastern tip of the county. The roads winding through the sparsely settled, rolling farmlands of Calhoun County may provide some of the most peaceful and memorable cycling you'll experience anywhere (unless you ride them during commuting hours, when traffic can be substantial).

Four miles after disembarking the Brussels Ferry you'll pedal through an overgrown levee then, less than a mile later, encounter a right-hand turn for the mile-long side trip to **Two Rivers National Wildlife Refuge** (HCR 82, Brussels, IL 62013; 618–883–2201). Extending from the small visitor center here, an observation deck overlooks a mix of ponds and wetlands. Spring at the refuge is alive with the sights and sounds of migrating waterfowl, shorebirds, and warblers; in late summer and fall, you can experience large migrations of waterfowl and raptors, including bald eagles. White-tailed deer, ring-necked pheasants, and northern bobwhites are among the full-time residents of the refuge.

Ferry crossing number two takes you across the Mississippi River into Missouri. You'll board the ferry beside **Kinder's Restaurant and Lounge** (Box 48 RR, Golden Eagle, IL 62036; 618–883–2586), whose sign brags of the best catfish and chicken around and offers a bit of river-rat humor: ON AND SOMETIMES IN THE MISSISSIPPI RIVER.

You'll join up with the Katy Trail at St. Charles, but only after exploring downtown historic districts that could keep you off your bike for hours—or even days. The **Trailhead Brewing Co.** (921 South Riverside Drive, St. Charles, MO 63302; 636–946–2739; www.trailheadbrewing.com), located kitty-corner from where you access the trail, could cause some delays, as well. Don't miss the **First Missouri State Capitol Historic Site** (200–216 South Main Street, St. Charles, MO 63301; 636–940–3322; www.mostate parks.com), a pair of adjacent Federal-style brick structures that served as the seat of government from 1821—when Missouri became the twenty-fourth state as a result of the Missouri Compromise on slavery—until 1826, when the newly built capitol building in Jefferson City was ready for occupation.

The oldest part of the city, the Frenchtown Historic District, predates by more than forty years the future state's territorial status, which Missouri gained in 1812 after being split from the Louisiana Territory. The Frenchtown District, which grew as a hub of the fur trade, is found at the north end of Second, Third, and Fourth Streets. Here you'll see French Colonial architecture of a type that St. Charles shares with only a few other old French settlements in North America, such as New Orleans and Quèbec City. Finally, before leaving St. Charles, you'll no doubt want to grab a bite in **Lewis & Clark's American Restaurant and Public House** (217 South Main Street, St. Charles, MO 63301; 636–947–3334), located in the Main Street Historic District.

En route to Marthasville on the Katy Trail, you'll pass through Defiance, near which is situated Daniel Boone's 1810 rock home; then you'll skirt the edge of Augusta, a hilly little town that's definitely worth leaving the trail to explore. Founded in 1836 by Leonard Harold, by 1980 Augusta was honored as the first official U.S. Wine District. The **Augusta Winery** (5601 High Street, Augusta, MO 63332; 888–667–9463) is located at the corner of Jackson and High Streets.

Mileage Log

0.0 Ride onto the bike trail opposite the entrance to Lewis and Clark State Memorial Park. Merge briefly onto road, then bear right to cross bridge.

2.0 Downtown Hartford is to the right.

8.0 Merge left onto Discovery Parkway, then immediately bear left back onto the bike path. Pass under the spectacular Clark Bridge. Now in Alton, empty into a parking lot, aiming toward the Alton Belle Casino and a grain elevator.

9.0 Walk bike across highway to visitor center, then ride northwest on State Road 100.

11.0 Bear right onto the bike path near big holes in the cliffs.

15.5 Separated bike path changes to shoulders on both sides of highway.

19.5 Elsah.

24.0 Turn left onto Grafton Hills Drive at the south end of Grafton, following bike route signs. Turn right 1 block later.

25.5 Continue straight after stop sign onto signed bike path.

26.0 Bike path crosses to east side of the road.

28.5 At Père Marquette riding stables, turn left from path and head south on SR 100.

29.0 Turn right into Brussels Ferry landing. After disembarking ferry, continue straight on Illinois River Road toward sign that reads BRUSSELS 8 MILES.

35.5 Turn left onto Golden Eagle Road/County Road 1945E.

36.0 Bear left where Gun Club Road goes right.

37.5 Turn right onto Mississippi River Road/CR 240N.

38.5 Turn left onto Gun Club Road at the T.

40.5 Ride straight onto ferry. Cross the Mississippi River and enter Missouri. Disembark, riding onto Hayford Road.

41.5 Turn left at the T onto unsigned CR B.

44.5 Turn right onto Seeburger Road.

46.0 Go right onto Airport Road.

47.5 Pass under SR 370; road becomes Elm Avenue, St. Charles.

49.0 Turn right onto Pam Avenue. One block later turn left onto Sibley Street.

50.0 Ride across busy King's Highway; the route becomes Washington Street. One block later go right onto Ninth Street then, in 1 more block, left onto Jefferson Street.

51.0 Turn right onto Main Street and begin riding on a rough brick surface through historic downtown St. Charles.

51.5 Turn left onto Boone's Lick Road. One block later, turn right onto the Katy Trail.

52.0 Ride under Interstate 70.

71.0 Defiance.

72.5 Matson.

78.5 Augusta.

86.0 Dutzow.

89.5 Marthasville.

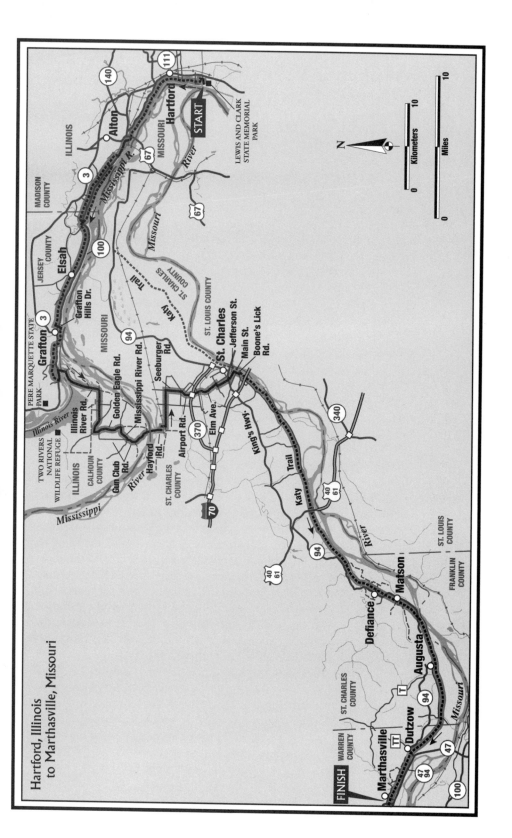

Hartford, Illinois
to Marthasville, Missouri

2
Marthasville to Boonville, Missouri
113 miles (202.5 miles cumulative)

". . . a Short distance above the mouth of [a] creek, is Several Cou-
rious paintings and carving on the projecting rock of Limestone in-
lade with white red & blue flint, of a verry good quallity, the
Indians have taken of this flint great quantities . . ."
    —CAPT. WILLIAM CLARK
    Thursday, June 7, 1804
    At Moniteau Creek in present-day Rocheville

The route between Marthasville and Boonville is entirely along the Katy Trail. Widely considered the queen of America's rails-to-trails projects, the Katy traces a former route of the Missouri-Kansas-Texas Railroad—the MK&T, or Katy for short—between St. Charles and Sedalia. (The Union Pacific contributed the southernmost portion, between Sedalia and Clinton.) A pathway perfect for quiet reflection and nature study, the Katy Trail serves thousands of self-propelled travelers each year, who come from around the country—indeed, from around the world—to make their way amidst bottomland forests, sycamore-smothered bluffs, brackish backwaters, flat crop fields, and beautiful farms carved into rolling hills. It's a toss-up as to which season is better for traveling the trail—spring, with its choruses of songbirds and promise of new life, or autumn, which in the Missouri River Valley erupts into a kaleidoscope of colorful shrubs and hardwoods, including the firey red of sugar maples. (For greater detail on the Katy Trail and the towns lining it, pick up a copy of Brett Dufur's *The Complete Katy Trail Guidebook*.)

Whereas much of the Katy Trail to the east is in the open and exposed to the hot sun, more of this portion—generally beginning west of Treloar—is blessed with shade provided by bluffs and timber. It retains its flat character, though, particularly if you compare it with the hilly terrain tackled by State Road 94, which is often in close proximity to the trail.

South of the Katy Trail and the Missouri River, by way of the SR 19 bridge *(hazardous; call the Hermann Visitor Center at 573–486–2744 for information on shuttles and/or vehicle-escort services)*, is Hermann, one of the most popular tourist destinations in Missouri. To give you some idea of just how popular, the town of fewer than 3,000 residents boasts more than three dozen B&Bs. Hermann was settled early in the nineteenth century by German immigrants—specifically, the German Settlement Society of Philadel-

Near Rocheport, the Katy Trail skirts sycamore-smothered bluffs.

phia—who intended for the town's residents to remain self-supporting and to "stay German" rather than lose their native language and culture as had so many other Germans in America. If you're cycling through in the fall, be aware that Hermann celebrates Oktoberfest in a big way—on every full weekend of every October!

In Mokane a town-renaming contest in 1893 (it was originally known as St. Auberts) drew the winning submission, which derived from letters in Missouri, Kansas, and Eastern, a railroad line that would become part of the MK&T. Mokane is one of several miniscule towns lining the Katy Trail whose residents, because of their fortuitous trailside locations, enjoy having the world come to them. Many of these same towns' riverside locations worked against them in 1993, when they were severely damaged by the great floods.

As you approach Jefferson City from the east, you'll see the dome of the state capitol building protruding above the treed horizon, along with a couple of water towers: It seems a uniquely midwestern scene. Continuing west from where U.S. Highway 54 crosses the river into Jefferson City, the Katy Trail penetrates a wilder, less roaded country than what you've experienced east of here. The 9 miles between McBaine and Rocheport—an alluring small town teeming with B&Bs and pre–Civil War homes—is perhaps the most appealing stretch of the entire trail. Just west of McBaine, the MK&T Fitness Trail branches off to the northeast, making a side trip into Columbia easy and practical. It's 9 miles into the heart of the city, home to the University of

Missouri. A couple of miles past that junction you'll see a marker commemorating the Lewis and Clark campsite of June 6, 1804. Watch as you pedal along for birds like redheaded woodpeckers perched in immense cottonwood snags. As you approach the din of the high Interstate 40 bridge, watch for swallows darting about the bluffsides and for the more surprising sight of Canada geese nesting on rock ledges. Steep, junglelike drainage ravines dissect private lands to your right, while to the left the Missouri River is right there—wide, deep, and brown, full of twirling whirlpools and bobbing branches and logs.

When Lewis and Clark traveled up the Missouri in 1804, the river and its floodplain comprised a complex of braided channels, bottomland forests, wet prairies, and prolific wetlands. Today the Missouri is a much different animal, having been subdued by a network of dams, dikes, and levees. It is faster flowing than originally, owing to channelization that has separated the river from its natural floodplain. Just before reaching Rocheport, on the far (south) side of the river in the distance, you can see the Overton Bottoms North, part of the Overton Bottoms Mitigation Project. Here the U.S. Army Corps of Engineers and U.S. Fish and Wildlife Service are trying to set the clock back, working to rejoin a small segment of the river with its historic floodplain. Among the agencies' goals are re-creating and enhancing habitats for wildlife that depend on wetlands for survival, including such endangered species as the pallid sturgeon and piping plover. The project is one of six sites between Hermann and Kansas City that together make up the Big Muddy National Fish and Wildlife Refuge. Established only in the mid-1990s, the refuge is predicted eventually to encompass 60,000 acres of river bottom.

Mileage Log

0.0	Continue west from Marthasville on the Katy Trail.
3.5	Peers.
6.5	Treloar.
23.0	McKittrick.
27.0	Rhineland.
33.0	Bluffton.
38.0	Portland.
43.5	Steedman.
47.0	Mokane.
53.0	Tebbetts.
59.5	Wainwright.
65.0	Cedar City.
71.5	Claysville.
75.5	Hartsburg.
79.0	Wilton.

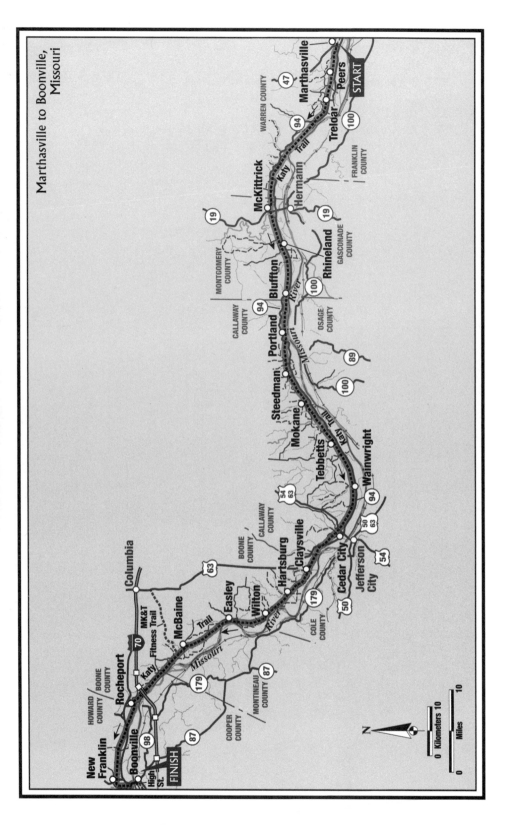

Marthasville to Boonville, Missouri

84.0	Easley.
91.0	McBaine.
100.0	Rocheport.
110.0	New Franklin.
112.5	Turn left onto SR 87.
113.0	Turn right onto U.S. 40/SR 5. Cross Missouri River bridge and enter Boonville. Turn right onto High Street.

3 Boonville to Henrietta, Missouri
92 miles (294.5 miles cumulative)

". . . The Ticks & Musquiters are verry troublesome."
—CAPT. WILLIAM CLARK
Saturday, June 17, 1804

At Boonville you bid adieu to the Katy Trail as it leaves the protected Missouri River floodplain to course southwesterly through sun-drenched, wind-whipped uplands. Immediately west of town you'll pedal over a delightfully smooth, low-traffic road that rolls through hills covered in crops of hay and corn and which serves as a component of the Santa Fe National Historic Trail.

The Santa Fe Trail began its role as a commercial highway for trade between the United States and Mexico in 1821, the year in which Missouri became a state and Mexico gained independence from Spain. The trail began at Franklin, not far from Boonville, then crossed to the south side of the Missouri and eventually split into a mountain route and more southerly cut-off route. Until 1848, when the Treaty of Guadalupe ended the Mexican-American War and New Mexico fell under U.S. military rule, the terminus was a Mexican city known as La Villa Real de Santa Fe de San Francisco de Asis. That city's name, mercifully, has since been shortened to Santa Fe.

In addition to hosting hundreds of freight wagons, each of which took approximately two months to travel from Franklin to Santa Fe, the trail was traced by soldiers, fur trappers and traders, would-be gold miners headed to Colorado and California, and a host of other wanderers. It continued serving as an important overland route until the railroad reached Santa Fe in 1880.

Swing in to have a look at the venerable settlement of Arrow Rock, and you'll sense that the days of wagons storming down the Santa Fe Trail are not that long gone. Here you can walk along streets bordered by carved-limestone gutters and fronted with boardwalks and canopied structures housing enterprises such as antiques shops and general stores. The name-sake Arrow Rock bluffs were an important landmark along the Missouri for several decades before Lewis and Clark came through, first appearing as *pierre a fleche* ("rock of arrows") on a 1732 French boatmen's map. The Corps of Discovery passed the site on June 9, 1804, when Clark noted *". . . Several Small Chanels running out of the River below a Bluff & Prarie Called the Prarie of Arrows where the river is confined within the width of 300*

Arrow Rock's streets are bordered by carved-limestone gutters and fronted with creaking boardwalks.

yds. . . ." As is the case with many present-day river hills of the Midwest, these bluffs are more heavily timbered than they were in presettlement times, when wildfires kept the land cleared. The "prairie" of arrows is largely forest today.

With the establishment of the Santa Fe Trail, travelers setting out from Howard County on the north side of the river would cross the Missouri on the Arrow Rock ferry, then stock up on water at a spring that still flows today (it's located behind the Old Tavern). A town, originally called New Philadelphia, was platted in 1829; that name quickly devolved back into Arrow Rock, which, by the mid-1800s, claimed more than 1,000 residents. As railroads, then highways began lacing the landscape, the Missouri became less important as a travel corridor, and the town's population dwindled. Fewer than one hundred persons call Arrow Rock home today. In 1964 the entire town was given National Historic Landmark status, with a smaller portion designated as the **Arrow Rock State Historic Site** (Arrow Rock, MO 65320; 660–837–3330; www.mostateparks.com). The state historic site encompasses several old structures, including the Old Tavern, whose life began way back in 1834, and a fine new visitor center (open 10:00 A.M. to 5:00 P.M. daily) with displays covering such topics as the Little Osage and Missouri tribes that formerly resided in this part of the state.

As you walk through open forest over the high boardwalk connecting the parking lot and the visitor center, listen for the distinctive call of an American cardinal, whose looks rival his brilliant melody. The bright-red male of the species creates a magnificent contrast against the subdued backdrop of greenery. Also, while walking or cycling around Arrow Rock, don't miss inspecting the trench known as Godsey's Diggings, which was excavated beginning 1840 and abandoned around 1860 before ever reaching its intended goal of the Missouri River. Missouri's state-park system is one of the best in the country, and this park claims an extremely pleasant primitive campground nestled amidst hardwoods.

You can ruminate on another important chapter of Missouri's complex history in the Higginsville and Lexington areas. The 135-acre **Confederate Memorial State Historic Site** (Route 1, Box 221-A, Higginsville, MO 64037; 660–584–2853; www.mostateparks.com), just off the route north of Higginsville, commemorates the more than 40,000 Missouri soldiers who fought for the Southern cause in the Civil War. The grounds include several historic buildings, small ponds, stately stands of old trees, sprawling lawns, and a cemetery holding the remains of some 800 of Missouri's Confederate soldiers. The Confederate Soldiers Home of Missouri was established here toward the end of the nineteenth century, with the first ailing veteran admitted in April 1891. He was followed over the ensuing six decades by more than 1,600 veterans and their relatives. In 1950 the final surviving Missouri Confederate soldier, 108-year-old Johnny Graves, died at the home.

As the Civil War heated up, Missouri was a state divided. In 1860 some 115,000 slaves made up nearly 10 percent of Missouri's population, and most rural white Missourians were Southern sympathizers. What largely saved the critically located state for the Union were the approximately 65,000 antislavery German immigrants living in the St. Louis area. For the siege of Vicksburg, Missouri furnished thirty-nine regiments—roughly half of them Confederate and the other half Union. Today the National Cemetery in Springfield is the only cemetery where Union and Confederate forces are buried side by side. And although the state did ultimately go with the Union, one of the thirteen stars on the Confederate flag represents Missouri.

In Lexington don't miss visiting the **Battle of Lexington State Historic Site** (P.O. Box 6, Lexington, MO 64067; 660–259–4654; www.mostateparks. com). The visitor center is open Monday through Saturday from 9:00 A.M. to 5:00 P.M. The Confederacy's September 1861 victory here, at what also was known as the "Battle of the Hemp Bales" (you'll learn why if you visit), helped persuade Gov. Claiborne F. Jackson to come out of exile and call a special legislative session in Neosho, where his fellow pro-Confederates passed an Ordinance of Secession—even as pro-Union legislatures were meeting in Jefferson City to declare loyalty to the Union.

The bridge linking Lexington and Henrietta is a nasty affair, with a hair-raising gap at the outside of the lane where the curb has eroded away. Your best strategy is to capture the lane and let traffic pass once you exit the bridge.

0.0   Go west on High Street. Turn left onto Second Street and wind around to ride on the west side of the old depot

1.0   Turn right onto Spring Street, which becomes Santa Fe Trail.

1.5   Bear right to stay on Santa Fe Trail.

7.0   Turn right onto Old Highway 41.

7.5   Ride straight onto State Road 41.

10.0 Lamine.

21.0 Arrow Rock.

25.0 Hardeman.

35.0 Bear right onto County Road O ramp. In a quarter mile, turn left and ride under the highway.

36.0 Ride straight onto Lafayette Avenue, Marshall.

36.5 Turn right onto Arrow Street.

37.0 Route becomes SR 20.

46.5 Continue straight on SR 20; SR 127 joins route then leaves it 1 mile later.

53.5 Blackburn.

56.5 Alma, just off route to south.

62.0 Corder, just south off route.

67.0 Turn left at T to continue on SR 20.

68.0 Higginsville. Turn right onto Nineteenth Street.

69.5 Ride straight onto CR FF.

77.5 Turn right onto CR O.

83.0 Ride straight onto SR 13.

85.5 Lexington. Turn left to continue on SR 13; SR 224/Main Street joins route.

86.0 Follow SR 13/SR 224/Broadway. In 0.3 mile, bear right to continue on SR 13 as SR 224 leaves route. Cross the Missouri River.

92.0 Henrietta. Turn left onto CR H.

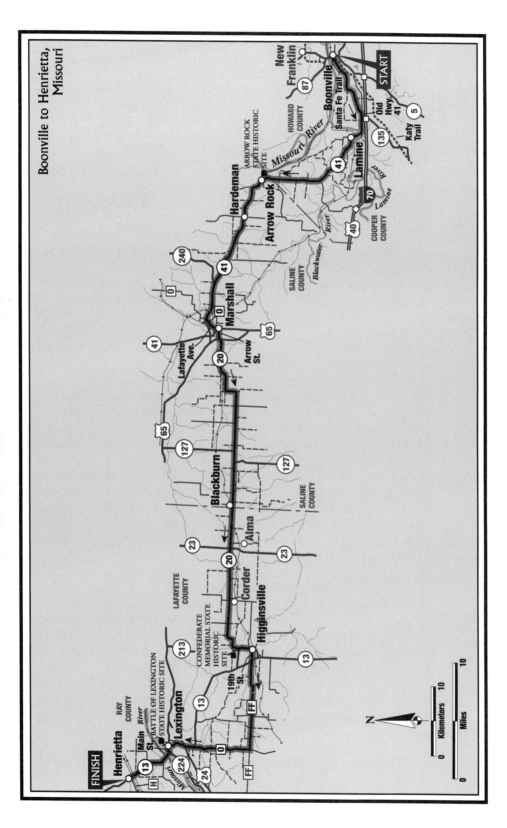

Boonville to Henrietta, Missouri

4 Henrietta to Weston, Missouri
86.5 miles (381 miles cumulative)

"The water we Drink, or the Common water of the missourie at this time, contains half a Comn Wine Glass of ooze or mud to every pint . . ."

—CAPT. WILLIAM CLARK
Thursday, June 21, 1804

As you've no doubt noticed, provided you're bicycling rather than armchair traveling, up to this point the route in Missouri is quite rural in nature and generally low on traffic. Conditions begin changing somewhere around Lawson, where, in addition to the still-abundant farms, you'll start noticing growing numbers of large new homes sprouting amidst ranchettes. Many of these are residences belonging to city commuters. By the time you hit County Road HH heading toward Platte City, traffic will be substantial, and you might feel as though you're racing those low-flying jets overhead, which are either approaching or just leaving the Kansas City International Airport, located only 3 or 4 miles south, as the 747 flies.

Among the little towns lining this stretch of the route is Camden, founded in 1836 near the site of Bluffton, which was settled twenty years earlier by families from Virginia, Kentucky, and Tennessee. At Mile 62, just before Smithville, if you go left rather than right at the T and proceed for 2 miles off the route, you'll come to Smiths Fork Park, a campground pleasantly situated adjacent to some athletic fields and behind the dam that impounds immense Smithville Lake. The reservoir, which reached full pool in 1982, is an exceedingly popular destination for anglers, who come to fish for largemouth bass, walleye, crappie, and other species. Higher and typically drier, wild turkeys and white-tailed deer may be seen in the timber stands thickly cloaking the lake's banks. A short distance farther up the main road from the campground sits the U.S. Army Corps of Engineers' **Jerry L. Litton Visitor Center** (U.S. Army Corps of Engineers, 16311 DD Highway North, Smithville, MO 64089; 816–532–0174), named for a late Missouri Sixth District congressman. Litton won the Democratic primary for the U.S. Senate election on August 3, 1976—only to be killed in a plane crash that same day, along with his wife and children, while en route to a victory celebration in Kansas City. Among several exhibits at the visitor center is a display of the lavish silver trophies won by the Litton family's prize Charolais cattle.

From the junction of State Road 273 and CR JJ (Mile 84.5), it's less than a mile south off the route to **Weston Bend State Park** (P.O. Box 115, 16600

Highway 45 North, Weston, MO 64098; 816–640–5443; www.mostateparks. com), another gem in the Missouri state parks system. It comes highly recommended as a spot for pitching your tent (have a gander at sites 32 and 33). A hilly, 1,133-acre mosaic of meadowed ridgetops and timbered ravines, Weston Bend provides one of the best panoramas of the river Missouri in the state of Missouri (watch for the huge tree growing out of the middle of an observation deck, and you'll know you've arrived at the overlook). The park's several large old barns owe their existence to the fact that the Weston area was, and is, a center of the Missouri tobacco-farming industry. The first crop was shipped down the Missouri and Mississippi Rivers in 1839, and today around seven million pounds of tobacco are raised and sold annually in Platte County.

At the park you also can learn a bit about the county's prehistoric residents, who can be traced back as far as the Middle Archaic Period, approximately 5,000 to 3,000 B.C. Subsequently, from around the time of Christ until the Europeans arrived, the Kansa and other tribes settled in villages, hacking out small farming operations in the larger valleys. They abandoned the area due to disease and warfare not many years before Lewis and Clark passed through.

Nearby Weston is a picturesque and historic village built on the trade of tobacco and hemp. Here, whiskey—to accompany the vice of tobacco, one supposes—has been produced at the McCormick Distillery since 1858. (Samples are available in a company store downtown.) Speaking of whiskey, three days before the Corps of Discovery visited the Weston Bend of the river, on the last of three nights at a camp at the mouth of the Kansas River (at the site of present Kansas City, Kansas), privates John Collins and Hugh Hall were caught dipping into the expedition's whiskey supplies while on guard duty. They stood court-martialed and were sentenced, respectively, to one hundred lashes and fifty lashes to the bare back.

There's a pair of historical museums you might want to visit to learn more about this corner of Missouri: the **Ben Ferrel Platte County Museum** (Third and Ferrel Streets, Platte City, MO 64079; 816–431–5121; open Tuesday through Saturday from noon to 4:00 P.M., March through October) and the **Weston Historical Museum** (601 Main Street, Weston, MO 64098; 816–386–2977; open year-round Tuesday through Saturday from 1:00 to 4:00 P.M. and Sunday from 1:30 to 5:00 P.M.)

Mileage Log

0.0 In Henrietta, ride west on CR H.
3.5 Turn left at the T onto CR T.
5.0 Camden.
7.5 Fleming.
10.5 Turn left onto SR 210.

11.5	Orrick. Turn right onto CR O.
22.5	Wood Heights. Turn right onto SR 10.
23.5	Turn left onto CR M.
26.5	Vibbard.
29.5	Ride straight onto CR C.
31.0	Turn left onto CR D.
33.5	Lawson. Turn left onto Pennsylvania Avenue.
34.0	Turn right onto Moss Street.
34.5	Turn left onto Salem Road.
35.0	Turn right onto CR MM toward Hidden Valley Golf Course.
40.5	Turn right onto CR BB.
42.0	Turn left onto 188th Street.
42.5	Road curves right to become Scott Street, left to become 189th Street, right to become Outer Road, left to become 192nd Street, then right to become Shanks Road.
44.5	Holt. Turn left onto unsigned SR 33.
46.0	Ride straight onto CR CC.
49.0	Turn left onto CR C.
51.5	Turn right onto CR W.
55.0	Paradise.
59.0	Turn left onto CR F.
61.0	Turn right, then left to remain on CR F.
62.0	Turn right at T to continue on CR F.
63.5	Smithville. CR F curves right to become First Street. At stop sign, turn right onto unsigned U.S. Highway 169 spur. After 0.1 mile turn right onto U.S. 169.
64.0	Turn left onto CR KK.
69.0	Turn left onto CR B.
70.0	Turn right onto North Winan Road.
72.5	Turn hard right onto unsigned Interurban Parkway toward Basswood RV Resort.
74.0	Turn left onto CR HH.
78.5	Ride over Interstate 29 and onto Main Street in Platte City.
79.0	Turn left onto unsigned Second Street. In 0.2 mile turn right onto SR 92/Branch Street.
79.5	Cross Platte River.
80.0	Tracy. Ride straight onto Belt Street.
80.5	Bear left onto SR 273.
84.5	At stop sign, ride straight onto CR JJ, which becomes Walnut Street.
86.5	Weston. Turn left onto Main Street, right onto Spring Street, then right onto Washington Street.

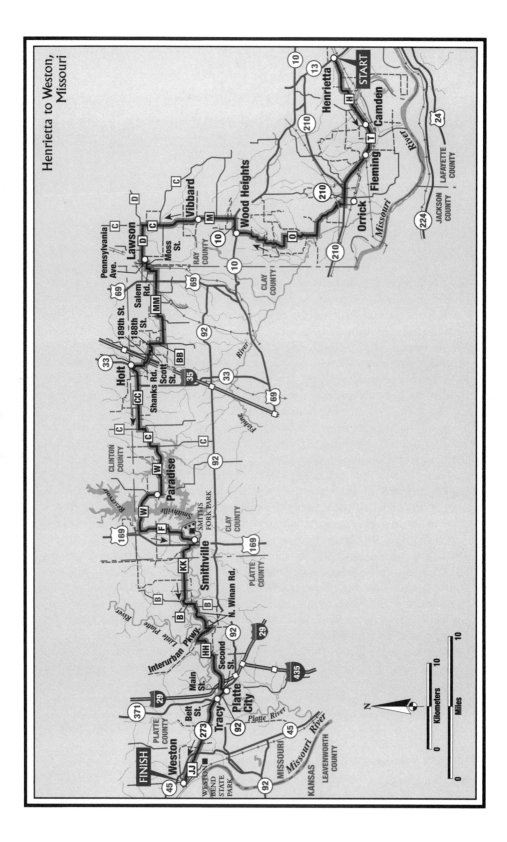

Henrietta to Weston, Missouri

5 Weston, Missouri to Falls City, Nebraska
75 miles (456 miles cumulative)

*". . . I had an extensive view of the Serounding Plains, which af-
forded one of the most pleasing prospects I ever beheld!"*
—CAPT. WILLIAM CLARK
Thursday, July 12, 1804

Not long after leaving Weston, you'll pass what could be termed a geographical oxymoron: a ski area in Missouri—specifically, the Snow Creek
Ski Resort. (Hopefully it will be green and not white when you zip by.) Later,
about 12 miles into the section, you'll skirt Lewis and Clark Village,
Missouri, population 142. It's the only town in the United States named after
the two explorers. Adjacent to the village is **Lewis and Clark State Park**
(801 Lake Crest Boulevard, Rushville, MO 64484; 816–579–5564; www.
mostateparks. com), where the camping is serviceable (but not nearly as
nice as that at Weston Bend State Park).

Soon you'll cross a narrow bridge spanning the Missouri and enter the
bustling minicity of Atchison, Kansas, where just north of town the Missouri
River welcomes Independence Creek to its waters. The creek was named by
Lewis and Clark in honor of their camping here on July 4, 1804, the twenty-
eighth birthday of the United States. If you want to look hard and long
enough in Atchison, you'll find at least five good museums. One of them celebrates an American explorer who traveled by air rather than water: Aviator
Amelia Earhart was born in her grandparents' house in Atchison on July 24,
1897, and grew up in the area. The **Amelia Earhart Birthplace Museum**
(223 North Terrace Street, Atchison, KS 66002; 913–367–4217) is open year-
round Monday through Saturday, 10:00 A.M. to 4:00 P.M., and Sunday, 1:00
to 4:00 P.M. To learn about the other museums in town, drop in at the visitor information center housed in the restored Santa Fe Depot (you ride right
by it, so you can't miss it).

As you get back into the country, you may suddenly notice that nearly
everyone driving a vehicle waves as he or she passes—Kansas has garnered
a reputation among touring cyclists as the friendliest state in the country,
and rightly so. North of Atchison, the route is characterized by rather steep
hills holding terrace farming, big barns, small country cemeteries, and the
occasional ornate but worn-down Victorian farmhouse. This northeast corner of Kansas is the state's glaciated region; it was covered by at least two of
the dozen or so glaciers that advanced across much of the northern United
States during the Pleistocene Epoch. A bedrock of limestones and shales is

sometimes buried beneath deep deposits of glacial drift, or soils, that the glaciers left behind as they retreated.

At Troy leave the route and ride 0.5 mile to the downtown district to view the classic town square with its streets of brick surrounding the century-old, Romanesque-style Doniphan County Courthouse. On the south side of the grand brick-and-block structure awaits a special treat: Peter Wolf Toth's *Tall Oak*, which the artist carved in 1978 from a huge bur oak log. Toth's goal was to complete at least one monument to a Native American tribe in every state of the nation—a goal that he's reached, and then some. This was the Hungarian native's twenty-ninth in a series of more than sixty sculptures (he's done more than one in some states and has also branched out into Canada). It is unique from the others in that the feathers, neck broach, and headband represent composites of the styles worn by this region's Iowa, Kickapoo, Pottawatomie, and Sac and Fox Indians.

At Sparks (Mile 44.5) leave the route and go 2 miles west on 240th Street, then turn north onto Elgin to reach the **Native American Heritage Museum** (1727 Elgin Road, Highland, KS 66035; 785-442-3304). Open Wednesday through Saturday from 10:00 A.M. to 5:00 P.M. and Sunday from 1:00 to 5:00 P.M., the site is maintained by the Kansas Historical Society. Housed in the old Highland Mission, a former Sac and Fox Indian mission situated along a branch of the Oregon Trail, the museum contains a wealth of crafts, artwork, interactive exhibits, and other information on the peoples who called this region home before Lewis and Clark came through—from the Paleoindians of some 12,000 years ago to the tribes that still reside on Kansas reservations.

Continuing north from Sparks, you'll come up against high river bluffs where loess *(luss)* soils like those you'll be seeing off and on for the next few hundred miles are well exposed; then, before reaching White Cloud, you'll come in right beside the muddy Missouri. At the Kansas-Nebraska border, stop to read the sign interpreting the history of how and when the area was first surveyed. Above this point, a cast-iron monument was erected in 1855, establishing the baseline of the important fortieth parallel.

Tiny Rulo, Nebraska, is in the vicinity of the Corps of Discovery's camp of July 13, 1804. Off route, across the river and about 4 miles back into Missouri, you'll find **Big Lake State Park** (204 Lake Shore Drive, Craig, MO 64437; 660-442-3770; www.mostateparks.com), where you can make like Lewis and Clark and camp alongside one of the Missouri River's largest remaining oxbow lakes.

Mileage Log

0.0 Ride north on Washington Street in Weston.
1.0 Turn left onto State Road 45.
7.0 Iatan.

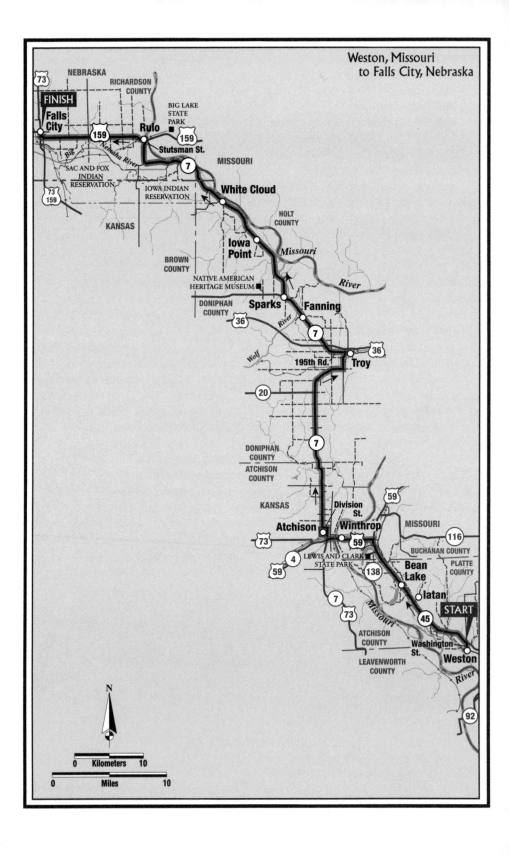

Weston, Missouri
to Falls City, Nebraska

9.0	Bean Lake.
12.5	Lewis and Clark State Park on left.
14.0	Turn left onto U.S. Highway 59.
16.5	Winthrop.
17.5	Enter Kansas.
18.0	Atchison. Turn right onto SR 7.
19.0	Turn left onto Division Street.
19.5	Turn right onto SR 7.
25.5	Enter Doniphan County.
35.5	Turn left to continue on SR 7.
37.0	Troy. Turn left onto West Locust, which becomes 195th Road.
39.0	Ride straight onto SR 7.
42.0	Fanning.
44.5	Sparks.
50.5	Iowa Point.
55.0	White Cloud.
56.5	Enter Iowa Indian Reservation.
57.5	Enter Nebraska.
61.5	Leave Iowa Indian Reservation.
66.0	Turn left onto Stutsman Street, Rulo. Ride straight onto U.S. 159.
75.0	Falls City. Turn right onto U.S. 73/Harlan Street.

6 Falls City, Nebraska to Council Bluffs, Iowa
99 miles (555 miles cumulative)

*". . . in this Situation the Storm which passd. over an open Plain
from the N. E. Struck our boat on the Starbd. quarter, and would
have thrown her up on the Sand Island dashed to pices in an
Instant, had not the party leeped out on the Leward Side and kept
her off with the assistance of the ancker & Cable, untill the Storm
was over . . ."*

—CAPT. WILLIAM CLARK
Saturday, July 14, 1804
Near present-day Indian Cave State Park

Falls City is several miles from the Missouri River, settled amidst a flat to
rolling landscape more typical of the Midwest than are the abrupt hills of
the river's valley. However, at a point 18 miles north of Falls City, you can
leave the route and ride east 5 miles on Spur 64E to a place that is anything
but flat: **Indian Cave State Park** (RR 1, Box 30, Shubert, NE 68437;
402–883–2575).

The 3,052-acre preserve is a gem—quite possibly, as the park brochure
proclaims, "Nebraska's Best Kept Secret." But be forewarned: If you leave
the route to camp here (a highly recommended activity), you might not get
back to the business of bike touring for a day or two. The park offers some
20 miles of hiking and mountain-biking trails winding along flat floodplains
and climbing up and over hills of loess. The elevation differential between
the highest hilltops and the river bottoms is an impressive 400 feet. A staggering variety of trees and shrubs thrive in the park's mix of dry upland,
damp slopeside, and flooded bottomland forests. You may learn to identify
red oak, bur oak, basswood, cottonwood, ironwood, bitternut hickory, green
ash, sycamore, and many other species. The park's diversity of habitats and
its location along the Central Flyway assure plenty of migrating birds in
spring and autumn, including waterfowl, shorebirds, raptors, and a host of
Neotropical songbirds, such as warblers and thrushes.

Find the trailhead for Trail #3, where an observation deck overhangs a
precipitous slope and provides a look down on an area not far from where
Lewis and Clark camped on July 14, 1804—on the banks of a Missouri that
was much more braided and unpredictable than today's relatively calm
river. Farther into the park, Trail #10 will lead you steeply to the top of
a knife-edge ridge, from which you can look south and west into a wild,

Meriwether Lewis, in spirit at least, still plies the waters of the lower Missouri River.

heavily forested piece of Nebraska that appears like something out of Willa Cather's early days. This is one of many places where the eastern hardwood forests meet the prairies of the West. Hit the right spot at the right moment, and you might hear, at the same instant, the muffled gobbling of wild turkeys emanating from a timbered north-facing slope below and a western meadowlark making its beautiful music in a high grassland clearing.

After descending along a road cut through hills of loess, you'll coast into Brownville, an antique of a town—among other "firsts" was the first telegraph office in Nebraska—then begin riding on the Steamboat Trace. The hiking-and-biking trail follows a grade that was abandoned by the Burlington Northern Railroad in 1992, then purchased by the Rails-to-Trails Conservancy (but only after a failed effort to launch a tourist train between Nebraska City and Brownville) and deeded in 1995 to the Nemaha Natural Resources District. The crushed limestone surface doesn't provide the smoothest of rides, but it's better than some of the gravel roads on any reasonable alternative routes! And the trail visits some quiet, seemingly pristine lowland environments.

The new Missouri River Basin Lewis & Clark Interpretive Trails and Visitor Center is slated to open in July 2004 just outside Nebraska City—the home, incidentally, of the founder of Arbor Day, J. Sterling Morton. The focus of the National Park Service facility will be on the 400 discoveries of flora and fauna made by the Lewis and Clark expedition. From Nebraska

City you'll cross the river into Iowa, where County Road L31 will have you flirting with Interstate 29 for several miles. Out there in the floodplain it seems like everyone's idea of what Iowa is—pancake flat. But not far to the east loom the Loess Hills, appearing like a mountain range relative to the terrain you'll be riding over.

This section ends at the Iowa West Trailhead in Council Bluffs, according to street signs a BICYCLE FRIENDLY COMMUNITY—a claim supported by the city's (as well as adjacent Omaha's) outstanding network of bike paths. From the trailhead you can follow one such bike path roughly 4 miles southwest to **Lake Manawa State Park** (1100 South Shore Drive, Council Bluffs, IA 51501; 712–366–0220). The 1,529-acre park encompasses its namesake oxbow lake, created after flooding in the early 1880s caused the Missouri River to shift its course and abandon the bend now making up the 660-acre lake. It's a fine place to camp, the buzzing of high-powered watercraft notwithstanding.

From the park it's 5 or 6 miles along a bike path to the **Western Historic Trails Center** (3434 Richard Downing Avenue, Council Bluffs, IA 51501; 712–366–4900). Open 9:00 A.M. to 6:00 P.M. daily, the low-profile, prairie-adapted stone-block and earth-berm structure backs right up against the Missouri River levee. Designed and built by the National Park Service, the center focuses on four east-to-west trails: the Lewis and Clark, Oregon, Mormon Pioneer, and California Trails. Outside, a footpath wends through alluvial lowlands adjacent to the Missouri River. While you won't see the grizzly bears, wolves, or elk that Lewis and Clark may have encountered here, you will get to view a large array of native flora and fauna still thriving in the area. You'll also see a marker commemorating Camp White Catfish, where Lewis, Clark, and company stayed for five nights during their upstream journey.

Mileage Log

0.0 Ride north from Falls City on U.S. Highway 73.
10.0 Turn right onto State Road 67.
16.5 Shubert off route 0.5 mile to west.
23.5 Nemaha.
27.5 Ride across U.S. 136 onto unsigned road, then curve right, dropping into Brownville. Ride across U.S. 136, then turn left onto the Steamboat Trace (suggested donation, $2.00 per riding day).
37.0 Peru.
49.5 Steamboat Trace Arbor Station Trailhead. Ride west on CR K.
52.5 Turn right onto CR 66. (Alternatively, to avoid gravel, ride 1 mile farther west on CR K, then turn right onto U.S. 75. After 1 mile, turn right onto SR 2, rejoining the route below at Mile 54.0 after riding east on SR 2 for 1 mile.)

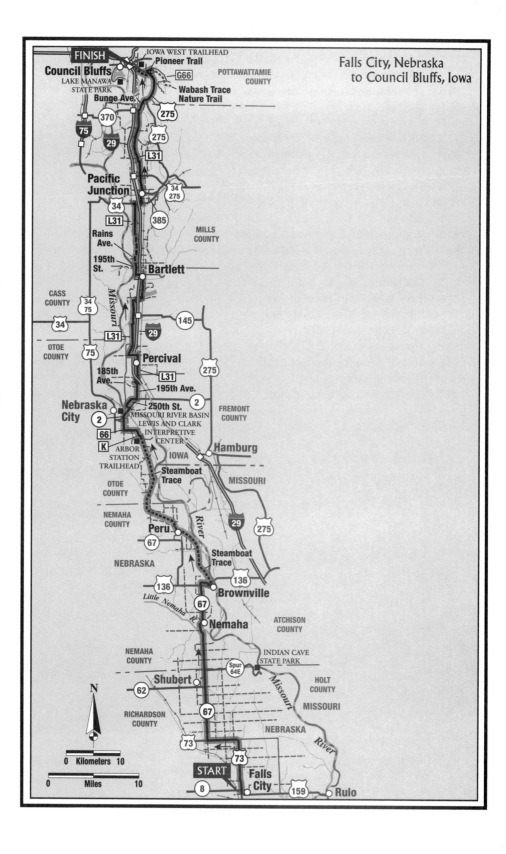

54.0	Turn right onto SR 2. Nebraska City just north off route. Missouri River Basin Lewis and Clark Interpretive Center on right.
55.0	Cross Missouri River into Iowa.
55.5	Turn left onto gravel 185th Avenue.
56.0	Turn right onto 250th Street.
57.5	Turn left at T onto 195th Avenue.
60.0	Ride over I–29. Route becomes CR L31.
61.5	Percival.
62.5	Turn left to cross over I–29, then go right to stay on CR L31.
63.0	Turn right to continue on CR L31.
72.0	Bartlett. Turn left to cross I–29, then right to continue on CR L31.
72.5	Route is gravel for next 3.5 miles.
80.5	Turn right to join U.S. 34 and pass under I–29, then go left to continue on CR L31.
81.5	Continue straight on Ellison Street/CR L31, Pacific Junction.
82.0	Turn right onto Lincoln Avenue/SR 385; in 0.2 mile turn left onto Front Street/CR L31.
90.5	Turn right onto Bunge Avenue/SR 370.
93.5	Turn left onto U.S. 275.
97.5	Turn right onto Pioneer Trail/CR G66; after 1 block turn right onto Wabash Trace Trail.
99.0	Iowa West Trailhead, Council Bluffs.

CHAPTER 2

Council Bluffs, Iowa to Pierre, South Dakota (486 miles)

L
ewis and Clark laid over for five nights, from July 22 through 26, 1804, at Camp White Catfish, located just south of present-day Council Bluffs. They did so not only to give the men rest and to get equipment repaired or replaced, but also to ready reports for shipment back to President Jefferson and, they hoped, to hold council with the local Oto Indians. Interpreter George Drouillard and Pvt. Pierre Cruzatte were dispatched to find Oto and Pawnee villages along the Platte River, which they did—but they found them empty, their inhabitants off hunting bison. The party finally met up with a group of Otos and Missouris on August 2, the day after Clark's thirty-fourth birthday. They had waited four days for the Indians, after a lone Missouri Indian informed them that he would bring in a small group of his fellows who were hunting elk nearby. Their official meeting took place on August 3 at a spot the captains called the Council Bluff (but which is well north of today's city of Council Bluffs), just outside Fort Calhoun, Nebraska. Clark wrote that the site was ". . . well Calculated for a Tradeing establishment," and, indeed, Fort Atkison was established there in 1819–20 to facilitate relations between the Indians and white fur traders.

It was the expedition's first, but by no means last, official meeting with indigenous peoples. Another first—and this was a first *and* a last for the entire journey—occurred seventeen days later, near today's Sioux City. On August 20 Sgt. Charles Floyd died of what Clark called a "Biliose Chorlick"— thought to be a ruptured appendix that led to infection. On August 22, by way of an election (the first one west of the Mississippi involving American citizens) held near Elk Point, South Dakota, Patrick Gass was chosen to replace Floyd as sergeant. On the next day, August 23, J. Fields killed the party's first bison—definitely not the last one they would kill and consume as they proceeded on their journey.

Between Council Bluffs and Sioux City, the riding tends to be either table flat or very hilly, depending on whether you're riding in the Missouri River floodplain or in the flanking Loess Hills. The roads around both of these Iowa cities can be very busy, so avoid riding them during the morning and afternoon commuting hours. From north of Sioux City to Yankton, South Dakota, the route follows a network of generally two-lane local roads with no shoulder, but which typically have sound surfaces and good sight distances. West of Yankton recreational vehicle traffic can be very heavy, as it can be around any of the lake/dam access areas (Fort Randall, Chamberlain, Fort Thompson). Road 1806 out of Fort Thompson, by comparison, carries less traffic while dishing up extreme climbs and dramatic vistas. The actual Lewis and Clark Trail through this area—the Missouri River, that is—is now less a river than a string of huge reservoirs, peppered with isolated communities and seasonal services. This trend continues into North Dakota and eastern Montana.

The section ends in Pierre, a midsized town of around 14,000 residents—making it the second smallest state capital in the United States, runner-up only to Montpelier, Vermont.

7 Council Bluffs to Onawa, Iowa
67 miles (622 miles cumulative)

"This being a good Situation and much nearer the Otteaus town than the Mouth of the Platt, we Concluded to delay at this place a few days and Send for Some of the Chiefs of that nation, to let them know of the Change of Government, the wishes of our government to Cultivate friendship with them, the Objects of our journy and to present them with a flag and Some Small presents."
—CAPT. WILLIAM CLARK
Sunday, July 22, 1804
At Camp White Catfish

As you head north the urban tentacles of Council Bluffs reach all the way to Crescent; north of there, though, you'll reclaim an Iowa that is more rural in character, a broad valley surrounded by low hills of loess. At one point you may spot the slopes of the Mount Crescent Ski Area far in the western distance. Then, about a mile before Honey Creek, you'll see a sign on the left marking the **Hitchcock Nature Area** (Pottawattamie County Conservation Board; 712–545–3283). The 806-acre preserve offers primitive camping and contains miles of hiking trails zigzagging through oak-hickory forests and along dry ridgetop prairies. The latter support mixed grasses more similar to the species found in western Nebraska than to those of the tallgrass prairies more often associated with Iowa.

Between Crescent and Honey Creek you'll pedal along a portion of the Old Lincoln Highway, the first transcontinental roadway in the United States. The plan for a motorway from New York City to San Francisco was laid out on September 1, 1912, by Carl G. Fisher, president of the Prest-O-Lite company and "father of the Indianapolis 500." Speaking at an Indianapolis dinner party attended by his colleagues in the auto industry, Fisher reportedly said, "A road across the United States! Let's build it before we're too old to enjoy it!" He predicted that it would take $10 million to build, and he solicited funds right then and there. A half hour after the rousing talk, Frank A. Sieberling of Goodyear cut Fisher a check for $300,000—without even consulting his board of directors. Or so the story goes, anyway. Others, such as Henry Ford, thought the idea was ridiculous and offered no help whatsoever. Ford believed that government, not industry, should finance construction of a road such as this.

Later, another supporter of the highway, Dr. Frank Crane, wrote, "It would be the path of progress, the river course of humanity, part of the golden girdle of the earth. It would liberate the farmer from the shackles of bad roads, as the Emancipation Proclamation freed the slaves," explaining in part, perhaps, why the road was named after Abraham Lincoln. Fisher over-optimistically believed the road would be finished in time for the 1915 Panama-Pacific International Exposition in San Francisco; in fact, what he called "America's Coast-to-Coast Rock Highway" wasn't completely paved until 1925.

One problem with a designated bicycle trail such as this is that the designers must always pick one road to the exclusion of others, yet the best route for cycling can't possibly lead past all the interesting sites in any given area. Such is the case north of Council Bluffs, where busy traffic precluded the route taking in one of most compelling sites along the entire Iowa-Nebraska border. Still, there is a way to get there, and if you are a birding or history buff, it is one side trip you do *not* want to miss. Just north of Loveland, turn left onto County Road G14, which passes under some railroad tracks and then over Interstate 680 to become State Road 362. After 6 miles on this oddly red-surfaced, low-traffic road, you'll enter **DeSoto National Wildlife Refuge** (1434 316th Lane, Missouri Valley, IA 51555; 712–642–4121; midwest.fws.gov/desoto). A half mile later you'll pass the left-hand turn into **Wilson Island State Park** (32801 Campground Lane, Missouri Valley, IA 51555; 712–642–2069)—which offers excellent camping, by the way—then loop around the southeastern end of the refuge lake and enter Nebraska. You'll come in alongside the Missouri River, reenter Iowa, and encounter the turn for the refuge visitor center at just under 12 miles since leaving the trail.

Inside you will discover one of the most incredible and priceless bounties of booty imaginable: goods that were being shipped aboard the steamboat *Bertrand* toward Fort Benton, Montana, in 1865—the last year of the Civil War, just sixty-one years after Lewis and Clark passed the spot—when the 178-foot stern-wheeler went down. It was one of more than 800 stern-wheelers and side-wheelers that sank or were otherwise stranded in the snag-strewn river between St. Louis and Fort Benton during the days of the steamboat. The *Bertrand* was quickly mired in mud, which served to protect its contents for more than a century until it was discovered on DeSoto NWR in 1968 and excavated a year later. Tools, clothing, liquor, canned goods, plates and cutlery, weapons, and much more can be viewed, all of it in excellent repair and sealed in airtight display cases to protect it from the elements. You can also visit the dig site, where the hull of the *Bertrand* still lies.

And then there's the wildlife, which appears to be a constant: The Corps of Discovery camped in the vicinity on August 3, 1804, when Clark wrote about the hordes of geese—and mosquitoes. Today upwards of 800,000 lesser snow geese stop at the refuge on migration, as do plenty of mallards, mergansers, canvasbacks, and other varieties of diving and dabbling ducks.

To return to the route, if you have a high tolerance for heavy traffic and big trucks, you can ride east on U.S. Highway 30 (it does have a small black-

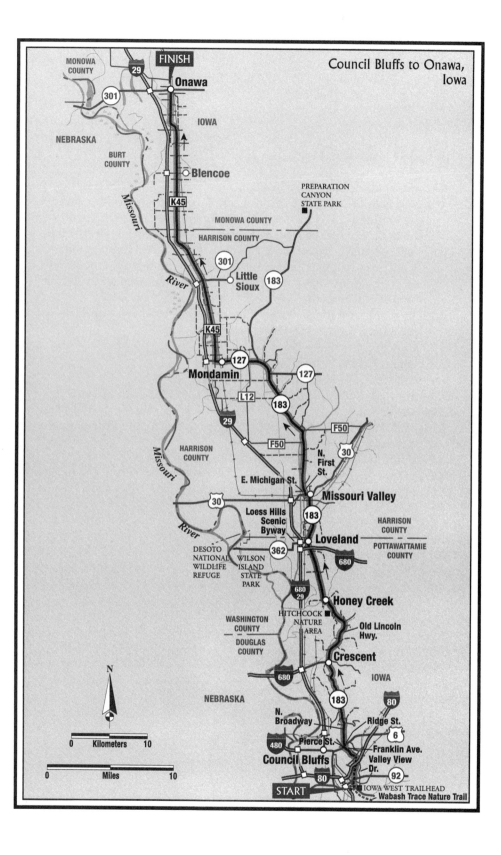

Council Bluffs to Onawa,
Iowa

top shoulder and adjacent gravel verge), which after 7.5 miles will take you to the trail in the town of Missouri Valley. Otherwise, backtrack the far more peaceful 12 miles to Loveland.

Mileage Log

0.0 Begin at the Iowa West Trailhead in Council Bluffs. To get into and out of the city, ride onto the path between the trailhead and Lewis Central High School. The path crosses the campus of the Iowa School for the Deaf, then parallels SR 92 for almost 0.5 mile before going north along Valley View Drive. After passing under I–80, go left along Mall Drive, then right onto Bennet Avenue, left onto Franklin Avenue (which becomes Lincoln Avenue), and right onto Pierce Street.

4.5 Turn left onto Ridge Street, then ride straight across Kanesville Boulevard onto North Broadway/SR 183.

11.5 Crescent.

17.5 Honey Creek.

22.5 Ride under I–680; Loveland.

27.0 Missouri Valley. Turn left onto SR 183/ U.S. 30/Sixth Street.

27.5 Turn right following SR 183. West Erie joins route; U.S. 30 leaves route. In 0.2 mile turn left onto East Michigan then jog right onto North First Street.

38.5 Continue straight on SR 183; SR 127 joins route.

40.0 SR 183 leaves route.

43.0 Mondamin. Route becomes Maple Street.

43.5 Turn right onto CR K45/Austin Avenue.

50.5 Little Sioux, off route 1 mile.

55.5 Enter Monowa County.

60.0 Blencoe. Route becomes Main Street/CR K45.

67.0 Onawa.

8
Onawa, Iowa to Vermillion, South Dakota
87 miles (709 miles cumulative)

". . . Serj. Floyd Died with a great deal of Composure, before his death he Said to me, 'I am going away' I want you to write me a letter.' We buried him on top of the bluff ½ Mile below a Small river to which we Gave his name . . ."

—CAPT. WILLIAM CLARK
Monday, August 20, 1804

If you tire of the flat and the wind, you can get some relief (in more than one sense of the word) by exploring those intriguing hills to the east that you've been looking at since the Kansas-Nebraska border. They truly are a world apart from the flats below. From Onawa it's easy to leave the route and access a portion of the **Loess Hills National Scenic Byway,** a network of roads that explore what many consider to be Iowa's finest natural treasure. Roughly 200 miles long, yet rarely wider than 10 miles, the Loess Hills stand along the western edge of Iowa like a high bunker. Loess (German for "loose"), a generic term for fine-grain loam deposited by the wind, is found in many locations across the globe; but only one other place on earth—in the Yellow River Valley of western China—can claim accumulations as impressive as Iowa's Loess Hills. The hills formed after fine, glacially ground soils were hauled in and deposited by the Missouri River then, over the course of thousands of years, driven by westerly winds into ever-growing dunes.

The stretch of the byway from Turin, east of Onawa, to where you would rejoin the main route at Sergeant Bluff, takes in an interesting part of Loess Hills. It winds through the settlements of Castana, Rodney, and Smithland before descending to meet State Road 982, which runs northwesterly directly along the point where the hills meet the Missouri River floodplain. Alternatively, you could experience a night in the Loess Hills without having to ride much in them by booking a room at the **Country Homestead Bed and Breakfast** (22133 Larpenteur Memorial Road, Turin, IA 51059; 712–353–6772), located a mile north of Turin

If you'd prefer to jump onto the byway even farther south, a good place to do so is at Mondamin (see previous map section, Mile 43.0). This allows you to visit peaceful **Preparation Canyon State Park** (c/o Lewis and Clark State Park, 21914 Park Loop, Onawa, IA 41040; 712–423–2829), with its ridgetop trails, walk-in campsites, and lofty overlook where an interpretive sign speculates on what the landscape below would have looked like when the Corps of Discovery viewed it. What were predominantly hillside and ridgetop prairies when the explorers came through is now a mosaic of crop fields, forests resulting from the suppression of wildfires and loss of grazing bison, and a few prairies that have hung on along the steep, sun-blasted southern slopes. More than 300 plant species grow in these hills, where the tallgrass prairie of the Midwest merges with the short- and mixed-grass prairies of the Great Plains. (Preparation Canyon's name, incidentally, derives from a small Mormon settlement that emerged near here in 1853, established as a "School of Preparation for the Life Beyond.")

The roughly 200-mile Loess Hills National Scenic Byway is made up of a paved spine, off of which branch numerous spurs and loops, both paved and gravel, penetrating the more inaccessible parts of the hills. A mountain bike is recommended for taking full advantage of the unpaved portions. For a detailed map/brochure, contact Golden Hills Resource Conservation and Development, 712 Highway 6 South, P.O. Box 189, Oakland, IA 51560; (712) 482-3029; www.goldenhillsrcd.org.

Back along the main route a few miles west of Onawa, then back off the route, is **Lewis and Clark State Park** (21914 Park Loop, Onawa, IA 51040; 712-423-2829). The park sits on Blue Lake, an oxbow formed by the Missouri. In addition to camping, hiking, and other activities, here you can inspect a full-scale replica of the *Discovery*, Lewis and Clark's keelboat, which was constructed in the park by volunteers, as well as reproductions of the party's two pirogues. The park also celebrates a Lewis and Clark Festival annually in mid-June.

As you make your way through Sioux City by way of a route that is . . . most interesting, as you will see, know that the **Sgt. Floyd Monument**, a tall obelisk marking the grave of the Lewis and Clark expedition member, is situated off U.S. Highway 75 at a point not far south of where you pass under that highway (Mile 44.5 below). Similarly, the **Sgt. Floyd Riverboat Museum and Welcome Center** is several blocks south of the route from Eighth Street and Hamilton Boulevard. Here the M.V. *Sergeant Floyd* contains displays on Lewis and Clark, the fur trade, and the storied roles in river transportation and trade that the Missouri River and Sioux City have played. The museum, located at 1000 Larsen Park Road, Sioux City, IA 51103 (712-279-0198; www.siouxcity.org/museum), is open daily 8:00 A.M. to 6:00 P.M. May through September and 9:00 A.M. to 6:00 P.M. the rest of the year. And brand new as of late 2002 in Sioux City: the **Lewis and Clark Interpretive Center,** located just southeast of the Sgt. Floyd Riverboat Center at 900 Larsen Park Road, Sioux City, IA 51101 (712-224-5242). The center, which focuses on such topics as Sgt. Floyd and the flora and fauna of the region, is open free-of-charge Tuesday through Saturday from 9 A.M. to 5 P.M. and Saturday noon to 5 P.M.

Even if you weren't up for heading into Iowa's own version of mountains earlier, you'll still get up close and personal with the Loess Hills as you head north from Sioux City on SR 12. The **Dorothy Pecaut Nature Center** (4500 Sioux River Road, Sioux City, IA 51109; 712–258–0838; www.woodbury parks.com), open Tuesday through Saturday 9:00 A.M. to 5:00 P.M. and Sunday 1:00 to 5:00 P.M., is a modern, barn-inspired structure that houses outstanding displays on the flora, fauna, and geology of the Loess Hills. Here you can pick up all sorts of little-known facts; for example, a layer of volcanic ash found within the Loess Hills resulted from eruptions more than 700,000 years ago. Another display features a cutaway of the hills and adjacent floodplain, demonstrating how they interact with and affect each other. Outside, nature trails wend through forest and prairie.

Back on the highway and just north of the nature center is **Stone State Park** (5001 Talbot Road, Sioux City, IA 51103; 712–255–4698). In addition to pleasant primitive camping, the park encompasses roads and trails—the latter including some for mountain biking—that climb high and proffer long-range views of the surrounding hills and river plain.

Mileage Log

0.0   Continue north from Onawa on County Road K45.
1.0   Turn left onto CR K42.
4.0   Ride over Interstate 29.
12.5 Turn left at T to continue on CR K42 (160th Street goes right, over the interstate and into Whiting).
14.5 Berry Avenue.
20.5 Enter Woodbury County. Route becomes CR K42/Charles Avenue.
21.5 Turn right onto SR 141.
22.0 Ride over I–29.
23.0 Turn left onto CR K45; Sloan.
29.5 Salix.
35.5 Turn right onto CR K29/Lakeport Road; Sergeant Bluff.
40.0 Turn left onto Southern Hills Drive.
40.5 Turn right onto South Lakeport Street; Sioux City.
42.5 Turn left onto Morningside Avenue.
43.0 Continue straight onto Transit Avenue.
44.5 Turn left onto Cunningham Drive. Ride under U.S. 75 and railroad tracks.
45.5 Turn left onto Dace Avenue.
46.0 Turn right onto Virginia Street
46.5 Turn left onto Sixth Street. In 0.1 mile turn right onto Jennings Street. Six blocks later, go left onto Eleventh Street; 3 blocks after that, head right on Nebraska Street and immediately left onto Twelfth Street. In 4 blocks turn left onto Summit Street, which curves right to become Bluff Street. Go right onto Eighth Street for 7 blocks, then left onto Fourteenth Street and immediately

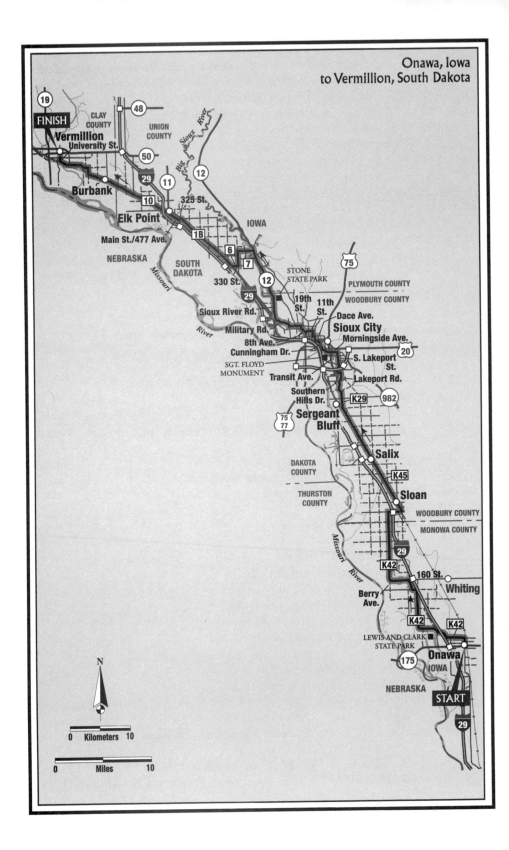

Onawa, Iowa
to Vermillion, South Dakota

right onto Center Street. Five blocks later turn left onto Nine-teenth Street then, a little over a mile later, right onto Casselman Street. In 0.5 mile turn left onto Military Road and about 1.5 miles later, right onto Riverside Boulevard. This becomes SR 12.

55.0   Enter Plymouth County.

60.0   Turn left onto unsigned CR 7. Enter Union County, South Dakota.

61.5   Turn left to stay on CR 7.

63.0   Turn right onto 330 Street/CR 6.

63.5   Jefferson. Turn right onto CR 1B.

71.0   Turn left onto 325 Street/CR 9. In 0.1 mile turn right onto Main Street/477 Avenue/I–29 Business Loop. Elk Point.

73.0   Ride under I–29 onto CR 10.

79.5   Enter Clay County.

81.0   Burbank.

83.0   Curve right over railroad tracks.

87.0   Vermillion. Curve right onto University Street.

9 Vermillion to Springfield, South Dakota
67 miles (776 miles cumulative)

". . . our Dog was so Heeted and fatigued we was obliged [to] Send him back to the Creek . . ."

—CAPT. WILLIAM CLARK
Saturday, August 25, 1804
Near Spirit Mound

Vermillion is an attractive little college town, home to the University of South Dakota. Fort Vermillion—whose moniker derived from the Sioux name for the Vermillion River, which alluded to the thickets of red willows growing along the river's course—was established here in 1835 by the American Fur Company, twenty-one years after the Corps of Discovery passed through. The low prairie hill known as Spirit Mound, located 7 miles north of town, is one of the most significant Lewis and Clark sites in all of South Dakota, as it is one of a handful of places where historians can point to a place where they know the explorers actually stood.

Known as *Paha Wakan* to the Sioux, the oddly isolated and symmetrical topographical feature was believed by the region's tribes to be the home of spirits that would kill any human that came close to it. The legend was apparently enough to make the intrepid explorers *want* to get close to it, and Lewis and Clark, along with their dog and eight or nine of their men, spent most of the sweltering day of August 25, 1804, hiking to and exploring Spirit Mound. The party encountered no miniature bow-and-arrow-wielding devils there, but from the top of the mound they did look down, according to Clark, on *". . . a most butifull landscape; Numerous herds of buffalow were Seen feeding in various directions . . ."* In 2002 a group of citizens in the Spirit Mound Trust succeeded in getting the private lands encompassing the site (a feed lot) under state control, and they've begun restoring it to a 320-acre native prairie.

If you're a fan of classical or world-beat music, you won't want to miss **The Shrine to Music Museum** (414 East Clark Street, Vermillion, SD 57069; 605–677–5306). Open Monday through Friday 9:00 A.M. to 4:30 P.M., Saturday 10:00 A.M. to 4:30 P.M., and Sunday 2:00 to 4:30 P.M., the museum is located on the campus of the University of South Dakota. Among more than 5,000 musical artifacts on display from the Americas, Europe, the Orient, the Middle East, and elsewhere are antique music boxes, an extremely rare Antonio Stradivari guitar, a beautifully hand-painted Persian drum, and a trombone shaped like a dragon. To find the museum, go 1 block after turning onto Main Street at Mile 0.5 below, then turn right onto Yale Street and continue for 3 blocks.

Situated several blocks north of the music museum, but still on the university campus (just west of Ratingen Street near the DakotaDome), is the **W. H. Over Museum** (605–677–5228; www.usd.edu/whover), open 9:00 A.M. to 5:00 P.M. weekdays and 1:00 to 4:30 P.M. weekends. The museum was named for paleontologist-archaeologist-naturalist William Henry Over, who, despite having only an eighth-grade education, served as the university museum's curator from 1913 to 1948, a period during which he cataloged holdings and vastly improved the museum's presentations. Over also conducted archaeological, fossil, and faunal investigations in the region under the auspices of the museum. The W. H. Over Museum includes displays on the prehistoric cultures of the region, as well as exhibits on fossil finds, flora and fauna, the Lewis and Clark expedition, and more.

Yankton was the capital of the Dakota Territory for more than twenty years, from 1861 until 1883, when the capital was moved to Bismarck. Yet, wrote author Ted Morgan in *A Shovel of Stars*, ". . . Yankton stagnated. It was less a capital than a campsite for traders, trappers, and land agents. . . . The Ash Hotel was notable for its dirt floors, its blanket partitions, and its bed sharing."

Today west of Yankton the Gavins Point Dam backs up Lewis and Clark Lake, the downstreammost in South Dakota's chain of large Missouri River reservoirs. If you leave the route to cross the nearly 2-mile-long bridge leading over the dam, look ahead into Nebraska and you'll see the **U.S. Army Corps of Engineers Visitor Center** (402–667–7873) sitting high on Calumet Bluff. It was at the base of the bluff where Lewis and Clark held their first council with friendly Yankton Sioux on August 29, 1804. To reach the visitor center, turn right onto State Road 121 after exiting the dam, then turn right again in 0.5 mile. Inside are some good displays, primarily on Lewis and Clark and other historical matters but also one explaining the local habitats of wetlands, bottomland forest, prairie, and river. Outside, a short trail winds through the Dorian Prairie Garden, with its native grasses and wildflowers.

Back in South Dakota and west of the Gavins Point Dam is the **Lewis and Clark Recreation Area** (43349 SD Highway 52, Yankton, SD 57078; 605–668–2985; www.state.sd.us/gfp/sdparks). Although the camping here is somewhat industrial strength, you can locate some primitive tent sites a short ways west of where you start to leave the park (at Mile 42.5 below). If you'd like something even less populated, continue on to the primitive **Sand Creek Campground** (South Dakota Department of Game, Fish, and Parks, 605–773–3391), found in a quiet, estuarial-like setting about 5 miles after turning onto Apple Tree Road (Mile 57.0 below), or, a few miles beyond that, the South Dakota Department of Game, Fish, and Parks campground in Springfield. (For yet another camping option in the area, see the next section's narrative.)

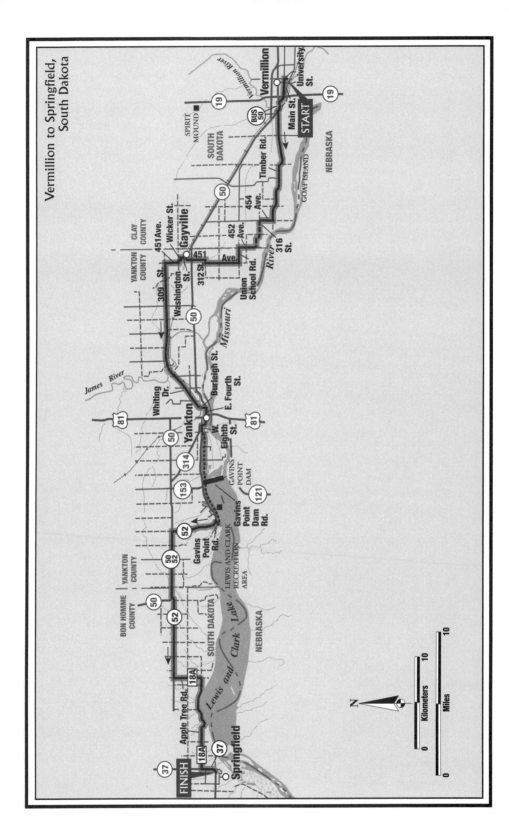

Vermillion to Springfield,
South Dakota

Mileage Log

0.0   Vermillion, begin riding north on University Street.

0.5   Turn left onto Main Street.

2.5   Turn left onto Business SR 50.

3.0   Turn left onto SR 19, then immediately right onto Timber Road.

11.5   Curve right onto 454 Avenue.

12.5   Turn left onto 316 Street. Route becomes hard-packed dirt and gravel.

14.5   Curve right onto 452 Avenue. Enter Yankton County; pavement resumes.

15.5   Curve left onto Union School Road.

16.5   Curve right onto 451 Avenue.

18.0   Curve right onto 312 Street, then immediately left back onto 451 Avenue.

20.0   Gayville. Cross SR 50 and curve right onto Brown Street, then turn left onto Washington Street.

20.5   Curve left onto Armstrong Street, then go right onto Wicker Street.

21.0   Curve left, then right to return to 451 Avenue.

22.0   Turn left onto 309 Street.

29.5   Route becomes Whiting Drive.

33.0   Yankton. At unsigned intersection, turn left onto Burleigh Street. Cross railroad tracks.

33.5   Turn right onto East Fourth Street.

35.0   Turn left onto West Eighth Street/SR 52.

35.5   Cross over and ride onto bike path paralleling south side of highway.

39.0   Bike path goes through the Lewis and Clark Marina and Resort then continues beyond the Gavins Point Dam Road.

41.0   Lewis and Clark Recreation Area Campground.

42.5   Bear right on the bike path, passing an entrance station. Climb for 0.3 mile on Gavins Point Road, then turn left onto SR 52.

46.0   Turn left following SR 52; SR 50 joins route.

50.0   Enter Bon Homme County.

51.0   Turn left following SR 52; SR 50 leaves route.

57.0   Turn left onto County Road 18A/Apple Tree Road.

66.0   Turn left onto SR 37.

67.0   Curve right to stay on SR 37; Springfield.

10 Springfield to Burke, South Dakota
94 miles (870 miles cumulative)

> *"At 9 I went out with one of our men, who had killed a buffaloe and left his hat to keep off the vermin and beasts of prey; but when we came to the place, we found the wolves had devoured the carcase and carried off the hat."*
>
> —SGT. PATRICK CASS
> Saturday, September 8, 1804

If you're willing to make a roughly 10-mile side trip (one-way), you'll find yourself in one of the most beautiful parks located anywhere along the Missouri River. From Springfield go to Mile 5 of the log below, then leave the route and continue south on State Road 37 to cross into Nebraska. Turn west onto SR 12 and go through tiny Niobrara, then cross the Niobrara River near its mouth and you'll come to the entrance of **Niobrara State Park** (P.O. Box 226, Niobrara, NE 68760; 402–857–3373). A 1,260-acre expanse of meadowed ridgetops, hardwood-embellished north slopes, and rich bottomlands, the park features tent-camping sites nestled in thickets of juniper, hackberry, and ash; cabins are also available to rent for the night (reservations recommended). As you bike or hike through certain parts of the park—the grassy ridgetops and south slopes in particular—you'll get a definite sense that you're getting into the West. Elsewhere, on the north slopes and in the bottomlands, things still appear quite midwestern in nature.

An option while visiting Niobrara State Park is to arrange for a two-hour guided river trip aboard the *Little Pearl*, an eleven-passenger motor-powered inflatable raft. After getting picked up in the park, you'll be shuttled upstream to Verdel Landing, then return by way of one of the wildest stretches of the Missouri River remaining east of Montana, in the company of a captain/interpreter. Call the park for additional information.

As you continue west toward Marty along excellent cycling roads, the landscape progressively turns drier. The hills surrounding Choteau Creek look as though they should be teeming with bison, but spotting a wild turkey is more likely. Looking south at the distant bluffs lining the Nebraska side of the river, you'll see that the north slopes are cloaked in timber and shrubbery, while the area you're riding through is quite barren, except in the protected, brush-choked draws. You'll then climb out of the dissected river country to ride amidst rolling crop fields as you approach Marty, home to the Marty Indian School, established in 1922 by Father Sylvester Eisenman.

The view from Chief Standing Bear Memorial Bridge, near Niobrara, Nebraska.

From 1948 until 1975 the boarding school was run by St. Paul's Catholic Church, a period during which it gained a reputation as one of the worst Indian schools. In 1998 the church formally asked for forgiveness from the American Indians who attended the school during those years, many of whom suffered beatings and other humiliations from priests and nuns. The school is still in operation, now run by the Yankton Sioux Tribe; the spot seems eerily serene today.

Forty-eight miles into the day's ride you'll cross the **Fort Randall Dam,** where tours of the power plant are available thrice daily Memorial Day through Labor Day (625–487–7845). The dam was begun in 1946 and completed ten years later, to the total tune of $200 million. As you ride across the dam, look to your left and you'll see the Missouri River; to the right you'll see Lake Francis Case. Named after a former South Dakota congressman, the lake reaches upstream for more than 100 miles, all the way to the Big Bend Dam near Fort Thompson.

On the far side of the dam, drop down to the left to visit the site of the Fort Randall Military Post, established one hundred years before the completion of the Fort Randall Dam for the purpose of helping maintain peace on the rolling plains of the Missouri Plateau. Among the "guests" here was the great Sioux warrior Sitting Bull, who was held prisoner of war for nearly two years at Fort Randall after surrendering to U.S. troops on July 19, 1881.

Sitting Bull had been a wanted man since Custer's 1876 defeat at the Little Bighorn. Fort Randall was abandoned in 1892, yet you still can visit the site of the parade ground and view the evocative ruins of the fort's 1856 chalkstone chapel.

To the southeast lies the **Karl E. Mundt National Wildlife Refuge** (Lake Andes NWR Complex, 38672 2912st Street, Lake Andes, SD 57356; 605–487–7603), which encompasses one of South Dakota's last remaining stretches of natural Missouri River bottomland. Waterfowl, shorebirds, and songbirds—warblers, grosbeaks, orioles—flock in by the thousands during the annual spring and fall migrations. In winter several hundred bald eagles gather in the refuge to fish the open waters of the Missouri. In fact, the growing congregations of our national bird were what spawned the creation of the refuge. As dams were completed along the Missouri, more and more native habitat was inundated; here, however, in the open tailwaters of the Fort Randall Dam, eagles found a veritable smorgasbord of fish and waterfowl, as well as adjacent stands of mature cottonwoods perfect for roosting. In a partnership involving 7-Eleven Food Stores and the National Wildlife Federation (NWF), the former raised a quarter million dollars though the sale of endangered species drinking cups. The money was transferred to the NWF, which in turn used it to purchase 780 acres of river bottom. Administration of the preserve was transferred to the U.S. Fish & Wildlife Service in December 1974. Because of the sensitive nature of the habitat and its occupants, the refuge is closed to public use; regardless, the eagle population peaks in December and January, when you're least likely to be cycling through.

It was a few miles downstream of today's Fort Randall Dam, incidentally, that the Corps of Discovery took aboard a new member: a live prairie dog. The men had captured the "barking squirrel" after coercing it out of its subterranean quarters by pouring several barrels of water down a burrow hole.

Mileage Log

0.0   Springfield. Ride west on SR 37.

5.0   Ride straight onto County Road 18.

12.5 Cross Choteau Creek; enter Charles Mix County. Route becomes CR 2.

21.5 395 Street becomes 310 Avenue.

27.5 Turn right onto 390 Avenue.

34.5 Marty. At T turn left onto CR 22/303 Street. In 0.1 mile turn right onto 388 Avenue/CR 21.

40.5 Turn left onto SR 46/297 Street.

46.0 Ride straight onto U.S. Highway 18/281; SR 46 ends. Pickstown.

47.0 Cross Missouri River. Fort Randall Dam.

58.5 Continue straight on U.S. 18; U.S. 281 leaves route.

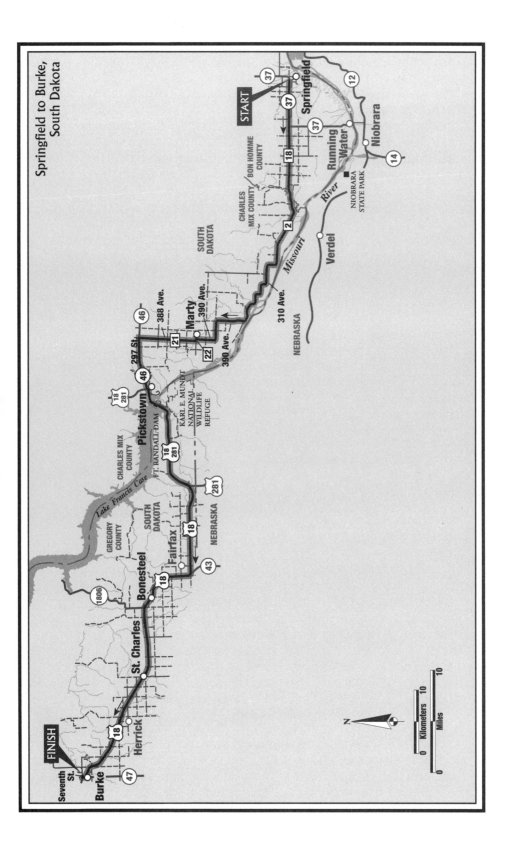

Springfield to Burke, South Dakota

67.5 Turn right to continue on U.S. 18.

69.0 Fairfax, 1 mile off route.

73.0 Bonesteel.

74.0 SR 1806.

81.0 St. Charles.

87.0 Herrick, 1 mile off route.

94.0 Burke. Turn right into town; 0.1 mile later turn right onto unsigned Seventh Street.

11 Burke to Fort Thompson, South Dakota
93.5 miles (963.5 miles cumulative)

". . . this senery already rich pleasing and beatiful was still farther hightened by immence herds of Buffaloe, deer Elk and Antelopes which we saw in every direction feeding on the hills and plains."
—CAPT. MERIWETHER LEWIS
Monday, September 17, 1804

Burke Lake Recreation Area (South Dakota Department of Game, Fish, and Parks, 605–773–3391), 2 miles east of Burke, is a surprising, well-protected oasis of pines and hardwoods featuring primitive camping sites and a sheltered lake. To find it, leave the route at Mile 1.0 below by going straight rather than bearing left. You'll reach the right-hand turn into the recreation area in a mile, then come to the campground after another 0.5 mile.

The vistas garnered along State Road 1806 prior to where you descend toward SR 44 and Lake Francis Case (in the Mile 16.0 range) are nothing short of superlative: big waters encompassed by a beautiful rumpling of high hills that are green for a brief spell in late spring and early summer but are more typically brown. The days of Lewis and Clark somehow seem within grasp as you savor the views. Once you reach the water, on the far side of the bridge you'll see the **Snake Creek Recreation Area** (605–337–2587), another terrific spot to camp, with some sites situated right along the waterfront.

Not far from here is where Pvt. George Shannon, missing for more than two weeks, finally rejoined the rest of the Corps of Discovery on September 11, 1804. According to Capt. Clark, Shannon, who at eighteen was the youngest member of the expedition, hadn't eaten anything in twelve days other than a rabbit and some wild grapes. To say that he was happy to hook back up with the others is most likely a world-class understatement.

In Chamberlain a must-visit on the campus of the St. Joseph Indian School is the **Akta Lakota Museum** (Chamberlain, SD 57326; 605–734–3452), open Monday through Saturday 8:00 A.M. to 6:00 P.M. and Sunday 1:00 to 5:00 P.M. Memorial Day through Labor Day, closed weekends the rest of the year. It is among the best, if not *the* best, American Indian cultural centers you can visit along the entire Lewis & Clark Bicycle Trail. Thoughtfully displayed artifacts and artwork, video presentations, and surrounding sounds and images bring to life the culture of the Sioux Nation. You'll walk away with greater understanding of what the bison meant to the Plains Indians and how the Sioux, from historic to modern, view the world.

Sprawling views and big waters typify the Lewis & Clark Bicycle Trail in the vicinity of Chamberlain, South Dakota.

Also in town is the **Lewis & Clark I–90 Information Center** (Chamberlain, SD 57325; 605–734–4562), open 8:00 A.M. to 6:00 P.M. daily, whose balcony overlooking the Missouri River and surrounding hills is shaped like Lewis and Clark's keelboat. Inside, displays trace the Corps' travels through the future state of South Dakota. A few miles downstream from here, on September 14, 1804, Clark shot his first "wild goat," or pronghorn antelope, adding yet another species to their collection of animals unique to the West.

Mileage Log

0.0 Ride out of Burke on Seventh Street.
1.0 Bear left onto unsigned County Road 6.
8.5 Curve right, following main road.
11.0 Route curves to the left.
11.5 Lucas.
14.0 Turn right following pavement.
16.0 Turn left onto SR 1806.
19.5 Turn right onto SR 44.

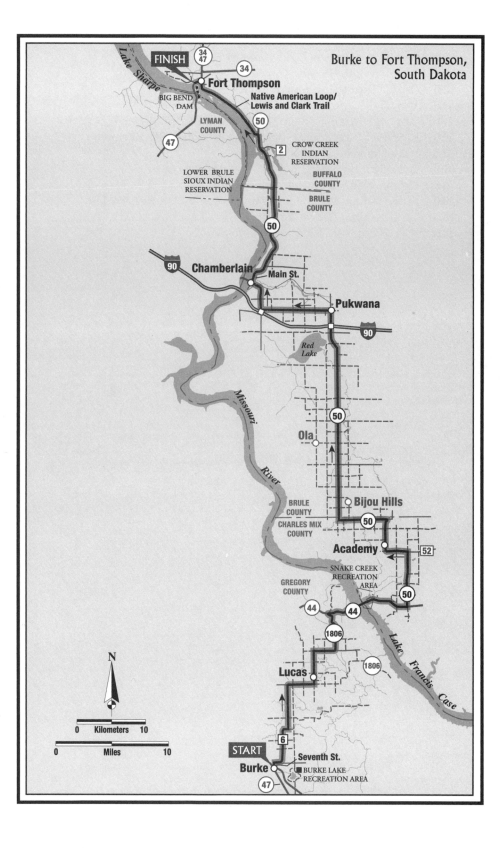

Burke to Fort Thompson,
South Dakota

22.0	Cross Lake Francis Case/Missouri River.
27.0	Turn left onto SR 50.
32.0	CR 52. Turn left to remain on SR 50.
34.0	Turn right to remain on SR 50; Academy.
41.0	Turn right to remain on SR 50. Enter Brule County.
59.0	Ride over Interstate 90 onto unsigned road. SR 50 ends.
60.5	Pukwana just off route to right.
67.0	Turn right onto SR 50.
70.0	Chamberlain. Turn right onto Main Street/SR 50.
80.0	Enter Buffalo County and Crow Creek Indian Reservation.
85.5	Turn left onto Native American Loop/Lewis and Clark Trail.
93.5	Fort Thompson. Ride south onto SR 47.

12 Fort Thompson to Pierre, South Dakota
77.5 miles (1,041 miles cumulative)

> ". . . three Souex boys Came to us Swam the river and informd
> that the Band of Seauex called the Tetongues of 80 Lodges were
> Camped at the next Creek above, & 60 Lodges more a Short dis-
> tance above . . ."
>
> —CAPT. WILLIAM CLARK
> Sunday, September 23, 1804

Between Chamberlain and Pierre, while riding on the **Native American National Scenic Byway,** you'll cross the one-hundredth meridian, that invisible line of demarcation where the East ends and the West begins. This, the one-hundredth longitudinal line west of Greenwich, England, was highlighted by legendary explorer-surveyor Maj. John Wesley Powell in his 1879 report to the U.S. Geological Survey. Powell recognized the one hundredth meridian as the division line between the moist eastern United States and the arid West. In general, east of the line, where annual precipitation is greater than 20 inches, crops can be grown without the aid of irrigation; west of it, with less than 20 inches annual precipitation, irrigation and cultivation techniques unique to dry lands are generally required. Directly related to the less abundant precipitation is the fact that you are now firmly planted in the mixed-grass prairie of the Great Plains, having left behind the tallgrass prairies of Missouri and the Iowa-Nebraska border country.

On the far, north side of the river is the Crow Creek Indian Reservation, which you rode through as you approached Fort Thompson from the south. When the reservation was established in 1863, Santees from Minnesota were moved there; later, Yankton and Teton Sioux moved in as well. Subsequently, the Santees moved on to Nebraska and the Tetons traveled to the south side of the river. Today the 122,531-acre reservation is occupied by Yankton Sioux peoples. The area through which you are now riding, on the south side of the river, is within the Lower Brule Indian Reservation. The Lower Brule Sioux are related to the Tetons who showed Lewis and Clark such an interesting time as they visited the future site of Pierre (read ahead). The reservation, approximately the same size as the Crow Creek Reservation, covers nearly 80 miles of Lake Sharpe shoreline.

Things are more complex when you look at them from the Native Americans' perspective. What the U.S. government, and most Americans, refer to as the Sioux are more accurately called the Lakota/Dakota people, which

The Lewis and Clark Trail crosses the Lower Brule Indian Reservation, a landscape of mix-grass prairie spreading beneath a broad canopy of sky.

means "friend" (Sioux is a shortening of the Chippewa word *Nadowesioux,* meaning "enemy," or the exact opposite of friend). Within the Lakota Nation the Lower Brule Sioux Tribe is known as the *Kul Wicasa Oyate.* Together with the Rosebud, or Upper Brule Sioux, they make up the *Sicangu Oyate,* the Burned Thighs. (The name *Brule* came from early French traders.) The Lakota Nation, which also includes several other tribes, among them the Oglala and Hunkpapa, were primarily buffalo hunters. The Yanktons—or *Wicayela* or Middle Sioux—speak a different Siouan language dialect from the Lakota. Another thing differentiating them from the Lakota is that, in addition to being buffalo hunters, the Yanktons also did some small-scale farming.

While following the Native American National Scenic Byway through the Lower Brule Reservation, you'll skirt the Big Bend of the Missouri River, a feature that is clearly visible (as part of Lake Sharpe) by eyeing a South Dakota state road map. Capt. Clark estimated that to negotiate the bend, the party's three boats covered 30 miles; by land they could have connected the same two points by walking a little more than a mile!

The terrain surrounding the byway is classic ranching country. Golden hills—occasionally green—are dissected by minicanyons, embellished with dispersed cattle herds and explosions of dark-green timber, and teeming with wild turkeys and ring-necked pheasants. It's easy to imagine yourself as a member of the Corps of Discovery as you come in alongside the river, at approximately Mile 47.0 below, in an area of drowned snags. Returning to higher ground, in these wide-open spaces you can spot Pierre when it's still a good 15 miles away.

At the mouth of the Bad River, in today's Fort Pierre, the Corps had their first meeting with the fearsome Teton Sioux on September 25, 1804. Both this and a farewell get-together a few days later nearly erupted into battle. Hindering communications and complicating matters were the expedition's lack of a good interpreter and the fact that the two main Teton chiefs with whom Lewis and Clark dealt were themselves mired in a power struggle. Rumor had it—a rumor coming from some Omaha Indians recently captured during an attack by the Tetons—that the latter intended to annihilate the expedition members. Therefore, although things may not have gone quite as well as President Jefferson would have hoped—establishing friendly relations with the Tetons, who served as important middlemen in the fur trade, was a primary goal—Lewis and Clark probably considered themselves lucky to have made it past the Teton Sioux and continued their quest for the Pacific Ocean.

Plan to lay over at least a day in Pierre; there's lots to see, some of which is highlighted in Chapter 3, map Section 13. Note that free camping is available at Griffin Park; reach it by going southeast along the riverfront trail, which you can access by going 2 blocks south from Dakota Avenue. Near the park, legend has it, a steamboat returning from Fort Benton filled with Montana gold went down in the 1860s and was never recovered.

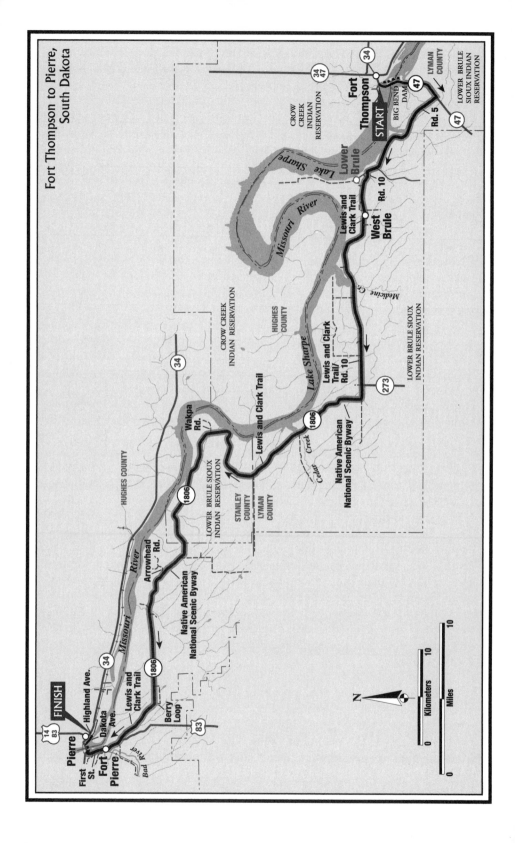

Fort Thompson to Pierre, South Dakota

0.0   Fort Thompson. Ride south onto State Road 47.

1.0   Ride onto Big Bend Dam.

2.0   Enter Lyman County and Lower Brule Sioux Indian Reservation.

6.0   Turn right onto Road 5.

13.0   Bear right onto Road 10.

13.5   Turn left onto Lewis and Clark Trail/Road 10 toward West Brule. Lower Brule is just off route.

16.5   West Brule.

23.0   Medicine Creek Bridge.

30.5   SR 273. Ride straight onto SR 1806.

37.5   Cedar Creek Lake Access.

48.0   Wakpa Road.

57.0   Leave Lower Brule Sioux Indian Reservation.

60.0   Arrowhead Road.

69.5   Berry Loop.

73.0   Turn right onto U.S. Highway 83.

74.5   Bad River Bridge; Fort Pierre. Route becomes First Street.

75.0   Route becomes Deadwood Street.

75.5   Turn right, following bike route signs to bridge. Use sidewalk bike path crossing bridge.

76.5   Pierre. Turn right onto Dakota Avenue.

77.5   Section 2 ends at the corner of Dakota and Highland Avenues.

CHAPTER 3

Pierre, South Dakota
to Williston, North Dakota
(510 miles)

T he arrival of autumn brought with it chilly nights and shortening days as the Corps of Discovery pushed north from the Bad River and into the wilds of future North Dakota. Game was abundant, though, and the men fared well on bison, elk, and deer that were fat and healthy from a long summer of grazing. After their nearly disastrous meeting with the Teton Sioux, the captains took greater care in subsequent meetings with Indians, and as they proceeded upstream relations proved friendlier and more fruitful. The Arikara impressed Lewis and Clark with their skillful negotiating of the wind-whipped, whitecapped waters of the Missouri River in bullboats, fashioned from bison skins stretched across frames of willow branches. After the Arikara, they encountered people of the Mandan and Hidatsa tribes, who lived in the area where the expedition members would build Fort Mandan and spend their first winter on the trail.

In November a French-Canadian named Toussaint Charbonneau visited the under-construction fort to offer Lewis and Clark his services as an interpreter; they accepted. Despite that she didn't speak English, one of Charbonneau's two Shoshone wives, Sakagawea, would also be accompanying him and the group, and the captains rightly believed that she would prove beneficial when it came to communicating with and relating to Indian tribes to the west. Also joining the expedition would be Charbonneau and Sakagawea's two-month-old infant boy, Jean Baptiste Charbonneau, whom Capt. Lewis helped deliver on February 11, 1805.

Throughout the winter, expedition members performed myriad duties and activities, including hunting, commingling with the Mandan women, dancing, putting up food supplies, building canoes, coaxing navigational information from Indian and white visitors, preparing journals and animal specimens, and simply trying to stay warm and avoid frostbite. By April 7 spring breakup on the river was complete, and it was time to move on. The keelboat, loaded with reports, plant and animal specimens (including a live prairie dog and four live magpies), rocks and minerals, Native American artifacts, and other items, headed downstream back toward St. Louis. The dozen-plus men aboard included Corp. Richard Warfington, who was in charge of the return float, and John Newman, a private who had been found guilty the previous October of "expressions of a highly criminal and mutinous nature." (His flogging, a common military practice of the time, was a foreign concept to the local Indians, and it greatly disturbed the Arikara chief who witnessed it.) Meanwhile, the permanent party of around thirty men, along with one woman, one baby, and one dog, boarded two loaded-down pirogues and six equally burdened canoes to continue the upstream explorations.

As you head north from the capital city of South Dakota toward Bismarck, North Dakota's counterpart, you will ride through high, rolling bluff country that is typically some distance away from the river corridor but which occasionally offers amazing views of a big body of water below. The drier the air and land become as you continue west, the wetter that big expanse of water looks. You'll probably find yourself either praising or cursing the ever-present wind, depending on which way it is blowing in relation to the way you're trying to go. Plenty of river/lake access is offered via gravel roads as you ride along State Road 1804, which you follow off and on all the way from Pierre to Williston. Potentially heavy recreational and agricultural traffic on the road is countered by generally good sight distances. Services are few and far between, a situation you will find continuing into and through much of Montana. Because the availability of camping—or lack of it—can make for tricky logistics, a suggested schedule for dividing up the riding days, with each day ending at a campground, is outlined in the following text.

The section ends in Williston, just a few miles east of the Montana border.

13 Pierre to Akaska, South Dakota
92.5 miles (1,133.5 miles cumulative)

". . . The Chief on board was So fritened at the Motion of the boat which in its rocking Caused Several loose articles to fall on the Deck from the lockers, he ran off and hid himself . . ."
—CAPT. WILLIAM CLARK
Sunday, September 30, 1804

You can't help but suspect that Pierre, which barely makes the list of the ten largest towns in South Dakota—a state, in turn, not known for its urban sprawl—was designated the state capital by virtue of its central location. Or perhaps it stems from the important role the area has played through the decades, for more history is centered around Pierre—originally known as *Matto*, Lakota for bear—than anywhere else in the Dakotas.

As you enter the elbow-room-abundant community, turn south off Dakota Avenue onto Poplar Avenue. In short order you will arrive at the **Lewis and Clark Bicentennial Trail** at the point where the trail joins the road leading to **La Framboise Island Recreation Area** (605–224–5862; open sunrise to sunset). A foot trail and mountain biking trails web the island, an undeveloped nature preserve that makes a fine spot for birding or simply collecting one's thoughts. It is believed to be the same river-surrounded plot of land that William Clark called "bad humered Island," a reference to the mood he was in after his party's initial meeting with the Teton Sioux. The main trail around the island features interpretive signs detailing Lewis and Clark's visit to the area and also offers a good look across the Missouri River—which here actually retains the characteristics of a river—at the mouth of the Bad River, where that nearly calamatous meeting took place on September 25, 1804.

Back on the mainland, the Lewis and Clark Bicentennial Trail continues southeasterly out of town for approximately 4 miles to the **Farm Island State Recreation Area** (South Dakota State Parks, 523 East Capitol, Pierre, SD 57501; 605–773–3391), with its campground, rental cabins, and nature trails. The Bicentennial Trail passes wetlands and stands of riverside cottonwoods and other native flora en route to the island, where Pvt. John Colter shot several elk as the expedition passed through. In doing so, Colter was honing skills that later would help him become one of the greatest and best-known mountain men of the Rockies.

A South Dakota still life, north of Pierre

As you're heading out of town on the route, 0.1 mile after turning onto Euclid, turn right onto Fourth Street to go around the upper end of the open parklands extending from the state capitol building. About a half mile after turning, pull left into the parking area of the **South Dakota Cultural Heritage Center** (900 Governors Drive, Pierre, SD 57501; 605–773–3458). The low-slung underground structure was designed to evoke the spirit of the Arikara earth lodges that once dotted the Missouri River Valley. Sporting "wings" sticking out above, the building encompasses 63,000 square feet and is covered with native sod taken from Jones County southwest of Pierre.

The Cultural Heritage Center is home to several entities, including the **Museum of the South Dakota Historical Society** (605–773–3458), open 9:00 A.M. to 4:30 P.M. Monday through Friday and 1:00 to 4:30 P.M. Saturday and Sunday. Outstanding exhibits detail the prehistoric and historic cultures of the state, with an emphasis on the Lakota. One of many items displayed is an Arikara bullboat similar to those described by Capt. Clark on October 9, 1804, as "Canoos of Skins." Another highlight is the Verendrye Plate, which was buried on a hilltop just north of the Bad River and west of the Missouri in March 1743 by the brothers Louis and Chevalier Verendrye, the first known European explorers in the region, who were claiming the Missouri River Valley for France. The lead plate was uncovered nearly two centuries later, in 1913, by some schoolkids.

If you'd like to delve more deeply into the area's long and colorful human history, pick up a copy of the *Pierre/Fort Pierre Historic Sites Driving Tour* pamphlet. One place it's available is the **South Dakota Discovery Center & Aquarium,** occupying the old Pierre City Power Plant (805 West Sioux, Pierre, SD 57501; 605–224–8295; www.sd-discovery.com) and open 10:00 A.M. to 5:00 P.M. Monday through Saturday and 1:00 to 5:00 P.M. Sunday. If you'd like to get a look at the land from the perspective of the river, sign on with **Missouri River Kayak Tours** (511 West Dakota, Pierre, SD 57501; 605–224–6572). Trips ranging from a half day to three days are available, led by guides who will interpret the landscape, the wildlife, and the history of the Lewis and Clark expedition.

The Missouri River and its tributaries have carved the earth surrounding Pierre into a terrain that appears almost mountainous when looked at from the bottom up. That illusion is quickly dispelled as you leave the city and climb out of the valley to reclaim flat to rolling mixed-grass prairies dotted with glacially deposited rocks and boulders. Conceivably, it could have been the inspiration for the saying "the middle of nowhere." You'll note an abundance of historical markers as you ride along State Road 1804 above the river, which, backed up behind the Oahe Dam, suddenly becomes a lake again, with arms of light-colored sand reaching into its dark blue waters.

Bob's Resort (HCR 3, Box 84, Gettysburg, SD 57442; 605–765–2500; www.bobsresort.com), with its commercial campground (also featuring cabins and motel rooms), is located at Mile 55.5 below. It's a natural for night one out of Pierre, as it is the first conveniently located campground

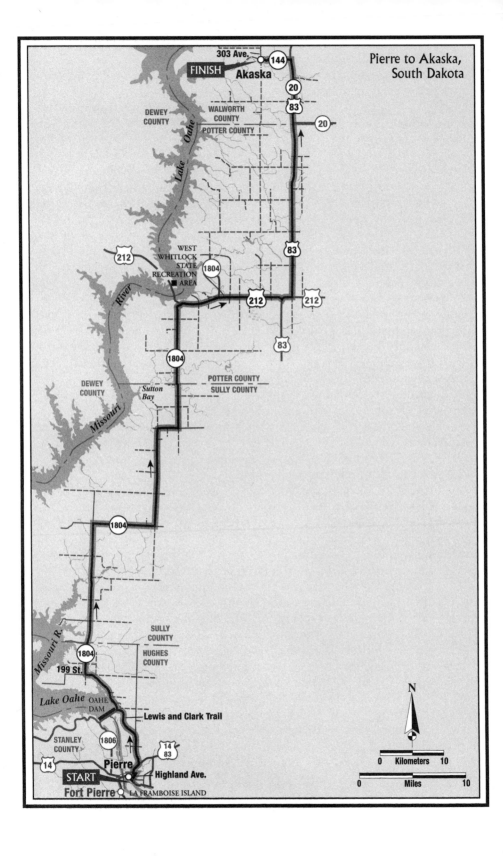

encountered since leaving the capital city. Or you could continue up the route 4 miles and take the side trip along SR 1804 to **West Whitlock State Recreation Area** (HC 3, Box 73A, Gettysburg, SD 57442; 605–765–9410). It likewise features camping and cabins, along with a well-done reproduction of a dome-shaped Arikara earth lodge.

Mileage Log

0.0   From the corner of Highland and Dakota, go north on Highland Avenue.

1.0   Turn left onto Second Street then right onto Euclid Avenue/U.S. Highway 14/83.

2.0   Turn left onto SR 1804/Lewis and Clark Trail.

13.0   199 Street; turn right following SR 1804/Lewis and Clark Trail.

27.5   Turn right to remain on SR 1804/Lewis and Clark Trail.

33.5   Turn left to remain on SR 1804/Lewis and Clark Trail.

42.5   At sign reading SUTTON BAY LAKESIDE USE AREA, curve right to remain on SR 1804/Lewis and Clark Trail.

44.5   Turn left following SR 1804/Lewis and Clark Trail.

55.5   Turn right following SR 1804/Lewis and Clark Trail. U.S. 212 joins route.

59.5   Ride straight to remain on U.S. 212/Lewis and Clark Trail. SR 1804 leaves route.

66.0   At T, turn left to remain on U.S. 212/Lewis and Clark Trail. U.S. 83 joins route.

67.0   Turn left to remain on U.S. 83/Lewis and Clark Trail. U.S. 212 leaves route.

83.5   Enter Walworth County. SR 20 joins route.

89.5   Turn left onto SR 144.

92.5   Akaska. Turn right onto 303 Avenue.

14 Akaska to Pollock, South Dakota
66 miles (1,199.5 miles cumulative)

*". . . Those Indians wer much astonished at my Servent, they never
Saw a black man before . . . he Carried on the joke and made him-
self more turribal than we wished him to doe."*
— CAPT. WILLIAM CLARK
Wednesday, October 10, 1804
Meeting with the Arikara

Soon after leaving Akaska you'll commence riding one of the relatively rare
unpaved stretches of the Lewis & Clark Bicycle Trail. As you listen to the un-
accustomed sound of tires popping across gravel, you'll gaze up at grassy
swales that look as though they're just waiting for a huge bison herd to come
storming over the top, warriors on horseback in close pursuit. As the pavement resumes, though, and you descend toward the big waters of Lake
Oahe, you're snapped out of the nineteenth century and returned to the
twenty-first; still, the lake's waters ripple against the base of ancient, crum-
pled hills typically so brown that they appear like gigantic sand dunes.

Mobridge, the "Oasis of Oahe," was named by those building the Mil-
waukee Road early in the twentieth century, in honor of the bridge constructed to carry the tracks across the Missouri River. Located about 65
miles from the previously recommended overnight, Mobridge and surroundings offer several camping options. **Indian Creek** (U.S. Army Corps of
Engineers, P.O. Box 278, Mobridge, SD 57601; 605–845–2252) is south off
the route, about 3 miles east of town.

The Corps of Discovery spent four days in and around a trio of Arikara
villages that were situated just upstream from the mouth of the Grand River,
which flows easterly into the Missouri opposite present Mobridge. The first
of the three villages occupied an island that now lies beneath the waters of
Lake Oahe. These villages, each home to several hundred residents living in
permanent earth lodges, were what remained of nearly three dozen similar
villages that thrived in the area prior to the early 1780s, when a smallpox
epidemic killed thousands of Arikara and members of other tribes. Primarily farmers by summer, raising corn, beans, squash, and other crops, many
Arikara transformed into tepee-dwelling nomads come winter, following the
trail of bison and other game.

Across the bridge from Mobridge is a memorial to Sitting Bull that was
carved by the late Korczak Ziolkowski, a self-taught sculptor who devoted

South of Pollock you'll ride through S-turns amid rolling hills covered in short- to mid-height grasses.

more than three decades at the end of his life to planning and beginning the ambitious Crazy Horse Memorial in South Dakota's Black Hills. (Since Ziolkowski's death in 1982, several of his ten children have been carrying on his dream.) Also nearby is a memorial to Sacagawea, located near the site where the Shoshone woman *may* have died just six years after the Lewis and Clark expedition ended. At the **Klein Museum** (West Highway 12, Mobridge, SD 57601; 605-845-7243) in Mobridge, you will find, among many other displays dedicated to homesteaders and Native Americans, a collection of photos of Sitting Bull and his relatives. The museum is open April through October from 9:00 A.M. to 5:00 P.M. on Monday and Wednesday through Friday and weekends 1:00 to 5:00 P.M.; it's closed on Tuesday.

Another 40 miles up the road from Indian Creek is the quiet little town of Pollock. At the north end of town, the **Lake Pocasse Recreation Area** (U.S. Army Corps of Engineers and the City of Pollock; 605-889-2301) offers primitive camping alongside a lake named for the chief of one of the three Arikara villages visited by Lewis and Clark. Nearby, as detailed on a roadside sign, was the site that Capt. Clark noted on October 13, 1804, as "a Creek on the S.S. [starboard side] 18 miles above the Ricaras [Arikara] I call Stone Ido(l) Creek . . ." He went on to explain that he'd named the creek for a pair of stones resembling human figures, along with a third that looked

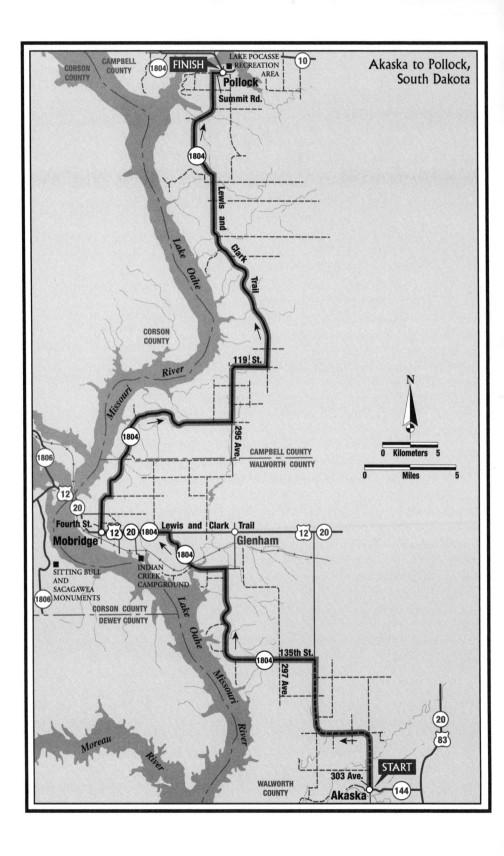

like a dog, that were the principles of an Arikara legend: a Romeo-and-Juliet-like story of a man in love with a woman whose parents wouldn't permit the two to marry. The pair, accompanied by the dog, wandered off to mourn, and all three eventually turned to stone.

Mileage Log

0.0 Akaska. Ride north on 303 Avenue.

1.0 Ride straight onto wide, unsigned gravel road.

3.0 Curve left toward State Road 1804.

6.0 Curve right toward SR 1804.

8.0 Unsigned gravel crossroad.

10.0 Turn left onto 135th Street toward SR 1804. Pavement resumes.

12.0 297 Avenue. Continue straight onto SR 1804.

20.0 Turn left following SR 1804. Glenham, off route 2.5 miles.

24.5 Turn left to remain on SR 1804. U.S. Highway 12/SR 20/Lewis and Clark Trail join route.

28.5 Mobridge. Turn right onto Fourth Street/SR 1804/Lewis and Clark Trail. U.S. 12/SR 20 leave route.

31.0 Turn left following pavement to remain on SR 1804.

33.5 Enter Campbell County.

42.0 295 Avenue. Turn left to remain on SR 1804/Lewis and Clark Trail.

45.0 Turn right to remain on SR 1804/Lewis and Clark Trail. 119 Street joins route.

47.0 Turn left to remain on SR 1804/Lewis and Clark Trail. 119 Street leaves route.

65.5 Turn right onto Summit Road/SR 1804/Lewis and Clark Trail. Pollock.

66.0 Turn left onto B Avenue South/SR 1804.

15 Pollock, South Dakota to Bismarck, North Dakota
85.5 miles (1,285 miles cumulative)

". . . I observe near all large gangues of Buffalow wolves and when the buffalow move those animals follow, and feed on those that are killed by accident or those that are too pore or fat to keep up with the gangue."

—CAPT. WILLIAM CLARK
Saturday, October 20, 1804

Nine miles after leaving Pollock you'll enter North Dakota, which at first looks very similar to South Dakota. As you ride roughly parallel to the Missouri, the roller coaster of a road you're on repeatedly drops into then climbs out of drainages sloping down to meet the river. At just under 60 miles into the day's ride, you'll come to **Hazelton Campground** (U.S. Army Corps of Engineers, P.O. Box 278, Mobridge, SD 57601; 605–845–2252), the last conveniently located place to pitch a tent before Bismarck. The alternative is to continue another 30 miles—making for a long-in-the-saddle day of 85 miles— to **General Sibley Park** (Bismarck Parks and Recreation District; 701–222–1844). Located on the southern outskirts of Bismarck about 0.5 mile south off the route where Forty-eighth Avenue and Washington Street meet (Mile 84.5 below), the park includes a primitive tents-only camping area.

Bismarck-Mandan boasts an outstanding network of bike/pedestrian trails. After accessing the system at its southern end (at Mile 85.5), the Lewis & Clark Bicycle Trail follows a progression of separated pathways that skirt Sertoma Park and the Dakota Zoo and then parallel the Missouri River to the junction with River Road (Mile 6.0 in the next map section). Backing up, not far past the Dakota Zoo, you can take another trail spur west across Memorial Bridge and the Missouri River to Mandan, then find your way west and south on bikeways to **Fort Abraham Lincoln State Park** (4480 Ft. Lincoln Road, Mandan, SD 58554; 701–663–9571; www.state.nd.us/ndparks). Encompassing 1,006 acres of prairie hills and timbered riverbanks and more than 400 years of history, the park holds nature trails and a pleasant campground, settled riverside in groves of timber.

This, the granddaddy of North Dakota state parks, got its start in 1907 when President Theodore Roosevelt—ever bully on the Roughrider State (although it wasn't known by that T.R.-related moniker until the 1960s)— deeded seventy-five acres to the State Historical Society. In the 1930s the Civilian Conservation Corps (CCC) developed much of what you see today, including the park's museum and shelters and the quartet of earth lodges,

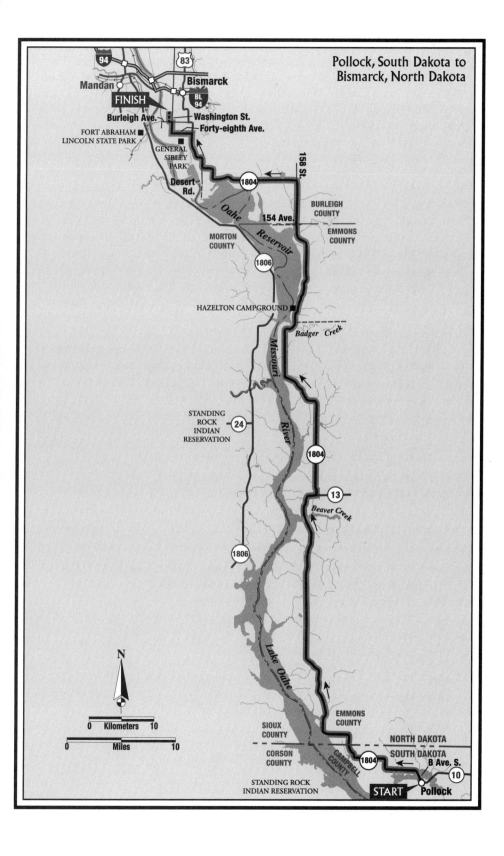

Pollock, South Dakota to
Bismarck, North Dakota

three of which are family sized and the fourth a huge council lodge. These were reconstructed from some of the ruins of On-a-Slant Indian Village, which was occupied by Mandan farming people from the late 1500s until 1781. By the time William Clark and his expedition passed through, On-a-Slant had been deserted for twenty-three years; on October 20, 1804, Capt. Clark noted it as ". . . the old remains of a village on the Side of a hill."

On June 14, 1872, an infantry post was established here at the confluence of the Missouri and Heart Rivers; a year later a cavalry post was added to the compound. The first commander in charge of the cavalry was none other than Lt. Col. George Armstrong Custer, and it was out of Fort Abraham Lincoln that Custer and his 7th Cavalry rode on May 17, 1876, bound for their demise the following month along Montana's Little Bighorn River. The fort closed for good in 1891, but there's plenty remaining to recall the military days, including the post cemetery (located adjacent to the old Infantry Post) and Calvary Square, which includes the Victorian-style home where Custer and his wife resided. Finally, don't miss the park's museum, with its encapsulation of Mandan history and culture; be sure to scan the schedule of upcoming presentations and festivities.

If you visit only one other site in Bismarck, make it the **North Dakota Heritage Center** (612 East Boulevard Avenue, Bismarck, ND 58505; 701–328–2666; www.state.nd.us/hist/hcenter.htm), open 8:00 A.M. to 5:00 P.M. Monday through Friday, 9:00 A.M. to 5:00 P.M. Saturday, and 11:00 A.M. to 5:00 P.M. Sunday. Here, the official state museum located on the grounds of the state capitol, you can learn about the prehistoric Indians of North Dakota, the era of change following first European contact up to the reservation period, the Settlement Period of 1870–1915, and the years covering World War I, the Great Depression, and World War II.

Mileage Log

0.0   Pollock. Continue riding on B Avenue South/State Road 1804.
1.0   Turn left, following SR 1804/Lewis and Clark Trail.
9.0   Enter Emmons County, North Dakota.
33.5   Cross unsigned Beaver Creek.
36.5   SR 13.
54.5   Cross unsigned Badger Creek.
65.0   154 Avenue. Enter Burleigh County.
69.0   158 Street Southeast. Bear left, following SR 1804.
79.0   Desert Road.
82.5   Turn left onto Forty-eighth Avenue.
84.5   Turn right onto Washington Street. Bismark.
85.5   At Burleigh Avenue, on the west side of Washington Street, access the tarmac bike/pedestrian path. Continue north, paralleling Washington Street.

The Katy Trail skirts sycamore-smothered bluffs, brackish backwaters, and beautiful farms carved into rolling hills.

The Klondike Bluffs outside Augusta, Missouri

The hills surrounding the lower Missouri River are more heavily timbered than in pre-settlement times, when wildfires kept the ridges in prairie.

Conversing with a fellow hard-shelled critter

The northeast corner of Kansas was covered by at least two of the glaciers that advanced across North America during the Pleistocene Epoch.

At Lewis and Clark State Park outside Onawa, Iowa, you can inspect this full-scale replica of the Corps of Discovery's keelboat.

Broad skies and puffy whites accompany this modern-day explorer outside Chamberlain, South Dakota.

Storm clouds brewing over Lake Oahe, outside Mobridge, South Dakota

Fort Abraham Lincoln State Park, which holds 1,000
acres of river hills and 400 years of history

Battening down the hatches in a North Dakota breeze, east of Williston

The White Cliffs of the Missouri River, outside Fort Benton, Montana

The Lewis and Clark State Memorial, in Fort Benton, Montana, was sculpted by the late Bob Scriver.

Gates of the Mountains outside Helena, Montana

Parker Homestead State Park near Three Forks, Montana ▶

Camp Fortunate overlook at Clark Canyon Reservoir, southwest of Dillon, Montana

The narrow gravel road plummeting westward into Idaho from Lemhi Pass

Cliffs of hardened lava mark the route west of Clarkston, Washington

Much of the bicycle trail between Clarkston and Walla Walla follows the approximate overland route taken east by the Corps of Discovery in early May 1806.

Weather-worn outbuildings occupy the flats below rolling golden hills west of Pomeroy, Washington

Harvest time in the wheatfields surrounding Walla Walla, Washington

Flat Rock State Park's namesake, one of several volcanic plugs that resisted erosion during the Spokane Flood, was noted by Capt. William Clark in his journal.

The Maryhill Museum of Art, in Washington state's Klickitat Hills, claims a surprisingly diverse collection of American and European art.

You'll get up close and personal with this, the aptly named Vista House, a 1917 creation that recently underwent renovation.

Those choosing to follow Capt. Clark's 1806 east-bound travels will encounter scenes like this along the Yellowstone River.

Pompeys Pillar National Monument, along the Yellowstone River northeast of Billings, Montana, preserves the signature of Capt. William Clark, which he carved into the feature's sandstone face.

previous page:
Would Lewis and Clark recognize the Columbia River as it appears today, flowing through Portland, Oregon?

16

Bismarck to
Pick City, North Dakota
87 miles (1,372 miles cumulative)

"This Morning at Daylight I went down the river with 4 men to look for a proper place to winter proceeded down the river three miles & found a place well Supld. with wood, & returned . . ."
—CAPT. WILLIAM CLARK
Friday, November 2, 1804
Near the site of Fort Mandan

In the Dakotas history and prehistory are far more than mere fodder for textbooks. That sense of a tangible past will only intensify as you explore this section of the route. It is, in fact, one of the most historically vivid sections of the entire Lewis & Clark Bicycle Trail; for this reason you might want to plan on making your way slowly through the area.

Double Ditch Indian Village (701–328–2666), encountered about 8 miles after leaving Bismarck on River Road, is among the most obvious transformations of a native landscape by prehistoric people that you'll see anywhere in the United States outside the desert Southwest. It's right up there with the work of the mound builders of the Mississippi and Ohio River valleys. This large earth-lodge village perched high above the river was inhabited by Mandan Indians from the early 1500s through 1781, the year smallpox wiped out thousands of natives in the upper Missouri River region. Today, more than 220 years later, the remains of two fortification ditches, dug to keep out enemies, along with hummocks and depressions remaining from earth lodges and midden mounds, are clearly visible. It is believed that, combined, this and the six or seven other Mandan villages existing near the mouth of the Heart River claimed more than 10,000 residents prior to 1781. That number that was reduced to scarcely more than 1,000 Mandan by the time Lewis and Clark visited twenty-three years later.

As you walk the trail leading from one interpretive sign to the next, listen for the sweet call of a western meadowlark—while keeping a vigilant ear to the ground for the ominous buzz of a prairie rattlesnake. One sign explains that at its zenith, Double Ditch Village boasted approximately 2,200 residents—larger than 95 percent of the towns in North Dakota today!

The Corps of Discovery began getting snowed on as they headed north from today's Bismarck on October 22 and 23, 1804. The men were cold, and rheumatism was affecting several of them; also, the river was low, and its channel was becoming difficult to discern. After conducting peaceful meetings with Mandan chief Sheheke and Arikara chief Eagle's Feather, they

A re-creation of Fort Mandan, outside Washburn, North Dakota

camped on October 24 just south of present-day Washburn and the next day began looking for a place to spend the winter. They found it a few days later at a spot about 14 miles upriver from Washburn on the north side of the river, opposite a Mandan village on the southern shore. Here, over an often-frigid six weeks, they built Fort Mandan—a grandiose name for a rather humble affair boasting just 1,600 square feet of living space. The U.S. flag was first hoisted at Fort Mandan on Christmas Day.

Today, just off the route near Washburn, you'll find the stunning new **North Dakota Lewis & Clark Interpretive Center** (P.O. Box 607, Washburn, ND 58577; 701-462-8535; www.fortmandan.com), open 9:00 A.M. to 7:00 P.M. daily Memorial Day through Labor Day and 9:00 A.M. to 5:00 P.M. the rest of the year. Displays inside do an admirable job of exploring the lack of understanding that Lewis and Clark exhibited toward the native cultures. There's much more, too, including a carved-out cottonwood-log canoe similar to the half dozen canoes fashioned by expedition members at Fort Mandan, where they spent nearly half a year. Other highlights are reproductions of Capt. Clark's famous map of the West and Karl Bodmer's historic paintings. In the company of Prince Maximilian of Germany, Bodmer, a Swiss artist who was twenty-three years old at the time, ventured west up the Missouri in 1833, getting approximately as far as present-day Great Falls, Montana. Traveling by steamboat and keelboat with the American Fur Company, during the thirteen-month journey Bodmer captured some of the first, and most important, images of the Great Plains region and its indigenous peoples.

The interpretive center's $5.00 entry fee also gets you into **Fort Mandan Historic Site** (open sunrise to sunset; call the interpretive center for information on tours and group camping). The site is located farther off-route, 2.5 miles west of the interpretive center on pavement. Managed by the North Dakota Lewis & Clark Bicentennial Foundation (as is the interpretive center), this replicated version of Fort Mandan lies about 10 miles east of where the Corps actually spent the winter of 1804–05. All sorts of reenactments and festivities are planned here for the Lewis and Clark Bicentennial years; call ahead to find out what will be happening during your visit.

Other camping options in the area include **Cross Ranch State Park** (1403 River Road, Center, ND 58530; 701–794–3731; www.ndparks.com/parks/crsp.htm), lying 10 miles off the route but well worth the extra effort needed to get there. Turn south onto pavement just west of Hensler and follow the signs. The park protects one of the most riverlike sections of the Missouri River remaining in North Dakota, with an active floodplain blanketed in cottonwoods and willows. On sandbars protruding into the waters, you might glimpse a threatened piping plover, recognizable by its orange legs and pale upper body. Rising away from the river, drier uplands of mixed grasses are interrupted by damp, chiseled draws supporting shrubs, tallgrass species, and bur oaks and other trees. More than 15 miles of interconnected hiking trails wind through the diverse habitats of the state park's units—including the Lewis and Clark Backcountry—and the adjacent grasslands preserve maintained by The Nature Conservancy, where you might spot a resident bison herd. Exhibits in the park's River Peoples Visitor Center focus on the natural and human history of the region. Canoe rentals are available there, too, and river trips ranging from 2 to 41 miles can be arranged, including upstream drop-off or downstream pickup.

Alternatively, in a pinch you might stay at the primitive **West Arroda Lake Recreation Area,** located 7 miles west of Hensler on the south side of the road (take the second turn). With its surprising little lake embraced by low hills and brushy ravines, it is a wonderful wildlife-viewing area; clear, flat tent sites, however, are as rare as ravens' teeth. **Fort Clark State Historic Site** (701–328–3567; open sunrise to sunset), a couple of miles farther west on State Road 200A and then three-quarters of a mile north, protects what remains of one of a handful of major fur-trading forts that were established on the upper Missouri. A self-guiding trail leads through the area of the trading post and adjacent Indian village, where Karl Bodmer drew sketches of Mandan, Hidatsa, and Arikara Indians.

And the best is yet to come: **Knife River Indian Villages National Historic Site** (P.O. Box 9, Stanton, ND 58571; 701–745–3300; www.nps.gov/knri), located about a mile north of Stanton. The park's visitor center features displays of cultural items of the Hidatsa, who settled in the area possibly as early as A.D. 1300. The cutaway cross-section of an underground food cache is particularly interesting, revealing stashed corn, beans, squash, and sunflower seeds. The Indians raised these crops in floodplain gardens that were central to the Hidatsa way of life: They made it possible for these Plains Indians, typically nomads who followed the bison herds, to settle in one place more or less permanently for centuries.

Behind the visitor center, which itself echoes the earth-lodge form, is a beautiful reproduction of a Hidatsa earth lodge. You can see for yourself how comfortable it would have been to live in and feel how well insulated it is. From there, a trail leads to the remains of two villages, Awatixa Xi'e and Awatixa Village. When Lewis and Clark came through, five earth-lodge villages near the mouth of the Knife River held some 4,000 people. Especially when taken in sum with the Mandan villages downstream, it's clear that this was no deserted frontier. Rather, it was an area holding a thriving civilization. Awatixa Village, the only one of the three villages inside the park that was occupied when Lewis and Clark visited, was home at the time to Toussaint Charbonneau and sixteen-year-old Sakagawea. Four or five years earlier, the Lemhi Shoshone girl had been kidnapped by the Hidatsa during a raid in the area of Three Forks, Montana. After Lewis and Clark accepted Charbonneau's offer to serve as an interpreter for the expedition, he and Sakagawea moved to Fort Mandan for the winter.

Mileage Log

0.0 Continue north on the bike path paralleling Washington Street. Bismarck.
0.5 Bear left to parallel Riverwood Loop.
1.5 Bear right to parallel Riverwood Drive.
2.5 Turn hard left to ride on pathway between Missouri River and Sertoma Park.
4.0 Pass under Business Route 94, paralleling River Road.
6.0 Turn left onto unsigned River Road in front of large Ducks Unlimited regional office.
10.0 At T, turn left onto SR 1804/Lewis and Clark Trail.
13.5 Double Ditch Loop.
15.0 Double Ditch Loop.
26.5 266 Avenue Northwest.
31.5 Enter McLean County.
37.0 Turn left onto U.S. Highway 83.
42.5 County Road 22. Washburn.
44.0 Turn left onto SR 200A.
45.0 Cross Missouri River. Enter Oliver County.
48.0 Hensler.
56.0 Fort Clark.

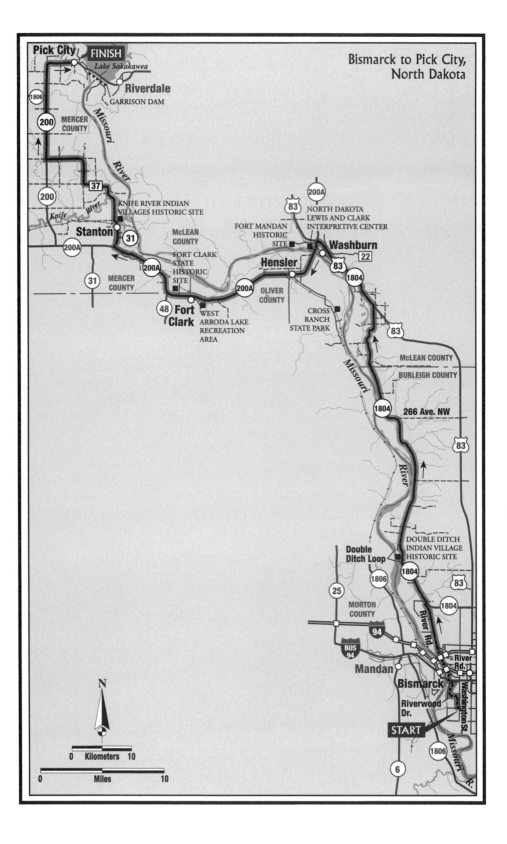

58.5 SR 48.

65.0 Turn right onto SR 31.

66.5 Stanton. SR 31 ends. Ride straight onto CR 37.

77.0 Turn right onto SR 200.

82.0 SR 1806.

87.0 Pick City.

17 Pick City to Parshall, North Dakota
86.5 miles (1,458.5 miles cumulative)

". . . when we halted for dinner the squaw busied herself in serching for the wild artichokes which the mice collect and deposit in large hoards. this operation she performed by penetrating the earth with a sharp stick about some small collections of drift wood. her labour soon proved successful, and she procured a good quantity of these roots . . ."

—CAPT. WILLIAM CLARK
Tuesday, April 9, 1805
On Sacagawea's food gathering

A couple of fine campgrounds lie off the route just east of Pick City, which you'll reach 45 miles after leaving Washburn. After zipping past town establishments such as the Dam Bar and **Tailrace Adventures** (canoe, kayak, and raft outings; 701–487–3357), you'll see a left-hand turn leading into **Sakakawea State Park** (P.O. Box 732, Riverdale, ND 58565; 701–487–3315; www.ndparks.com). The primitive camping area is reached about 1.5 miles after making the turn. Within the park is the western terminus of the **North Country National Scenic Trail,** a footpath that, once completed, will extend all the way from upstate New York to here, a distance of approximately 3,200 miles.

A short way farther east along the main route, as you're riding on the dam and looking to your right over rough, broken terrain, you'll see a right-hand turn descending toward the **Downstream Campground** (U.S. Army Corps of Engineers, P.O. Box 527, Riverdale, ND 58565; 701–654–7411). The campground is reached by riding 3 miles off the route, after passing the power plant and Garrison Dam National Fish Hatchery. This campground, sitting in cottonwood-shaded bottomlands, offers a somewhat more pleasant setting than that of the state park campground; the obvious drawback is that you can't see the lake from this side of the dam. A heavily timbered wildlife management area lies adjacent to the campground, and a trout pond sits between it and the river.

Garrison Dam holds back the waters of Lake Sakakawea, the largest reservoir in the country in terms of surface area: 178 miles long and boasting 1,530 miles of shoreline, it covers approximately 368,000 acres. The lake was christened Sakakawea in honor of the important contribution made to the Lewis and Clark expedition by Sakagawea, whose name, which means

"Bird Woman" in Hidatsa, is commonly spelled three different ways: Sakakawea, Sacagawea, and Sacajawea. The stated purpose of the dam and reservoir—and the same wording could be used to explain the reason for being of most any U.S. Corps of Engineers dam in the West—is "the generation of hydroelectric power, flood control, irrigation, recreation, municipal and industrial water supply, and downstream navigation." Several tours of the dam and power plant are offered daily from Memorial Day through Labor Day (call 701–654–7441 for more information).

About 3 miles north of Coleharbor you'll pass a road going right into the **Audubon National Wildlife Refuge** (3275 Eleventh Street Northwest, Coleharbor, ND 58531; 701–442–5474). Lake Audubon is at the center of the refuge, established in 1957 to partially mitigate the loss of vital bird habitat caused by construction of the Garrison Dam. The visitor center is situated a little less than a mile after turning onto the road mentioned above. Bicycles are permitted on the refuge's 7.5-mile scenic loop, which winds through an area of rolling hills and wetland potholes located within the glaciated Missouri River Plateau.

From Garrison, it is 3 miles south off the route to **Fort Stevenson State Park** (1252A Forty-first Avenue Northwest, Garrison, ND 58540; 701–337–5576; www.ndparks.com), another fine place to set up camp and absorb some Dakota Territory history. The site of the original fort, which served as a supply depot for the region's military posts, lies covered in the waters of Lake Sakakawea at a point approximately 2 miles southwest of the park. In addition to camping, the park has a marina and camp store and maintains three rental cabins. It is known as a place of celebration and living history, with annual events that include the annual Skydance Sakakawea kite-flying festival in late May and Fort Stevenson Military Days in late June. In early August some 350 bicyclists from North Dakota and beyond gather here to begin the weeklong, 450-mile Cycling Around North Dakota in Sakakawea Country, or CANDISC, which also ends at the park.

From Garrison to a point roughly 30 miles west, the route traverses relatively humdrum McLean County farm country, the sort of landscape that typifies many an outsider's view of what North Dakota should look like. The county *was* pretty much strictly farm country until the 1954 completion of the Garrison Dam, which paved the way for recreation to become an important component of the local economy. In some instances the demographics of McLean County reflect those of greater North Dakota; in other cases they do not. The median household income in the county is $32,129, very close to the $31,764 average for the state. The percentage of Caucasians in the county, 92.5 percent, is virtually identical to that of North Dakota overall, while the Native American population of 5.9 percent is just one percentage point higher than the state's 4.9 percent. However, the average square mile in McLean County holds just 4.4 residents, making it less than half as "crowded" as North Dakota in general, which averages 9.3 persons per square mile. Partially explaining this is the fact that, while North

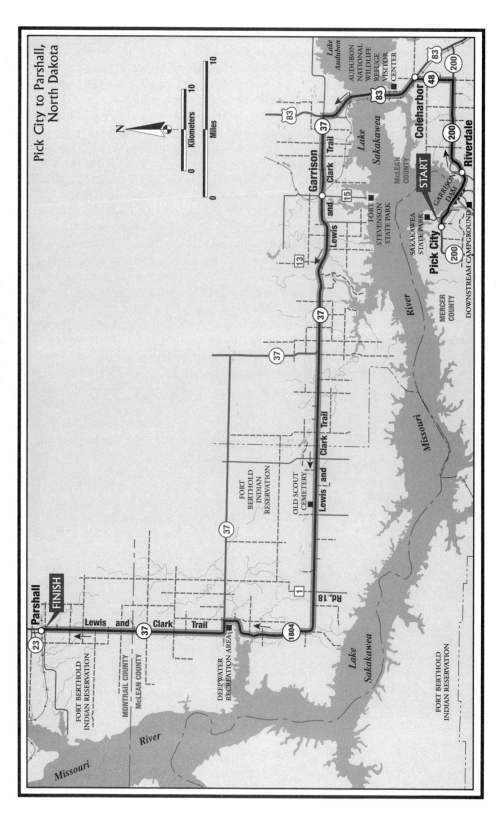

Pick City to Parshall, North Dakota

Dakota's population grew between 1990 and 2000—albeit just barely, by 0.5 percent—McLean County's declined by an alarming 11 percent.

A few miles after entering the Fort Berthold Indian Reservation, on the right you'll see the **Old Scout Cemetery** marked by a huge, simulated headdress turning with the wind. Established by members of the Arikara tribe, the site is dedicated first and foremost to chiefs White Shield (1798–1878) and Son of the Star (1813–1881). In addition to memorials to Spanish-American War veteran Eli Perkins and to Bloody Knife, who died at the Battle of the Little Bighorn in 1876 while fighting for the United States, you'll see the graves of many veterans of World War I, World War II, and the Korean War. Surnames such as Birds Bill, Young Bear, Little Owl, and Fox are common. It seems so isolated out here, yet at the same time peaceful and somehow comforting, with just the wind as a companion. And those tears welling up in your eyes may be from that wind, or from something else altogether.

Soon you'll curve north on State Road 1804 and, far below, see water coming back into view. Shortly after turning left onto SR 37 (at Mile 23.5 below), another left turn will take you down a mile of gravel to the **Deepwater Recreation Area** (U.S. Army Corps of Engineers, P.O. Box 527, Riverdale, ND 58565; 701–654–7411). It's open-country camping, but there is water—and it has been more than 70 miles since you left Pick City.

 Mileage Log

0.0   Pick City. Continue riding east on SR 200.
1.5   Cross Garrison Dam.
5.5   Riverdale.
12.0 Turn left onto SR 48.
15.0 Coleharbor. Turn left onto U.S. Highway 83.
18.5 Start across causeway.
20.5 End causeway. Continue straight on U.S. 83.
23.5 Turn left onto SR 37/Lewis and Clark Trail.
29.5 Garrison. County Road 15.
35.0 CR 13 on right.
42.0 Ride straight onto SR 1804.
49.0 Enter Fort Berthold Indian Reservation.
60.0 CR 1/Road 18.
71.0 Turn left onto SR 37/Lewis and Clark Trail.
79.0 Enter Mountrail County.
86.5 Parshall.

18 Parshall to Williston, North Dakota
92.5 miles (1,551 miles cumulative)

". . . Saw several buffalow lodged in the drift wood which had been drouned in the winter in passing the river."
—CAPT. WILLIAM CLARK ·
Saturday, April 20, 1805

If you follow the camping strategy outlined below (beginning at New Town), the morning after staying at Lewis and Clark State Park you can ride 20 miles to Williston and stock up on supplies before continuing another 25 miles to Fort Buford State Historic Site (described in Chapter 4). This relatively leisurely day will leave you time and energy for the highly recommended afternoon/evening side trip to Fort Union National Historic Site.

The **New Town Marina Campground** (New Town, ND 58763; 701–627–3900), 2 miles west of the route from New Town, is a short day's jaunt of about 35 miles from the previously recommended campground. A couple of miles farther west from there, across the Four Bears Bridge, you can visit the Fort Berthold Reservation's **Three Affiliated Tribes Museum** (HC-3, Box 2, New Town, ND 58763; 701–627–4477), open 10:00 A.M. to 6:00 P.M. daily. The museum displays historical artifacts and modern arts and crafts representative of the cultures of the Mandan, Hidatsa, and Arikara, the same three tribes that were friendly to the Corps of Discovery and helped them make it through the tough Dakota winter of 1804–05, through the trade of food and other acts. (The Three Affiliated Tribes also have a nearby interpretive center, focusing on the Mandan, Hidatsa, and Arikara and their interactions with the Corps of Discovery, on the drawing board. The intended opening date is the summer of 2006.)

When you're in New Town you're sitting relatively close to North Dakota's most extraordinary scenery. If you're undaunted by the prospect of adding an extra century ride to your adventure (it's 165 miles to Williston from New Town via this route versus 70 miles by staying on the trail), go west from New Town on State Road 23 for 11 miles, then ride south on SR 22 for 34 miles to **Little Missouri State Primitive Park** (c/o ND Parks & Recreation Department, 1835 Bismarck Expressway, Bismarck, ND 58504; 701–328–5357). The best, most secluded campsite in the small, rim's-edge campground is found by going to the north end of the short gravel road. The campsite is adjacent to the trailhead for the Travois and Indian Trails, hiking and horseback paths that drop into a bizarre never-never world of

The allure of the "open road" takes on a literal meaning in western North Dakota.

buttes, mesas, and arroyos carved by the Little Missouri River and its flash-flood feeder streams. Sheltered north-facing coulees act as moisture traps in the arid setting and teem with such vegetation as juniper trees and wildlife such as mule deer and wild turkeys.

From there, continue south for 19 miles to Killdeer, passing the diminutive Killdeer Mountains en route, then ride 20 miles west on SR 200 and 20 miles north on U.S. Highway 85. This will bring you to the entrance of the North Unit of **Theodore Roosevelt National Park** (P.O. Box 7, Medora, ND 58645; 701–623–4466; www.nps.gov/thro), where the Little Missouri River has performed a similar but even more spectacular job of sculpting 60-million-year-old Fort Union Group sediments into a geologic phantasmagoria. The Juniper Campground, located about 5 miles west off the highway, is reached via an absolutely beautiful cycling road. The distance to Williston from Theodore Roosevelt National Park is approximately 55 miles by way of U.S. 85 and U.S. 2.

If you're riding a mountain bike, you might want to check out the nearby **Maah Daah Hey Trail,** which is garnering a reputation as one of the premier fat-tire trails in the West. From a mile south of the entrance to the North Unit, just south of the river, turn west and go a mile to **CCC Camp-**

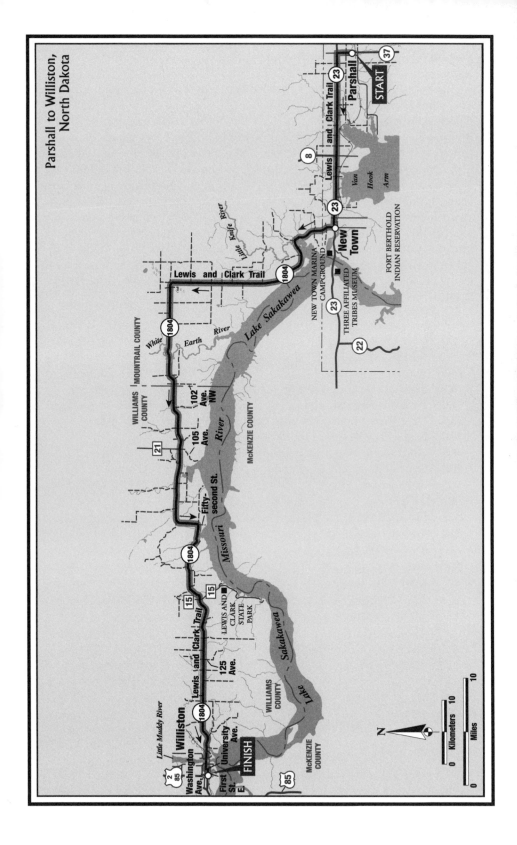

Parshall to Williston,
North Dakota

ground (U.S. Forest Service, 701–842–2392), where you'll find the northern terminus of the trail.

Back on the main route, the next recommended campground is **Lewis and Clark State Park** (4904 119th Road Northwest, Epping, ND 58843; 701–859–3071), 60 miles from the New Town Marina Campground. To find it, leave the route at Mile 74.0 below and zip 3 miles down a little badlands canyon full of cows, groves of timber, and grasses and shrubs. With its prolific wetlands lying at the base of protective hillsides, the park is right on the water's edge when Lake Sakakawea is at full pool. The Prairie Nature Trail leads through a fine remnant prairie supporting buffalo grass, little bluestem, and other native grasses. The Corps of Discovery camped not far away on April 17, 1805, as they were headed upstream in their two water-worthy pirogues and six new canoes. Once camp was set up for the night, it included a large bison-skin tepee, the mobile home of the Charbonneau family, who shared the spacious quarters with Lewis, Clark, and George Droulliard.

Mileage Log

0.0 Parshall. Continue riding north on SR 37.
1.5 Turn left onto SR 23/Lewis and Clark Trail.
18.5 New Town. Turn right onto SR 1804/Lewis and Clark Trail.
20.0 Leave Fort Berthold Indian Reservation.
49.5 102 Avenue Northwest. Enter Williams County.
56.0 County Road 21/105 Avenue.
65.5 Fifty-second Street.
74.0 CR 15.
80.0 125 Avenue.
90.5 Williston. Bear left onto University Avenue, then turn right onto First Street East.
92.5 Section ends at the corner of First Street East and U.S. 2 in Williston.

CHAPTER 4

Williston, North Dakota to Great Falls, Montana (538 miles)

As they proceeded on through Montana, which eighty-four years later, would become the forty-first state of the Union, the Corps of Discovery witnessed a magnificent countryside that in some areas has changed little to this day. In fact, the stretch of the Missouri River, along with the lands embracing it, between the James Kipp Bridge (north of Grass Range on U.S. Highway 191) and Fort Benton make up the wildest portion of the river corridor remaining. This meandering of river and drylands encompasses the Upper Missouri National Wild and Scenic River, six wilderness study areas, portions of two national historic trails (the Nez Percé and the Lewis and Clark), and the Missouri Breaks National Backcountry Byway. Unfortunately for the cyclist—but fortunately for the land and the critters living there, and for posterity—very few roads traverse the area. You won't actually lay eyes on the river for some 300 miles as you ride between Fort Peck and Fort Benton. That is not to say, though, that you won't experience some the most spectacular mountain-and-plains vistas in North America.

When you read in the journals of the Corps of Discovery's many harrowing encounters with grizzly bears—encounters that grew in number as they pushed into the future Montana—you might conclude that it is virtually unthinkable not one man was killed by a wounded bear. It's even more difficult to believe that not a single member of the party died in *any sort* of accident during their entire twenty-eight-month journey through largely uncharted territory filled with a multitude of hazards, both expected and unknown. How could that possibly have been, when seemingly every day in the news today we hear of people drowning, dying in mountaineering accidents, or getting killed while taking part in other outdoors activities? And this with help often just a cell-phone call away! These explorers were flawlessly prepared and incredibly self-reliant. That said, they also must have had one heaping helping of collective good luck.

Initially in Montana—especially if you're bucking headwinds—the riding might be characterized as "put your head down and grin and bear it" conditions. But after you turn south at Nashua and continue to Fort Peck, the riding and the scenery vastly improve. From Fort Peck to the junction with State Road 200, you'll enjoy fantastic cycling through rolling badland hills, along a fairly wide road with narrow shoulders. After turning west onto SR 200, you'll find that the road is quite narrow and very undulating. The wind will be a concern, too; it can affect your steering and make it hard, even impossible, to hear cars approaching from the rear. A rearview mirror, always a good idea, is strongly suggested in windy areas such as these.

From Lewistown to Fort Benton, you'll ride through the Montana of imagination—an idyllic scene that Charlie Russell, "America's Cowboy Artist," couldn't have bettered. Russell often called on his memories of some of these very landscapes to create paintings of the unfenced West of his younger years. Finally, from Fort Benton, a ride of about 40 miles will take you to Great Falls, a place that figured prominently in the travels of Lewis and Clark.

19 Williston, North Dakota to Poplar, Montana
95 miles (1,646 miles cumulative)

". . . my dog had been absent during the last night, and I was fear-
full we had lost him altogether, however, much to my satisfaction
he joined us at 8 oclock this morning."
>—CAPT. MERIWETHER LEWIS
>Thursday, April 25, 1805
>Near the Missouri-Yellowstone confluence

Approximately 23 miles after leaving Williston, the route passes close to **Fort Buford State Historic Site** (15349 Thirty-ninth Lane Northwest, Williston, ND 58801; 701–572–9034), open daily 9:00 A.M. to 6:00 P.M. mid-May through mid-September. Featuring a museum and primitive camping, the attraction is located just off the route from the junction of State Road 1804 and County Road 5.

Established in June 1866—and built in part from the dismantled Fort Union (see below)—Fort Buford was a military post strategically positioned at the confluence of the Missouri and Yellowstone Rivers. At its zenith the fort was the base of operations for six companies, including the black "buffalo soldiers" of the 10th Cavalry, who served at the post during its later years. Soldiers stationed there were charged with the mission of helping to keep peace on the buffalo-prairie frontier: They helped police the border between the United States and Canada, watched over steamboat traffic on the Missouri and Yellowstone Rivers, took part in the mid-1870s military campaign against nonreservation Indians, and, in the mid-1880s, helped protect the men who were toiling to extend the Great Northern Railroad through the region.

Indians who spent time, or *did* time, at Fort Buford included Sitting Bull, who turned himself in at the fort in July 1881, and Chief Joseph, who was brought to Fort Buford after surrendering on behalf of his Nez Percé people in the Bear's Paw Mountains of north-central Montana on October 5, 1877. The fort eventually proved unnecessary, as the surrounding countryside became more densely settled by whites and less populated with hostile Indians; it finally was abandoned in October 1895. Some of its structures still stand, however, including the commanding officer's quarters, a stone powder magazine, and the post hospital. If you happen to visit the site in mid-July, you can enjoy the Fort Buford 6th Infantry group's annual encampment and reenactment.

Fort Union Trading Post National Historic Site straddles the North Dakota-Montana border.

Located about a mile from Fort Buford, lying astride the North Dakota–Montana border, is **Fort Union Trading Post National Historic Site** (15550 Highway 1804, Williston, ND 58801; 701–572–9083; www.nps.gov/fous), open daily Memorial Day through Labor Day 8:00 A.M. to 8:00 P.M. and the rest of the year from 9:00 A.M. to 5:30 P.M. Only about a mile off the route, Fort Union is an absolute must-visit for any cyclist with an interest in American history, which describes just about anyone riding the Lewis & Clark Bicycle Trail.

Fur-trading companies took notice of this area after William Clark opined that whoever gained control of the Yellowstone-Missouri confluence would likely wind up commanding the fur trade of the entire Northwest. John Jacob Astor's American Fur Company established Fort Union here in 1828, under the supervision of a wily and ruthless Scot-Canadian named Kenneth McKenzie, who also served as the post's first manager, or *bourgeois*.

For the next thirty years, Fort Union was at the heart of the upper Missouri region's fur trade. Crow Indians from the upper Yellowstone, Blackfeet from the Missouri headwaters, Assiniboine from both sides of the Canadian border, and, from the east, Mandan, Hidatsa, and Arikara all traveled to the fort, hauling in beaver pelts and bison hides to trade for firearms, pots, clothing, and other goods. At its peak the fort employed approximately one hundred men, many of whom had Indian wives and children living there, too. In addition to black, white, and Native Americans, people from many other countries, including France, England, Germany, Russia, and Spain, found their way to the isolated fort, where the two main arteries draining the east slope of the northern Rockies became as one. Explorers who visited the frontier fort included the likes of artists George Catlin and Karl Bodmer and Father Pierre-Jean De Smet, whose long career of missionary and conversion work with western tribes began in 1838 when he established the St. Joseph's Mission for the Pottawattomies at Council Bluffs, Iowa. He went on from there to work with the Flathead, Blackfeet, Sioux, and many other tribes.

Trade—first for beaver pelts and then for tanned bison hides (after the demand for beaver dwindled in the mid-1830s, a victim of changing fashion tastes in Europe and the East Coast)—was strong until the steamboat *St. Peter* delivered a scourge of smallpox in 1837. This decimated many of the Indians, yet trade picked up again and remained robust until another smallpox epidemic hit in 1857. Activity dried up altogether during the Civil War, and in 1868 most of Fort Union's buildings were dismantled by soldiers and moved a mile downstream to be used in a burgeoning new army outpost called Fort Buford—an ironic turn of affairs when you consider that a primary impetus for establishing the military post was to provide Fort Union protection against the Sioux, who were becoming ever-more hostile toward both whites and other Indians.

Thanks to archaeological excavations and reconstructions that took place between 1985 and 1991, the fort has reclaimed much of its 1851 appearance, replete with stone bastions, an Indian trade house, and the impressive Bourgeois House, former quarters of the post manager. The prairie surrounding the fort, too, is being restored to its near-native condition to evoke the look of the mid-1800s, when the plain stretching a mile north provided plenty of room for Indians to erect their tepees at trading time. During those sessions, liquor illegally brought in by traders was used to lubricate the natives, who, once drunk, would sometimes turn violent. The violence typically was aimed not at whites but at other Indians, who often held age-old grudges against one another. Those days—sans violence, one imagines—are relived during the third week of June, when Fort Union hosts its yearly fur-trade rendezvous.

On entering Montana, don't forget to set your watch back an hour. At Mile 59 below, 23 miles into the state, you'll enter Culbertson, which has a free city park campground. The town was named for Alexander Culbertson, a bourgeois who succeeded Kenneth McKenzie at Fort Union. His namesake community popped up here on the prairie in 1887 with the arrival of the railroad.

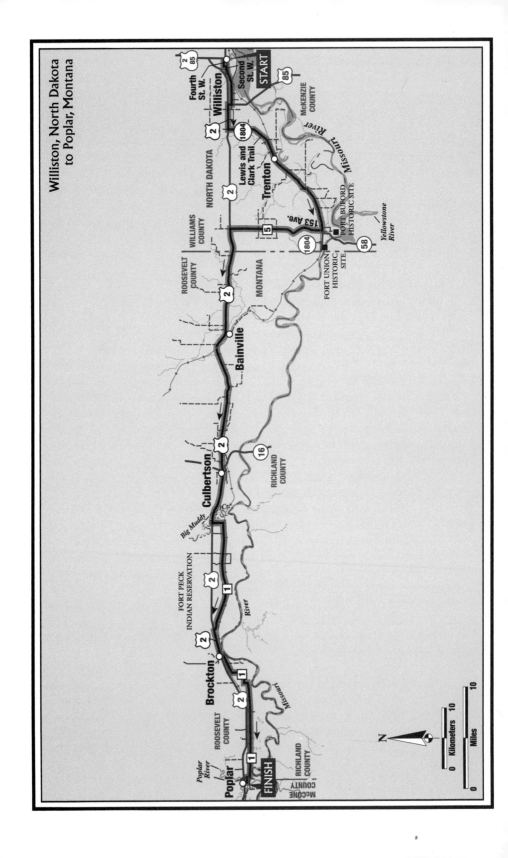

Williston, North Dakota
to Poplar, Montana

0.0 Williston. Ride west on First Street and turn right onto Washington Avenue, then left onto Fourth Street West. Twelve blocks later, turn left onto Fourteenth Avenue West, then right onto Second Street West.

1.5 Turn left onto the frontage road paralleling U.S. Highway 2/85.

5.5 Turn right onto U.S. 85. In 0.1 mile turn left onto U.S. 2.

8.0 Turn left onto SR 1804/Lewis and Clark Trail.

14.5 Trenton.

23.5 Turn right onto CR 5/153rd Avenue.

33.5 Turn left onto U.S. 2.

36.0 Enter Montana.

44.5 Bainville.

59.0 Culbertson.

64.5 Cross Big Muddy Creek and enter the Fort Peck Indian Reservation. Turn left onto CR 1.

77.0 Turn left onto U.S. 2.

80.0 Brockton. Turn left onto unsigned CR 1.

94.0 Turn right at T; after 0.2 mile turn left onto unsigned C Street.

95.0 Turn right at T onto unsigned Second Avenue. In 0.2 mile turn left onto F Street/U.S. 2. Poplar.

20 Poplar to Fort Peck, Montana
74 miles (1,720 miles cumulative)

*". . . a verry extraodernarey climate, to behold the trees Green &
flowers spred on the plain, & Snow an inch deep . . ."*
—CAPT. WILLIAM CLARK
Thursday, May 2, 1805
East of present-day Poplar, Montana

As you progress through this northeastern corner of Montana—alternately
ascending ridges then zipping down through drainages—your immediate
surroundings are low, rolling hills, with wheat fields in the bottoms and the
rugged breaks of the Missouri River visible not far to the south. Watch for
Amtrak's *Empire Builder* roaring by or for a flock of low-flying American
white pelicans aiming northeast toward the Missouri Coteau, a nearby proliferation of prairie pothole lakes occupying depressions left behind by
Pleistocene glaciers.

Soon you'll arrive in the largest town on the Fort Peck Indian Reservation, home to Sioux and Assiniboine peoples. The sign at town's edge reads,
WELCOME TO WOLF POINT—LEWIS AND CLARK SLEPT HERE, WHY DON'T YOU? Take
that advice to heart, because you've already ridden nearly 60 miles since
leaving Culbertson. One place where you can emulate Lewis and Clark is at
the **Rancho Motel & Campground** (P.O. Box 884, Wolf Point, MT 59201;
406–653–1382), located on the north side of U.S. Highway 2 a couple miles
west of town.

Capt. William Clark and George Droulliard killed a grizzly bear on May
5, 1805, the day the Corps of Discovery erected camp near present-day Wolf
Point. Wrote Capt. Lewis: ". . . it was a most tremendious looking anamal,
extreemly hard to kill notwithstanding he had five balls through his lungs
and five others in various parts he swam more than half the distance across
the river to a sandbar, & it was at least twenty minutes before he died . . ."
This particular beast measured more than 8½ feet from the back of its hind
feet to its snout. Clark estimated that it weighed 500 pounds, but Lewis
guessed the weight to be closer to 600 pounds.

Speaking of wildlife (wild life, that is), if you happen to be pedaling
through Wolf Point during the second full weekend of July, don't miss the
Wild Horse Stampede (406–653–2012), the granddaddy of Montana's
rodeos, with roots going back to the early 1900s. In addition to the expected
buckin' horses, barrel racing, and calf roping, associated activities include
Indian cultural displays and a carnival.

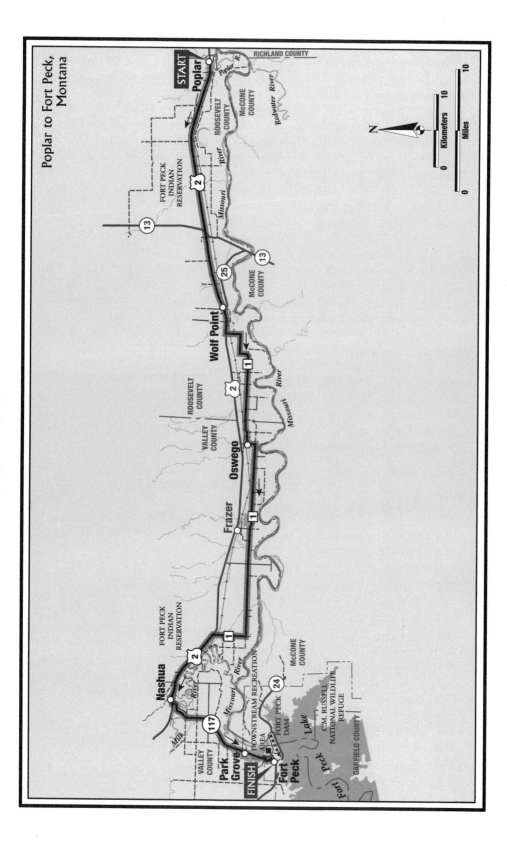

Poplar to Fort Peck, Montana

After you leave the Fort Peck Indian Reservation and turn onto State Road 117 at Nashua, to the left you'll see **Bergie's** (406–746–3441), a plain brown wrapper of a structure holding a 24-karat surprise in the form of homemade ice cream. Driving to Bergie's to sample the seasonal favorites is a time-honored tradition for Montana folks from miles around (not to mention visitors from North Dakota and Saskatchewan). Rhubarb and chokecherry are a couple of the more popular summertime taste treats.

Just south of Nashua you'll ride across the stream that, as described by Capt. Lewis on May 8, 1805, ". . . possesses a peculiar whiteness, being about the colour of a cup of tea with the admixture of a tablespoonfull of milk. from the colour of it's water we called it Milk river . . ." Lewis speculated that the river might offer a connection to the Saskatchewan River to the north. In reality it begins on the east slope of Glacier National Park and enters Alberta north of Cut Bank, Montana, then reenters the United States after looping through Writing-on-Stone Provincial Park. While flowing through a deep gorge in Canada, the river picks up the fine sediment responsible for its whitish color. Although it's true that the Milk carries an unusually large sediment load in the spring, the rumor that the mud is so thick you can walk across the river at that time of year is not true.

As you come into Park Grove, just a couple of miles before Fort Peck, you'll see a nice swimming beach off to the right. From there, rather than climbing the hill into Fort Peck you might want to continue straight off the route for a mile to locate the **Downstream Recreation Area** (U.S. Army Corps of Engineers, P.O. Box 208, Fort Peck, MT 59223; 406–526–3224), with its pleasant, cottonwood-shrouded campground.

 Mileage Log

0.0 Poplar. Continue riding west on U.S. 2.
15.0 Cross State Road 13.
22.0 Wolf Point.
24.5 Turn left onto unsigned County Road 1, the first paved road past Milepost 589.
28.0 Route bends right.
35.5 Oswego. Turn left at T, then turn right 0.75 mile later.
43.0 Frazer, 0.7 mile north off route.
52.0 Turn right to follow CR 1.
55.0 Turn left onto U.S. 2.
62.5 Leave Fort Peck Indian Reservation. Nashua. Turn left onto SR 117.
64.0 Cross Milk River.
71.5 Park Grove.
74.0 Downtown Fort Peck

21

Fort Peck to Jordan, Montana
96 miles (1,816 miles cumulative)

". . . the Indian woman to whom I ascribe equal fortitude and resolution, with any person onboard at the time of the accedent, caught and preserved most of the light articles which were washed overboard."

—CAPT. MERIWETHER LEWIS
Thursday, May 16, 1805
On the aftermath of a near-disastrous capsizing of the white pirogue, caused by Charbonneau's ineptitude as a boatman

Fort Peck is a surprisingly civilized-looking place, contrasting sharply with its wild and woolly surroundings. Enjoy the oasis of shade trees and green grass while you can, for it yields to 230 miles of some of the emptiest, driest country you'll ever see.

An independent municipality that retains the look of a government town, Fort Peck took its name and grew up a couple of miles from the site of Old Fort Peck. Built as trading post in 1867 by the company of Durfee and Peck, the modest structure of about 300 square feet, with 12-foot-high walls of vertically set cottonwood logs, sat along a rock ledge 30 or 40 feet above the Missouri River. The position made it an ideal landing for stern-wheeler steamboats; unfortunately, the location also resulted in the trading post being washed away when the river flooded in the 1870s.

Where you turn onto the dam near **West End Campground** (U.S. Army Corps of Engineers, P.O. Box 208, Fort Peck, MT 59223; 406–526–3411), you'll look out over deep, blue-green waters so expansive that you almost expect to see the tide coming in or going out. Dessicated fingers of land stretching into the colorful water bring to mind the Persian Gulf region or some similar exotic mix of water and desert.

After skirting the site of Old Fort Peck, you'll turn onto the Fort Peck Dam and ride for more than 3 miles before getting to the other side—it's that big. Construction of the dam was authorized by President Franklin D. Roosevelt in 1933, when the country was deep in the throes of the Great Depression. Ostensibly the goal of the project was to enhance river navigation and flood protection; in reality the creation of jobs was a more important factor. This, the largest earth-filled dam in the United States, was also the first dam-building project in the upper Missouri River basin. It attracted more than 10,000 men and women to work on the dam itself and thousands more to establish and staff businesses both essential (grocery stores, hardware stores) and nonessential (bars, brothels) that provided services for the dam workers and their families. At the peak, eighteen boomtowns claimed an estimated total 50,000 residents. And in this arid piece of Montana outback, a shipyard, of all things, was created to build the "Fort Peck Navy," which dredged and pumped the river-bottom slurry used to form the earthen dam. The final load was deposited in October 1940, and the turbines generated their first electricity about three years later.

One of the most appealing pieces of the dam-building era remaining is the Fort Peck Theatre, an attractive wooden structure built in the spirit of a large Swiss chalet. It opened as a movie theater in November 1934, screening *The Richest Girl in the World* with Fay Wray, Joel McCrea, and Miriam Hopkins. Movies ran seven days a week, twenty-four hours a day during the construction heyday. Although intended only as a temporary structure, it persevered and now houses the **Fort Peck Summer Theatre** (P.O. Box 973, Glasgow, MT 59230; 406–526–3534), where professional-quality shows are presented through much of the summer. Alongside several other buildings in Fort Peck, the theater resides on the National Register of Historic Places.

The **Fort Peck Power Plant Visitor Center and Museum** (Power Plant No. 1, Fort Peck, MT 59923; 406–526–3431) is found in the lobby of Power Plant No. 1, just off the route from near the east side of the dam. You can take a free guided tour (daily from Memorial Day through Labor Day) and gain an appreciation for the magnitude of the project that culminated in this immense dam and its associated waterworks. The museum also features fossils and skeletons collected in the area, including a triceratops skull.

Not long after exiting the dam, you'll see a pullout on the right with interpretive signs discussing various aspects of the Lewis and Clark expedition. One of them mentions that as the explorers traveled through this area, game was so abundant that the men could hardly look in any direction without seeing deer, bison, elk, or antelope. As you look out over Fort Peck Lake, it is impossible to discern exactly where the river they followed would have flowed. And as you gaze at the lake that the river has become, know that you won't glimpse the Missouri's waters again until Fort Benton, more than 300 miles away.

Proceeding south from the dam and lake, you'll negotiate a maze of river breaks—a subdued, earth-tone kaleidoscope of sediments that were horizontally deposited and subsequently sculpted by water into steep slopes and erosional-remnant knobs. Particularly in early morning and evening, keep an eye out for the monster mule deer known to hang out in and around the protected coulees. There's no question about it: You will feel like an explorer while cycling through this dreamscape.

Although you'd never guess it, private cabins line portions of the lakeshore just a few miles to the west, accessed by the occasional road you'll see going that way. One of them, Nelson Creek Road (45 miles from Fort Peck), leads about 7 miles off route to the primitive **Nelson Creek Campground** (U.S. Army Corps of Engineers, P.O. Box 208, Fort Peck, MT 59223;

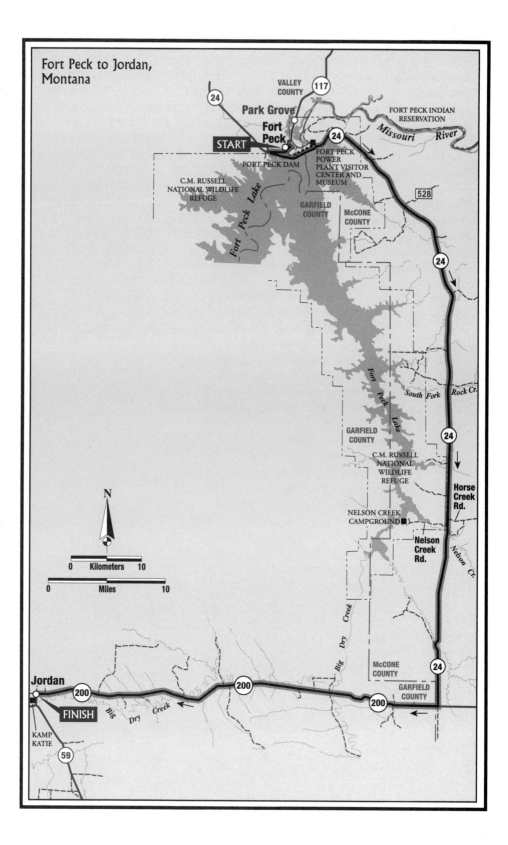

406–526–3411). Primitive "slop camping" is an option, too: Although you cannot legally free-form camp off Nelson Creek Road (it immediately enters the Charles M. Russell National Wildlife Refuge), you can if you continue south for a mile or two, where you'll be beyond the refuge border and on Bureau of Land Management lands. Free-form camping is fine there.

After some 60 miles of badlands bicycling, during which you may pass a handful of small cattle herds and even fewer residences—presto!—you'll have put enough distance between yourself and the river basin that you're into a rolling, unbroken terrain replete with plowed fields and farmhouses. Thirty-six miles after turning west onto State Road 200, you'll arrive in Jordan, the most isolated county seat in the lower forty-eight states. An option for camping here is the private **Kamp Katie** (P.O. Box 44, Jordan, MT 59337; 406–557–2851), located in a secluded setting just off SR 200 on the southern outskirts of town.

Mileage Log

0.0	Downtown Fort Peck.
1.0	Turn left onto SR 24.
2.0	Cross Fort Peck Dam.
9.5	Leave C. M. Russell National Wildlife Refuge.
15.5	County Road 528.
32.5	South Fork Rock Creek.
44.0	Horse Creek Road.
54.5	Timber Creek
60.0	Turn right onto SR 200.
82.0	Big Dry Creek.
96.0	Jordan.

". . . a handsome river of about fifty yards in width discharged itself into the shell river on the Stard. or upper side; this stream we called Sah-ca-ger we-ah or bird woman's River, after our interpreter the Snake woman."
> —CAPT. MERIWETHER LEWIS
> Monday, May 20, 1805
> At the Sacagawea River (a.k.a. Crooked Creek),
> near the mouth of the Musselshell

It was in the Jordan area in 1996 that the potentially dark side of western independence showed its hateful face, when a small contingent of Montana Freemen barricaded themselves in at a Garfield County farm. The Freemen, a loosely knit group of white supremists who believed that federal and state government had no authority over them, holed up following a multistate buying spree in which the members used their odd beliefs to justify buying cars, houses, and other high-ticket items with bogus checks. The Freemen were imports to the state of Montana, yet local sentiment in Jordan for their antigovernment views was generally sympathetic—until they started threatening public officials and exhibiting other sorts of deranged and paranoid behavior.

Delving much farther back into Jordan's past, the **Garfield County Museum** features displays on the important dinosaur finds in the vicinity of Nelson Creek and elsewhere in the area. (The museum, located at the east end of town, keeps irregular hours; call 406–557–2501 or 406–557–2517 for information.) The source of those dinosaur fossils is the Hell Creek Formation, a phrase that is known and respected by paleontologists worldwide; many of the finest dinosaur specimens ever found have come from the formation. Triceratops—pieces and parts of them, anyway—is the dinosaur most commonly found in the Hell Creek Formation. Other finds have included *Tyrannosaurus rex*, including the first nearly complete one, discovered in 1902 by paleontologist Barnum Brown of the American Museum of Natural History.

The Hell Creek Formation was deposited during the Late Cretaceous period, between sixty-eight and sixty-five million years ago, when the region was a vast low-lying, largely treeless plain bordering an inland sea. Rivers flowing eastward through the plain caused periodic flooding, which appears to have been responsible for trapping and concentrating large numbers of dinosaurs. The 300-foot-thick formation, representing three million years of deposition, ends abruptly at the K/T Boundary, which is the line of demarcation between the end of the dinosaur age and the beginning of the age of mammals. ("K" signifies the end of the Cretaceous period and "T" the beginning of the Tertiary.) The clearly discernible K/T Boundary in the Missouri River badlands north of Jordan was one of the most important finds supporting the theory first put forth in 1980 that the dinosaurs—along with an estimated 60 percent of all plant and animal species on the planet at the time—went extinct due to a cataclysmic event. That event, so goes the theory (one backed by strong evidence), was an immense meteor crashing into the earth at Chicxulub, Mexico, which resulted in worldwide acid rain and other devastating climate changes.

The name Jack Horner is likewise immediately recognized by paleontologists throughout the world. Horner is the paleontology curator for the Museum of the Rockies in Bozeman, Montana, whose collection accounts for nearly half the approximate two dozen *T. rex* individuals ever discovered. Several of the museum's specimens were found on recent forays into the Hell Creek area. Horner is an unorthodox bone man who has a history of turning "gospel truths" on their ear. One of his most ground-shaking assertions is that *T. rex*, widely considered the most terrible "terrible lizard" of all, was not the fearsome predator that the beast has been depicted in countless science-fiction movies. Horner and others determined that, due to its size, shape, and density, *T. rex* could not have stood upright, for such a posture would have broken its back; more likely, it stood bent over at the waist. This revelation, coupled with other findings such as the discovery that the dinosaur's arms were tiny and virtually useless, led Horner to the stunning conclusion that *T. rex* was not a savage killer but, like today's hyena and turkey vulture, a lowly scavenger!

After you visit remote Jordan—one of the few places in the nation where satellite radio might really make sense (electricity didn't get there until 1951; phone service, five years later)—and see the hardscrabble farmlands surrounding it, you may wonder how long the town can survive. Who will ever move there, other than temporary residents like first-year teachers and BLM employees? And will the kids who grow up there be willing to stay on the farm and try to eke out a meager living? Well, a small but growing series of movements—the Big Open and Buffalo Commons proposals are the best known—are attempting to persuade landowners here to consider ending the struggle of imposing their will on the land and go with the flow, by bringing back the short-grass prairie and its native species in great numbers— bison, elk, pronghorn, and other animals. Under this scenario these farmer-ranchers would stop growing hay and grazing Herefords on their lands and begin offering big-game hunting and photo safaris. To say that such proposals have not been met with open arms by the locals is a world-class understatement. But if the drought years continue, and if more and

Might these sheep grazing the Big Open outside Jordan some day be supplanted by bison and elk?

more ranchers continue going under, you never know what might happen. The 15,000-square-mile Big Open—an area considered to include all of Garfield County and portions of adjacent counties—might one day reclaim its role as the Serengeti of America, as it was when Lewis and Clark saw it.

As you ride west from Jordan, you'll begin appreciating the meaning behind Montana's nickname, Big Sky Country. Site distances improve as the creek drainages broaden and become shallower. If the day is partly cloudy, you might come over a hilltop to be struck by a singular mix of sun and shade on distant knolls and flat-topped buttes—some of them awash in light and others dark in shadow. What you see is constantly changing and will never look precisely the same again; it is just for you at this moment frozen in time.

Approximately 50 miles east of Jordan, you'll pass through a short stretch of timbered breaks where you might track down a primitive camping site. Some of the surrounding lands are private and others are managed by the BLM, but they're not necessarily signed as to which is which. To identify potential (legal) free-form camping areas, obtain the map of the area through the BLM (Lewistown Field Office, Airport Road, P.O. Box 1160, Lewistown, MT 59457; 406–538–7461). If you'd prefer to continue all the way to Winnett, camping is available there at the **Hilltop Campground** (P.O. Box 32, Winnett, MT 59087; 406–429–5321).

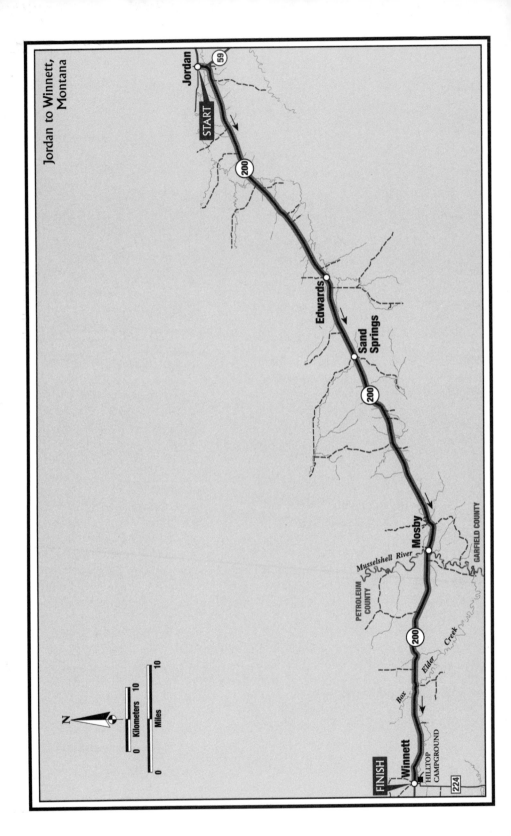

Mileage Log

0.0   Continue west from Jordan on State Road 200.

24.5   Edwards.

32.0   Sand Springs.

53.5   Mosby. Cross Musselshell River into Petroleum County.

67.0   Box Elder Creek.

76.5   Winnett.

23 Winnett to Lewistown, Montana
53 miles (1,945.5 miles cumulative)

". . . on arriving to the summit [of] one of the highest points in the neighbourhood I thought myself well repaid for my labour; as from this point I beheld the Rocky Mountains for the first time . . ."
—CAPT. MERIWETHER LEWIS
Sunday, May 26, 1805
Upstream from Cow Creek

Although you haven't glimpsed Fort Peck Lake since losing sight of it southeast of the Fort Peck Dam—you've been too far either to the east or the south—you have been pedaling parallel to the reservoir since leaving the dam. It's not until you travel a few miles west of Winnett that you're completely beyond the lake's westernmost reaches. Claiming a length of 134 miles and 1,520 miles of shoreline, the big pond is contained within the boundaries of the **Charles M. Russell National Wildlife Refuge** (P.O. Box 110, Airport Road, Lewistown, MT 59457; 406–538–8706), the largest unfragmented national wildlife refuge in the contiguous forty-eight states. A splendid mosaic of native short-grass prairie, brushy and timbered coulees, rich river bottoms, and arid badlands, the refuge encompasses a staggering 1.1 million acres, nearly a quarter of which are covered by Fort Peck Lake. The refuge is home to more than 200 species of birds and 60 mammal species, including mule deer, pronghorns, bighorn sheep, and one of the country's few remaining prairie elk herds. (Given a choice and a lack of human harassment, elk prefer the prairie, which is where Lewis and Clark encountered them.)

However, unless you have a boat suitable for big, windy waters—unlikely, since you're on a bicycle trip—for the most part the lands surrounding the lake are inaccessible. One place you *can* access them is along the gravel/dirt road shooting eastward from just north of the U.S. Highway 191 bridge (off the route 40 miles north of Grass Range). The road winds along a 20-mile stretch of river bottom just downstream from the west end of Fort Peck Lake, where the Missouri retains its riverlike qualities. Recommended side trips by motor vehicle are generally not within the realm of this book, but if you want to make one exception, this untamed tangle of terrain, with its heart-stopping views of the Missouri Breaks, might be the place to do it. If you're not blessed with a sag wagon, look into renting a vehicle in Lewistown (call Budget Rent-A-Car at 406–538–7701 or Hilltop Motors at 406–

538–4014). Before heading out, be sure to stop in at the BLM (Lewistown Field Office, Airport Road, P.O. Box 1160, Lewistown, MT 59457; 406–538–7461) for detailed information and travel advice, such as: Rains can make the gumbo-clay portions of the route temporarily impassable and unusable for bicycles and cars alike.

Beginning at the west end of the refuge is the newly designated **Upper Missouri River Breaks National Monument** (contact the BLM office listed above; www.mt.blm.gov/ldo/um); it's so new, in fact, that you'll see it depicted only on the newest of maps. In one of his final acts as President of the United States, Bill Clinton signed the proclamation creating the monument on January 17, 2001. He did so in the East Room of the White House, where two centuries earlier Thomas Jefferson had worked making plans for his Corps of Discovery's journey.

Like the also-new Grand Staircase–Escalante National Monument in southern Utah, Upper Missouri River Breaks is unusual among our national monuments in that it is administered by the Bureau of Land Management rather than the National Park Service. At the heart of the monument is the Upper Missouri National Wild and Scenic River, a 149-mile stretch of the Missouri between Fort Benton and the James Kipp Bridge that is still in a nearly natural condition. Here the wide, winding, cottonwood-hugged river yields to lofty multihued cliffs and to deeply etched feeder coulees supporting juniper, yucca, and other vegetation. Wrapped as it is in such an untrammeled landscape, this segment of the river and its adjacent breaks have changed less since Lewis and Clark's time than any other long portion of the Missouri River remaining.

As you will see on the approach to town, Lewistown and its surroundings paint the perfect western picture. It's as though all the natural assets of beautiful, broad-shouldered Montana come together here smack in the middle of the state: grassy meadows, timbered mountain ridges, trout-filled streams, badlands, lofty buttes, and big, big skies. If the atmospheric conditions are just right, you'll watch as wisps of virga whip down from the sky, evaporating before they ever have a chance to dampen the slopes of the Judith Mountains northeast of town.

The Judith Mountains, incidentally, along with other "Judiths" in the area—Judith River, Judith Basin, Judith Gap—are namesakes of Judith Hancock, the woman Capt. William Clark would marry on his return to the East. Lewistown, however, was not named after Capt. Meriwether Lewis but after Maj. William H. Lewis, whose name was given to a temporary army post established here in the mid-1870s for the purpose of protecting those traveling the Carroll Trail. Fort Lewis evolved into Lewistown, which today boasts one of the most attractive and best preserved downtown districts in all Montana, with numerous stone structures crafted by skilled Croatian immigrants who moved in around the turn of the twentieth century.

Compared with where you've been for the previous few hundred miles, Lewistown feels like the absolute heart of modern civilization—like

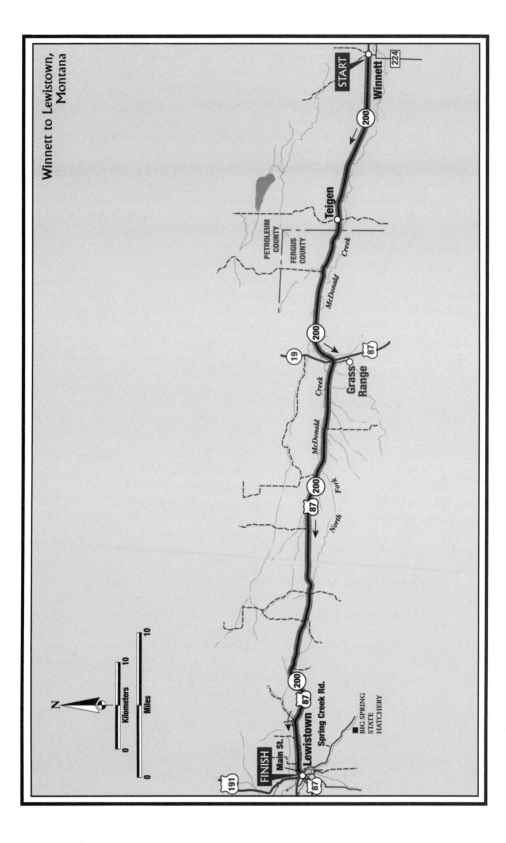

Manhattan, only way more laid back. If you choose to hang around the likable town for a day or two, be sure to make your way up Big Spring Creek to the **Big Spring State Hatchery** (406–538–5588), 6.5 miles south of Lewistown on Spring Creek Road. The peaceful park adjacent to the hatchery makes an ideal spot to spread a picnic or simply laze around.

Mileage Log

0.0   Continue riding west from Winnett on SR 200.
12.0 Teigen.
12.5 Enter Fergus County.
18.5 McDonald Creek.
23.0 U.S. 87 joins route. Grass Range, 1.0 mile south off route.
30.5 Cross North Fork McDonald Creek.
53.0 Route becomes Main Street in Lewistown.

24 Lewistown to Fort Benton, Montana
100 miles (2,045.5 miles cumulative)

> ". . . *Today we passed on the Stard. side the remains of a vast many mangled carcases of Baffalow which had been driven over a precipice of 120 feet by the Indians and perished . . . they created a most horrid stench. in this manner the Indians of the Missouri distroy vast herds of buffaloe at a stroke . . ."*
>
> —CAPT. MERIWETHER LEWIS
> Wednesday, May 29, 1805
> Near Arrow Creek, or "Slaughter River"

Leaving Lewistown, for 9 miles you will ride along U.S. Highway 191, part of the designated **Nez Percé (Nee-me-poo) National Historic Trail.** Only about 100 miles north of here, on October 5, 1877, the legendary trek of the Nez Percé came to a close at the Bear's Paw Battlefield. Although more than seventy years separated the two heroic journeys, the trek of the Nez Percé had indirect ties to the Lewis and Clark expedition.

"Do them no hurt," are the words attributed to Watkuseis, a Nez Percé elder addressing a council that had gathered to determine the fate of the white men who emerged cold, hungry, and sick with dysentery from the west slope of the Bitterroot Mountains in late September 1805. The Nez Percé opted to follow her advice, and the gracious Indians gave members of the Corps of Discovery food and navigational guidance, nursed them back to health, and agreed to keep their horses for the winter—horses the expedition would need the following summer to recross the Bitterroots.

The harsh realities the expedition had confronted in the Bitterroot Range killed any remaining hopes the captains may have harbored of finding an all-water Northwest Passage. But during the winter of 1805–06, while camped at Fort Clatsop, Capt. Lewis concocted a plan that he felt could salvage the expedition's primary mission of establishing a trade route to the Pacific: The Nez Percé and their nimble Appaloosa horses, he believed, would become a key link in a trade route passing directly through the northern Rockies.

It was not to be. Rather than becoming pivotal players in an important trading partnership, during the ensuing seven decades the Nez Percé suffered white missionaries, land grabbers, and gold seekers, who collectively squeezed the Indians into an ever-shrinking remnant of their home territory. Several chiefs, including Joseph, Looking Glass, and White Bird, determined that their peoples' last shot at leading a free and peaceful existence

The upper Missouri River courses beneath the foothills of the Highwood Mountains south of Fort Benton, Montana.

was to move them elsewhere. Beginning in June 1877, the chiefs led some 750 Nez Percé men, women, and children—accompanied by nearly 2,000 Appaloosas—on a circuitous, 1,170-mile trek lasting four months. While alternately fleeing from and defending themselves against pursuing U.S. Army troops under the command of Generals Howard, Miles, and Sturgis, the Nez Percé traveled through eastern Oregon, Idaho, Montana, Yellowstone National Park in Wyoming, and then back into Montana. The journey ended for most of the Indians along Snake Creek in the Bear's Paw Mountains, just 40 miles shy of Canada and their perceived liberation. Here Chief Joseph spoke those stirring and memorable words, "It is cold and we have no blankets. The little children are freezing to death . . . Hear me, my chiefs! I am tired. My heart is sick and sad. From where the sun now stands, I will fight no more forever."

This is by no means the last you will hear or see of the Nez Percé Trail, nor of the **Nez Percé National Historical Park** (39063 U.S. Highway 95, Spalding, ID 83540; 208–843–2261; www.nps.gov/nepe). The park—unusual in that it is as much a concept as it is a physical presence—encompasses more than three dozen sites scattered along the historic trail. The Bear's Paw Battlefield has no visitor center, but exhibits relating to the site can be found at the **Blaine County Museum** (501 Indiana Street, Chinook, MT 59523; 406–357–2590).

Back on the route, approximately 3 miles after turning onto State Road 81 you'll pass the entrance to **Gigantic Warm Spring** (admission fee; open from 10:00 A.M. until dark; 406–538–9825), a descriptively named enterprise located on the ranch of the Dave Vanek family. Here a pool holds water diverted from Warm Spring Creek; with its adjacent picnic ground, the scene makes a terrific place to stop for an early lunch.

Continuing on, you'll cross Warm Spring Creek, ride through a rimrock setting of yellow rock and beefy pine trees, and cross the Judith River. From there you'll climb for 3.5 miles before popping out into more of Charlie Russell's trademark high-plains country, where the views are endless and the lean of old barns reveals a lot about which way the prevailing winds blow. Soon you'll arrive at the settlement of Square Butte where, by leaving the route and riding a mile-plus on gravel and dirt, you'll come to the trailhead for the hike leading up the geologic feature of the same name. **Square Butte** (BLM Lewistown Field Office, Airport Road, P.O. Box 1160, Lewistown, MT 59457; 406–538–7461), an imposing, 2,000-foot-high volcanic laccolith, is home to an array of wildlife, including several species of raptors and a herd of shaggy white mountain goats. An official "outstanding natural area" in the view of the BLM, the butte offers rewarding views from its top, reached by a tough uphill hike of about a mile.

Camping options in this section include Denton, located just 38 miles from Lewistown, and Geraldine, 73 miles out. A drawback of camping at the latter is that it leaves only 27 miles remaining to Fort Benton, meaning that you might be tempted to push on another 43 miles to Great Falls on the same day. That would be a mistake; at least an afternoon and a night should be dedicated to Fort Benton, arguably the most history-rich community in Montana. If you do get there with plenty of daylight hours remaining, consider signing on with one of the numerous outfitters in the area, such as **Missouri Breaks River Co.** (406–453–3035; www.missouribreaksriver co.com), specializing in day trips on the Missouri via inboard jet boats; **Adventure Bound Canoe & Shuttle Co.** (877–538–4890; www.montanariver trip. com), offering canoe and kayak outings of various lengths on the Upper Missouri National Wild and Scenic River; and **White Cliff Tours** (406–728–2960; www.skybusiness.com/whiteclifftours), which runs day and half-day driving and driving-hiking tours to the magnificent White Cliffs of the Missouri, a scenic spectacle otherwise commonly viewed only by those making multiday canoe trips. If you'd like to dedicate a few days to off-bike adventure, call the **Upper Missouri River Keelboat Co.** (406–739–4333; www.mrkeelboat.com). They offer three- and four-day river expeditions aboard the 38-foot *Gen. Wm. Ashley* in the company of a crew properly outfitted for the pre-steamboat, fur-trade days.

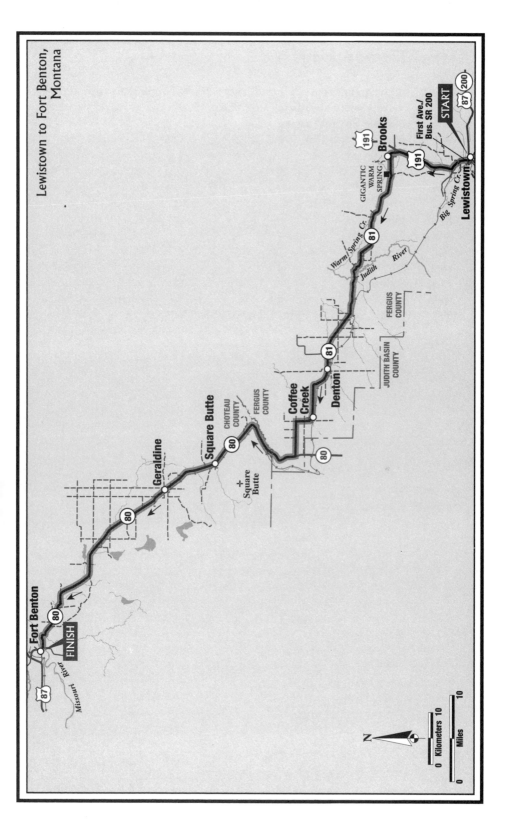

Lewistown to Fort Benton, Montana

Mileage Log

0.0 In Lewistown, cross railroad tracks and 0.1 mile later turn right onto First Avenue/Business State Road 20. U.S. 87 leaves route. Cross Big Spring Creek.

0.5 Turn right onto U.S. 191.

9.5 Turn left onto SR 81.

11.5 Brooks.

19.5 Warm Spring Creek.

27.0 Judith River.

38.5 Denton.

46.5 Coffee Creek.

52.0 Turn right onto SR 80.

66.0 Square Butte.

73.5 Geraldine.

99.5 Cross Missouri River.

100.0 Fort Benton. Turn right, following SR 80.

25 Fort Benton to Great Falls, Montana
43.5 miles (2,089 miles cumulative)

". . . An interesting question was now to be determined; which of these rivers was the Missouri . . . to mistake the stream . . . would not only loose us the whole of this season but would probably so dishearten the party that it might defeat the expedition altogether . . ."

—CAPT. MERIWETHER LEWIS
Monday, June 3, 1805
At the confluence of the
Missouri and Marias Rivers

Where Loma sits today (11 miles northeast off the route from Fort Benton), the weary and footsore Corps of Discovery faced a major conundrum: The river they'd been on for more than a year split into two forks of nearly equal size. They established a base camp at the confluence for more than a week, making exploratory trips up both forks to try to solve the puzzle. Initially, Lewis and six men followed the right-hand fork; Clark, with five others, explored the south. The captains concluded that the northerly fork was not the Missouri; most everyone else in the party, however, believed it *was*. For one thing, it was the muddier of the two, muddy like the Missouri they had become accustomed to. Lewis and Clark figured, rightly so, that the Missouri *should* begin running cleaner as they got close to the mountains. After the two parties regrouped, Lewis and four companions set off again, this time pushing farther upstream on the south fork than Clark had gone on his initial foray. In three days' time they reached the great falls, a major hurdle on the Missouri about which the Mandan had forewarned the explorers. The expedition leaders were correct: The south fork was the Missouri River.

Lewis named the other stream Maria's River (now spelled *Marias* and pronounced *Muh-RYE-us*) after his lovely cousin, Maria Wood, about whom he waxed absolutely poetically: ". . . it is true that the hue of the waters of this turbulent and troubled stream but illy comport with the pure celestial virtues and amiable qualifications of that loved fair one . . ."

The Missouri River upstream of its confluence with the Marias makes an impressive gash in the corrugated gray prairie surrounding Fort Benton. Stroll along the waterfront in the Birthplace of Montana—a.k.a. "the bloodiest block in the West" and "the world's most inland port"—and you will encounter a slew of interesting things to see. One of them is the *Mandan*, a

62-foot keelboat built for the 1951 production of Montana author A. B. Guthrie's *The Big Sky*, which was filmed in and around the Snake River in Jackson Hole, Wyoming. Other attractions include a monument to world-famous Shep the dog and the **Lewis and Clark State Memorial,** a stunning oversized sculpture of Lewis, Clark, and a kneeling Sakagawea, all three of them overlooking the waters of the river they'd become so intimate with—pondering, perhaps, which way to go at the Missouri-Marias confluence. Created by the late Bob Scriver, the sculpture was done as part of Montana's contribution to the 1976 American Bicentennial.

While in Fort Benton be sure also to visit the **Museum of the Upper Missouri** (P.O. Box 262, Fort Benton, MT 59442; 406–622–5316; www.fort benton.com/attract.htm) and the **Museum of the Great Plains** (1205 Twentieth Street, Fort Benton, MT 59442; 406–622–5316; www.fortbenton.com/attract.htm). Both are open Mother's Day through the last Sunday in September, daily from 10:00 A.M. to 5:00 P.M. At the Museum of the Great Plains, the official state agriculture museum, you can learn a lot about the past and present of Montana farm ways. Also exhibited there are the famous Hornaday Smithsonian bison, six animals that were displayed at the national museum in Washington, D.C., from 1887 until 1955. Likenesses of the big bull of the bunch appear on the buffalo-head nickel, on the National Park Service badge, and in several other prominent places.

Before leaving Fort Benton, duck in and have a look—for the entire night if your mood and budget are right—at the lavishly restored **Grand Union Hotel** (1 Grand Union Square, P.O. Box 1119, Fort Benton, MT 59442; 406–622–1882; www.grandunionhotel.com). The hostelry was reputed to be the finest accommodation between St. Paul and Seattle when it opened on November 1, 1882. You would certainly hope so, since it cost an outlandish $200,000 to build! Many of the hotel's rooms overlook the Missouri, and the enterprise features a brewpub and a good breakfast-dinner restaurant.

Busy U.S. Highway 87—try to avoid riding it during the morning and evening commuting hours—cuts through a gorgeous mix of mountains and plains en route to Great Falls. The peaks, the biggest you've encountered so far, rise above a classic central Montana landscape filled with fields of diagonal plow cuts and pastures teeming with grazing cattle.

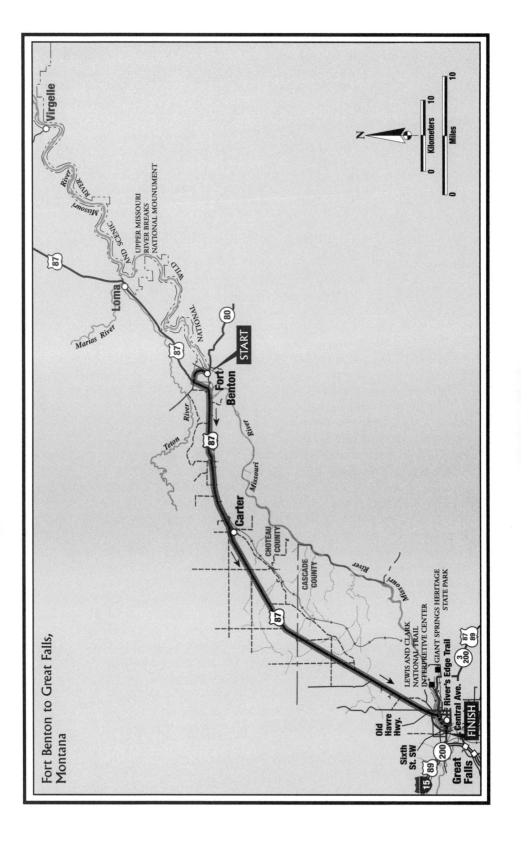

Fort Benton to Great Falls,
Montana

Mileage Log

0.0 Fort Benton.

0.5 Bear left following State Road 80.

2.0 Turn left onto U.S. Highway 87.

16.5 Carter.

27.0 Enter Cascade County.

40.0 Turn right onto unsigned Old Havre Highway. In a little over 1 mile, cross the Eagle Falls Memorial Bridge, riding onto the River's Edge Trail.

42.5 Turn right onto Central Avenue to cross river.

43.5 Section ends at corner of Central Avenue and Sixth Street Southwest in Great Falls.

CHAPTER 5

Great Falls to Missoula, Montana (479 miles)

After locating the great falls of the Missouri—and discovering that they actually consisted of a series of *five* major falls, with rapids separating one from the next, dropping the river some 500 feet in all—Lewis and Clark saw that they wouldn't be able to navigate this part of the river. After plotting a portage around the falls, the expedition members spent day after laborious day hauling thousands of pounds of gear and dragging their heavy canoes across the 18-mile overland route. As they went back and forth along the grueling portage, the men were battered by hail and rainstorms, molested by mosquitoes, and troubled by grizzly bears. To make matters worse, their feet were mercilessly punctured by prickly pear cactus and pummeled by the uneven footing that had resulted from buffalo hoofprints drying in the mud. On the plus side, bison, elk, and pronghorn were abundant, so the men ate very well—a good thing because after leaving the Missouri River, they would see very little game.

Finally, on July 14, 1805, they continued upstream in their dugout canoes, including two that were newly made. The month taken out of the middle of the summer to make such a short distance came close to costing the party dearly: They arrived at the eastern foot of the Bitterroot Range almost too late in the year to make a crossing.

As did the Corps of Discovery, south of Great Falls you will finally start getting into the canyons and mountains Montana is known for. A dividend of the terrific mountain scenery is that a large share of the lands are federally owned, so campgrounds become much more plentiful than they've been up to this point—so much so that it is generally no longer necessary to include suggested camping options in the text. Rather, plan your own days using the campground/motel information provided on Adventure Cycling maps.

At Three Forks, where the Gallatin, Madison, and Jefferson Rivers merge, you'll leave the Missouri River behind for good. Some of the finest cycling in southwest Montana lies between there and Dillon, south of which you'll ride for 20 miles in the Interstate 15 corridor. Between Clark Canyon Reservoir and Salmon, Idaho, the route incorporates one of its atypical stretches of gravel, 25 miles of it, as it goes up and over Lemhi Pass, the cresting of which was so important, both symbolically and actually, to the Corps of Discovery. It was there that the expedition crossed from the east to the west side of the Continental Divide, from future Montana into future Idaho, where they exited lands acquired through the Louisiana Purchase. Although they were far from being finished with mountain travel, they were now in the Columbia River watershed and, in a sense, on the downhill side of their journey.

26

Great Falls to Helena, Montana
95 miles (2,184 miles cumulative)

". . . from the singular appearance of this place I called it the gates of the rocky mountains."
— CAPT. MERIWETHER LEWIS
Friday, July 19, 1805

You should dedicate at least a day to checking out the sights in and around Great Falls; after all, the Corps of Discovery spent an entire *month* there— albeit covering a distance that they more typically made in just one or two days. In sharp contrast with the little-altered Missouri Breaks country of northeastern Montana, the Great Falls area has changed about as much in the past 200 years as any other place along the entire Lewis and Clark Trail. Consider, for example, that the falls that gave the city its name are a thing of the past, having been inundated in the interest of hydroelectic power generation. The community's nickname—"Electric City"—is a more apt moniker today than is Great Falls.

Making up at least in part for the transgression of obliterating those historic and once-spectacular falls is the city's magnificent new **Lewis and Clark National Historic Trail Interpretive Center** (4201 Giant Springs Road, Great Falls, MT 59403; 406–727–8733; www.fs.fed.us/r1/lewisclark/lcic.htm), open 9:00 A.M. to 6:00 P.M. daily. Operated by the USDA Forest Service, the center, sitting high above the Missouri River within Giant Springs Heritage State Park, is the preeminent Lewis and Clark interpretive facility on the entire trail. You can begin by viewing the thirty-minute orientation film, a Ken Burns–Dayton Duncan production, that is shown hourly in the 158-seat Montana Power Company Theatre. Next, lose yourself for half a day or more in the journey: A walk through the roomy, high-ceilinged center takes you from the beginning of the expedition to its close, with displays that pay particular attention to the Native American cultures the party encountered and to the difficult portage they made around the city's namesake falls. You may also find costumed docents on hand to answer questions and/or demonstrate the way certain things were done 200 years ago.

You can access the center by way of the heralded **River's Edge Trail** (P.O. Box 553, Great Falls, MT 59403; 406–788–3313; www.thetrail.org), a separated bike and pedestrian path that continues downstream through **Giant Springs Heritage State Park** (406–454–5840). The park is home to one of the world's largest cold freshwater springs—as well as to the world's shortest river: From the spring that William Clark noted on June 18, 1805,

Dugout canoe re-creation at the Lewis and Clark Interpretive Center near Great Falls, Montana

as "the largest fountain or spring I ever saw, and I doubt if it is not the largest in America known . . . ," the Roe River flows just 201 feet before reaching the Missouri. From the park, the River's Edge Trail continues eastward to the sites of Rainbow Falls and Crooked Falls; it is proposed eventually to extend all the way past Ryan and Morony Dams to Sacajawea Springs, not far from the beginning of the Lewis and Clark portage at Belt Creek.

Another attraction in Great Falls, not directly tied to the Lewis and Clark expedition but well worth visiting, is the **C. M. Russell Museum Complex** (400 Thirteenth Street North, Great Falls, MT 59401; 406–727–8787; www.cmrussell.org), which displays the largest existing collection of Charlie Russell's art and personal belongings. In addition to artwork by America's Cowboy Artist, works by his contemporaries—O. C. Seltzer, J. H. Sharp, and others—are displayed. Also on the grounds are the home and log-cabin studio of Russell, which is appointed in the style of the early 1900s, when he worked and hosted his many friends and visitors there. (On second thought, direct ties *do* exist between Russell and the expedition: For evidence, when you visit the capitol in Helena, go into the meeting room of the House of Representatives, where you can inspect the very large and impressive Russell painting *Lewis and Clark Meeting the Flathead Indians at Ross' Hole*.)

As you head south from Great Falls and approach imposing mountains, you'll pass the mouths of the Smith River, named by Lewis and Clark in honor of then-Secretary of the Navy Robert Smith, and the Dearborn River, named for Secretary of War Henry Dearborn. You'll pedal in the bottom of the Missouri River canyon beneath high walls of bare rock as you follow an outstanding progression of frontage roads paralleling Interstate 15. Terrific places to pitch your tent abound in and around the canyon; however, if you're in the mood for something a bit more exotic than sleeping on the ground, consider overnighting at **The Bungalow** (P.O. Box 168, Wolf Creek, MT 59648; 406–235–4276). The quaint yet stately structure, designed by Robert C. Reamer—the architect who built the Old Faithful Inn in Yellowstone National Park—is hidden in the hills off the route from just north of Wolf Creek (call for precise directions).

At Mile 76 below you'll pass I-15 exit 209, where a road leads about 3 miles east to the **Gates of the Mountains Recreation Area** (Helena National Forest, 2100 Poplar Street, Helena, MT 59626; 406–449–5490). Notwithstanding today's placid waters held at bay by the Holter Dam, the canyon appears much as it did when the Corps of Discovery passed through, with most of the same flora and fauna still thriving. Although the majority of historians believe that this is indeed the "gates of the rocky mountains" described in the journal of Meriwether Lewis, others assert that the site was actually farther north, between Cascade and Wolf Creek. There the river cuts through the black volcanic rock of the Adel Mountains, a terrain that better matches the setting as described by Lewis than do these cliffs of whitish limestone.

Regardless, the recreation area is a stunningly beautiful place: 1,200-foot-high cliffs rise above the water, and the area brims with wildlife, such as eagles, bighorn sheep, and Rocky Mountain goats. To get a good, close-up

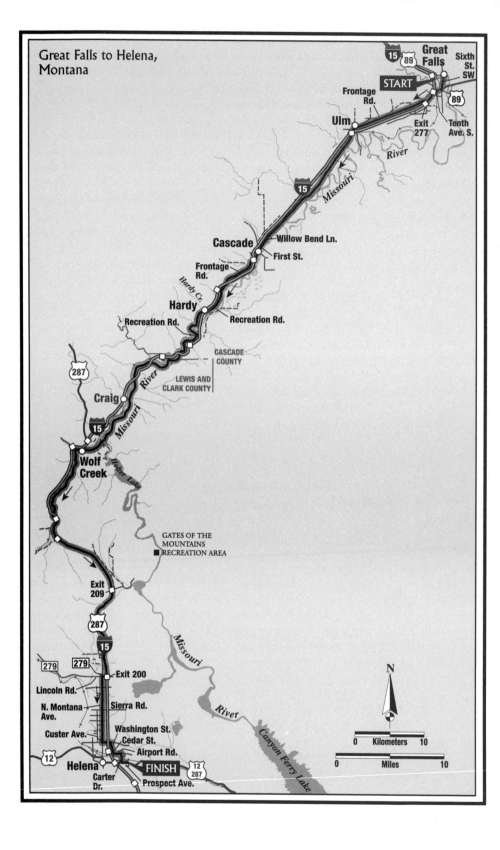

look at its many attributes, sign on with **Gates of the Mountains Boat Tours** (P.O. Box 478, Helena, MT 59624; 406–458–5241; www.gatesof themountains.com) for a cruise that lasts approximately two hours. Cruises are available from Memorial Day through mid-September.

Back on the route, as you near Helena—Montana's capital and the seat of the only Lewis and Clark County in the United States—you'll emerge from the sheer-walled river canyon into a pleasing scene that is characteristic of much of western Montana: a wide-open expanse of flat to rolling grasslands that give way to foothills and, finally, to timbered slopes hovering in the distance.

Mileage Log

0.0 Great Falls. Ride south on Sixth Street Southwest.

1.0 Sun River. In 0.1 mile turn right onto Tenth Avenue South/U.S. 89.

1.5 Continue straight onto I–15 South toward Helena.

2.5 Leave I–15 at exit 277. Bear right in 0.2 mile, then immediately left onto unsigned frontage road.

10.5 Ulm. At stop sign, turn left and ride under I–15.

25.0 Cascade. At stop sign, turn left onto unsigned First Street.

26.0 Ride under I–15 and, in 0.2 mile turn left onto Frontage Road.

29.5 Ride under I–15.

30.5 At stop sign, turn left to continue on Frontage Road.

33.5 Ride under I–15. Hardy.

36.0 Cross Missouri River.

38.0 Continue straight on Recreation Road.

40.0 Ride under I–15.

42.5 Enter Lewis and Clark County.

44.0 Ride under I–15.

47.0 Ride under I–15.

49.0 Craig, off route 0.5 mile to west.

58.0 Wolf Creek.

66.0 Ride under I–15. In 0.2 mile onto I–15 South.

76.0 Pass exit 209, which leads to Gates of the Mountains Recreation Area.

85.0 Leave I–15 at exit 200 (Lincoln Road). Turn right onto County Road 279. In 0.3 mile turn left onto unsigned North Montana Avenue.

91.5 Turn left onto Custer Avenue.

92.0 Turn right onto Washington Street.

92.5 Turn left onto Cedar Street, then bear left onto Airport Road.

94.0 Turn right onto Carter Drive.

95.0 Turn left onto Prospect Avenue/U.S. Highway 12. (Historic downtown Helena is to right.)

27 Helena to Three Forks, Montana
61.5 miles (2,245.5 miles cumulative)

"... our trio of pests still invade and obstruct us on all occasions, these are the Musquetoes eye knats and prickley pears, equal to any three curses that ever poor Egypt laiboured under ..."
—CAPT. MERIWETHER LEWIS
Wednesday, July 24, 1805

The capital city of Montana sits a few miles west of the Missouri River in a big, usually brown basin, backed by massive, dark mountains. The Missouri of today—Hauser and Canyon Ferry Lakes, that is—bears little resemblance to the waterfowl-abundant wetlands that Lewis and Clark experienced, where Lewis estimated that the outermost of a network of braided streams composing the river were as much as 3 miles apart.

Yet the past vividly lives on in Helena, a real treasure trove of nineteenth-century lore. It was here in the Prickly Pear Valley that a group of men known as the Four Georgians found gold on July 14, 1864, fifty-nine years almost to the day after the Corps of Discovery passed through the valley. Unlike the majority of southwest Montana's mining boomtowns, the Four Georgians' "Last Chance Gulch" flourished: Here, placer mining, a technique that could be carried out by solitary individuals, was replaced by the mining of underground quartz lodes, a far more labor- and equipment-intensive method of mining that required financial backing, cooperation among various interests, and long-range planning. Roads were built, corporations created, and banks established. Helena began looking like something more than the ragtag assortment of temporary quarters it started out as, and the city evolved into a center of trade, replete with permanent brick buildings and fine frame homes. It became the territorial capital in 1875, by which time the city's population stood at around 4,000, and the state capital fourteen years later when Montana became the forty-first state.

Today, **Last Chance Gulch** is an appealing car-free pedestrian mall, lined with renovated structures holding a variety of office spaces, cafes, and retail stores. Also be sure to check out **Reeder's Alley,** which branches off from the gulch at its upper end. The cluster of old brick bachelor-miners' shanties have similarly been spruced up into restaurants and other modern enterprises. And if you're a fan of Victorian architecture, by all means don't miss strolling or riding around the hilly streets west of downtown, a neighborhood that preserves a large share of the grandest, most lavish old homes in all Montana.

Setting up his home for the night outside Helena, Montana

In Helena for the first time (but not the last) on the Lewis & Clark Bicycle Trail, you'll skirt the Great Divide Mountain Bike Route. The Great Divide, Adventure Cycling's 2,470-mile bikepacking route that parallels the Continental Divide from Canada to Mexico, shoots southwest from historic downtown Helena by way of Grizzly Gulch, where it begins winding around a maze of Forest Service roads en route to the settlement of Basin.

At some point in or around Helena, you'll cross paths with the route taken by the 25th Infantry Bicycle Corps, a group of pioneer cyclists who participated in one of the most compelling bicycle tours in American history. Early in their trip, on June 16, 1897, the soldiers of the 25th Infantry descended from Mullan Pass to their overnight destination of Fort William Henry Harrison, situated on the northwestern edge of Helena. The 25th Infantry was one of a quartet of black Indian-fighting regiments—known as "buffalo soldiers" to the Native Americans—that was created by the U.S. Army following the Civil War and the emancipation of the slaves.

By 1897 the Indian wars were history, and the members of the 25th were stationed at Fort Missoula, where they spent time helping quell miner uprisings over in Idaho and performing various other duties. One of the regiment's white officers, Lt. James A. Moss, was an early-day cycling enthusiast who was convinced that the velocipede could, in some situations, prove to

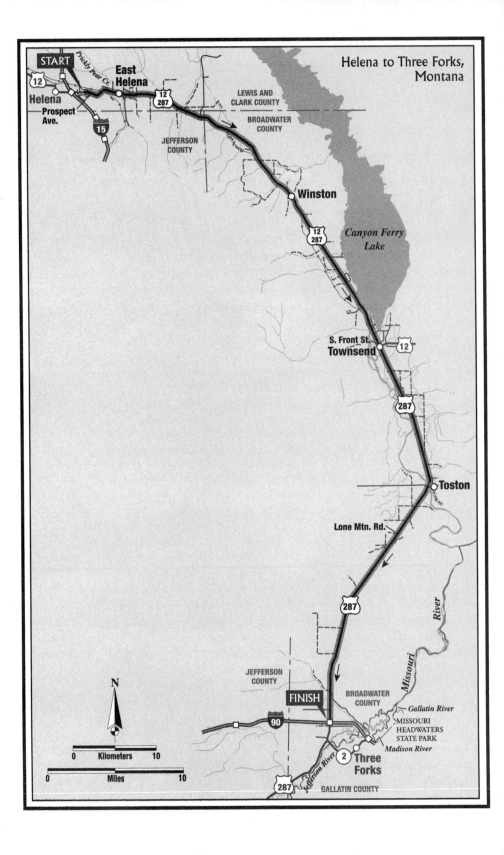

be a superior means of troop transport. "The bicycle," wrote Moss, "has a number of advantages over the horse—it does not require much care, it needs no forage . . . it is noiseless and raises little dust, and it is impossible to tell direction from its track."

Wishing to prove the legitimacy of his theory, Moss asked Gen. Nelson Miles for permission to organize a bicycle expedition that would traverse the largely untamed country between Fort Missoula and St. Louis, a distance of approximately 1,900 miles. Gen. Miles okayed the scheme, and Moss chose twenty black soldiers to ride with him on one-speed Spalding safety bicycles equipped with balloon tires and handlebar-mounted gear packs. The soldiers left Fort Missoula on June 14; on June 16, from near present-day Elliston, they pedaled up the Mullan Road, a wagon path that had been built in the early 1860s to link the port of Fort Benton with Fort Walla Walla, Washington. It was a wet and cold ascent to the Continental Divide, where 2 inches of fresh snow greeted the riders. The snow made the trip down muddy and slick, nearly as tough as the ride up had been.

East of Helena and Fort Harrison, the 25th Infantry rode on primitive trails, wagon paths, even over railroad ties. They dealt with many of the same dangers and inconveniences that Lewis and Clark had become all too familiar with as they traversed the wilderness, such as hordes of mosquitos, impassable wet gumbo clays, cloudbursts, searing heat, and sickening waters. Yet despite the hardships, the soldiers were in generally good condition when they pedaled into St. Louis on July 24, six weeks after departing Fort Missoula. Moss considered the trip a resounding success, but his fantasy of one day witnessing hundreds of bicycle-mounted troops never materialized.

Mileage Log

0.0 Ride east on Prospect Avenue.
2.5 East Helena. Cross Prickly Pear Creek. Ride straight onto U.S. 12/287.
7.5 Enter Jefferson County.
9.0 Enter Broadwater County.
18.5 Winston.
30.0 Cross Missouri River.
31.0 Townsend. Route becomes South Front Street; U.S. 12 leaves route. Ride straight, continuing on U.S. 287.
42.0 Cross railroad overpass. Toston. Cross Missouri River.
61.5 Interstate 90; Three Forks is southeast of route.

28

Three Forks to Dillon, Montana
86.5 miles (2,332 miles cumulative)

". . . the Indian woman recognized the point of a high plain to our right . . . this hill she says her nation calls the beaver's head . . ."
—CAPT. MERIWETHER LEWIS
Thursday, August 8, 1805

Near the junction of U.S. Highway 287 and Interstate 90 outside Three Forks, be sure to pop through the big silo and into the **Wheat Montana Farms & Bakery** (10078 Highway 287, Three Forks, MT 59752; 406–285–3614; www.wheatmontana.com). Here you can pick up any number of delectables, such as a deli sandwich or some healthy whole-grain cereal to haul along for hot breakfasts on the trail. The unique store is an enterprise of the Dale (father) and Dean (son) Folkvord families, who grow both red and white wheat on their 13,500-acre farm located a few miles away. Utilizing this bounty of grain, every day the business produces several thousand loaves of bread and hundreds of bags of bagels and buns; they also sell their chemical-free flour, cereal, and baked goods through grocery stores and independent bakeries, most of them in Montana and surrounding states.

In the early 1980s the Folkvords, having seen too many of their neighboring wheat farmers hurting or even going under, decided to stop selling their grain in the general market, a scenario that had made them overly susceptible to things they had no control over, such as fluctuating market prices. Instead they decided not only to "sow it and grow it," but also to "dough it," adding to their operations a bakery with their personal label and a distribution arm selling high-protein grain. Now not only are they more in control of their destiny, but they also gross far more money than they ever did as a traditional wheat farm. In a sense, their operation is a throwback to the local farm-to-market days of yore, which—considering the Folkvords' resounding success—people in our increasingly global economy obviously appreciate.

The Wheat Montana people also know how to market themselves and to get attention: According to the *Guinness Book of World Records*, a team of ten Wheat Montana bakers set a world record in September 1995 when they transformed standing wheat into thirteen (a baker's dozen) loaves of bread in just eight minutes and thirteen seconds!

Missouri Headwaters State Park (1400 South Nineteenth Street, Bozeman, MT 59715; 406–994–4042) is located about 7 miles off the route; to find it, from Mile 1.5 below, go 3 miles into Three Forks then inquire locally for directions. It is well worth the time and effort spent getting there, particularly in light of the vital role the confluence played during the Lewis and Clark expedition. It's also a good place to camp—provided you remember your bug dope. Here, where the Missouri River officially begins, a trio of fairly similar-sized rivers merge, and Lewis and Clark scratched their heads over which of the three they should follow. They named the waterways ". . . after the President of the United States and the Secretaries of the Treasury and state . . ."—Thomas Jefferson, Albert Gallatin, and James Madison. Gallatin, as Jefferson's Secretary of the Treasury, had played an important part in negotiating the Louisiana Purchase. Now also bearing his name is the county of which Bozeman is the seat of government, and both Madison and Gallatin have mountain ranges south of Bozeman bearing their names.

The three rivers still look much as they would have when the Corps of Discovery visited. Interpretive signs in the park point out various features related to the expedition, including one identifying Lewis Rock, which Capt. Lewis ascended for the purpose of mapping the confluence area. They camped upstream a couple of miles on the Jefferson, in the same place that Sacagawea's Shoshone people had been five years previously when she and several others were taken by Hidatsa raiders, who, according to her, also killed several Shoshones. It must have been encouraging for the captains to know that they were getting into the territory of Sacagawea's people, for they were depending on meeting the Shoshones to acquire the horses they would need to the cross the rugged mountains.

It was not the first time Sacagawea had been at the headwaters, nor was it the last time expedition members John Colter and John Potts would visit. Seduced by the wilderness and by the prospect of making his riches in beaver fur, Colter chose not to return with the others to St. Louis in 1806. He was granted the unusual request of an early leave, owing largely to the outstanding service he had provided the expedition. He turned back west in August 1806 from the Mandan villages of North Dakota to join forces with a pair of trappers from Illinois.

Subsequently Colter endured a pair of adventures that, added to the fact that he was part of the Lewis and Clark expedition, cinched his place in the history books. One of them was a solo trek of approximately 500 miles through the greater Yellowstone region during the deep of winter 1807–08; the other, an 1808 race from death that took him, barefoot and naked, from the headwaters to Fort Remon, Manuel Lisa's trading post at the confluence of the Big Horn and Yellowstone Rivers.

Charged with the mission of persuading area Indians to trade at Fort Remon, Colter, now accompanied by Potts, encountered a band of hostile Piegan (Blackfeet) warriors in the headwaters area. As legend has it—and no doubt the legend has grown over the years—Potts was killed immediately by the Indians, but Colter was given a slim chance at survival. After convincing a chief that he was a clumsy runner—in reality he was known among his fellows as being very fleet of foot—Colter was stripped of his clothes and footwear, given a short headstart, and permitted to run for his life. He was chased by the warriors over a rugged, rocky, and cactus-strewn terrain much like that which you'll see today at Missouri Headwaters State Park. He managed to lose them (after dispatching the lead Indian with the warrior's own spear!) by camouflaging himself in a tangle of brush and driftwood along the banks of the Madison. More than a week later, he emerged at Fort Remon, tattered, battered—and hungry.

Concerning the odyssey, H. M Chittenden wrote in his classic 1895 book *The Yellowstone National Park:* "The men at the fort did not recognize him at first and doubtless would not have believed his story if his terrible plight had not been proof of its truth." The adventure did much to enhance Colter's well-deserved reputation as the wiliest of the wild mountain men.

While pushing up the Jefferson River, the Corps of Discovery came close to, but apparently did not see, the entrance to Lewis and Clark Caverns. You can't *help* but notice the entrance to **Lewis and Clark Caverns State Park** (P.O. Box 949, Three Forks, MT 59752; 406–287–3541): It's located right beside the route, 16 miles into the day's ride. Particularly if the weather is hot, you'll relish the cool, constantly 50-degree temperature within the cave. In addition to cave tours, the park offers camping, rental cabins, hiking trails, and fishing access on the Jefferson River.

President Jefferson's namesake river is rather short, as you can see if you scan a map of the area. In the vicinity of Twin Bridges (Mile 59 below), the Jefferson emulates the Missouri by forming where three rivers meet to become one: the Beaverhead, the Ruby, and the Big Hole, the latter a name that is whispered quietly, with reverence and awe, by fly fishers the world over. (Lewis and Clark's choices of virtuous names for the rivers—the Philanthropy, Philosophy, and Wisdom—didn't stick.) Just as the explorers did, you'll take the middle fork, the Beaverhead. Where you cross that river at Mile 71.5 below you'll come close to Beaverhead Rock, a geographical feature that Sacagawea immediately recognized, helping to solidify her belief that the party would soon encounter some of her fellow Shoshones.

Mileage Log

0.0 Ride over I–90.

1.5 Go straight to continue on U.S. 287. Three Forks is 3 miles southeast of route on State Road 2.

6.0 Enter Jefferson County.

16.0 Lewis and Clark Caverns State Park on right.

21.0 LaHood.

23.5 Turn right at stop sign. Cardwell off route 0.5 mile to left. Ride under I–90, then curve left to stay on route.

25.0 SR 69 joins route.

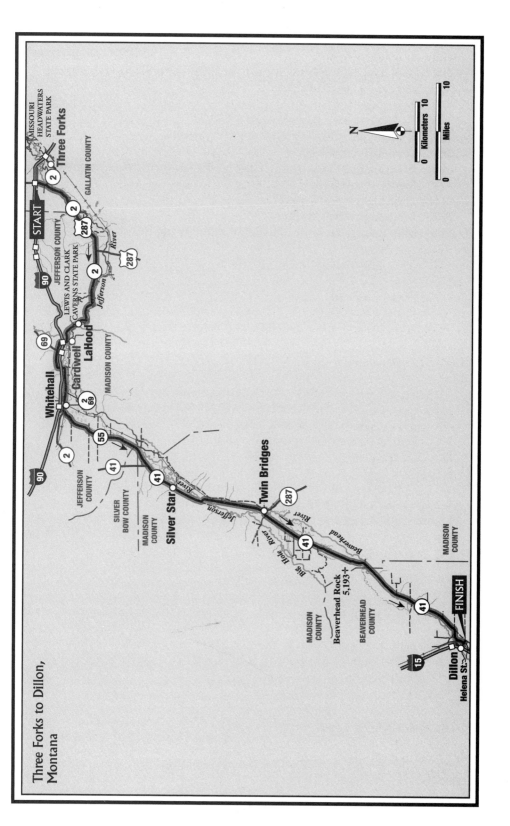

Three Forks to Dillon, Montana

27.0 Ride under I–90.

31.5 Whitehall. At west end of town, bear left onto SR 55 and immediately cross railroad tracks.

42.0 Enter Madison County.

44.5 SR 55 ends; ride straight onto SR 41.

48.0 Silver Star.

52.0 Cross Jefferson River.

59.0 Twin Bridges. Turn right to stay on SR 41, then cross Beaverhead River.

71.5 Cross Beaverhead River.

72.5 Enter Beaverhead County.

86.5 Dillon. Turn left onto Helena Street following Business I–15.

29 Dillon, Montana to Salmon, Idaho
88.5 miles (2,420.5 miles cumulative)

*". . . This day I completed my thirty first year, and conceived that
I had in all human probability now existed about half the period
which I am to remain in this Sublunary world. I reflected that I
had as yet done but little, very little, indeed, to further the hapiness
of the human race or to advance the information of the succeeding
generation . . ."*

—CAPT. MERIWETHER LEWIS
Sunday, August 18, 1805
At Camp Fortunate

From Dillon you'll ride south either on or parallel to Interstate 15 for about
20 miles before veering west at the Clark Canyon Reservoir on County Road
324. The man-made lake covers the site of Camp Fortunate, where Lewis
and Clark enjoyed the most fortuitous windfall of their entire expedition.
The timing couldn't have been better, either, because by this time a large
share of the men were lame, and morale was at a low point.

From Camp Fortunate, where the Red Rock River and Horse Prairie
Creek merged to create the Beaverhead River, upstream travel by canoe was
no longer an option; instead, foot and horseback would be the necessary
means of moving the troops into and over the mountains. It was paramount
to the success of the expedition that they meet up with Sacagawea's people
soon in order to obtain the horses needed both to transport gear and, if necessary, to serve as food. On an advance search for the Indians, Capt. Lewis
and three companions crested the Continental Divide at Lemhi Pass on
August 12, 1805. Of a spring that still flows near the pass, Lewis wrote that
he had found ". . . the most distant fountain of the waters of the mighty
Missouri. . . . I had accomplished one of those great objects on which my
mind had been unalterably fixed for many years." (In truth, he had not located the ultimate headwaters of the Missouri.) On surmounting Lemhi
Pass not only did the party cross the Continental Divide for the first time,
but they also passed from Louisiana Purchase lands into those still claimed
by European nations.

On the west side of the Divide, Lewis managed to track down Shoshone
chief Cameahwait then persuade him and his hungry, skittish people—they
feared they were being led into a Blackfeet ambush—to accompany Lewis
over the Continental Divide and back to Camp Fortunate to meet with the

The ride up Lemhi Pass is generally smooth and not overly steep, amid postcard-quality ranchlands lying below folded foothills and a distant backdrop of tall, dark mountains.

others. It was at this August 17 meeting that Sacagawea recognized Cameahwait as her brother! Wrote Nicholas Biddle, who transcribed the journals in 1814 with expedition member George Shannon at his side, of the meeting: ". . . She instantly jummped up, and ran and embraced him, throwing over him her blanket and weeping profusely: The chief was himself moved, though not in the same degree. . . ." The auspicious reunion enhanced the horse trading that followed, making this probably the most important contribution Sacagawea made to the success of the Lewis and Clark expedition.

The trip over Lemhi Pass takes you over gravel, through terrain that has changed very little in the past 200 years. If the weather is wet and/or you prefer to stay on pavement, you'll want to follow the Big Hole Alternate from south of Dillon; see the Adventure Cycling maps for this route. You'd be missing out on a treat, however. The ride up Lemhi Pass is generally smooth and not overly steep, through ranchlands holding barns, sideways-leaning outbuildings, and grazing black-whiteface cattle. Rounding out the scene are buck-and-rail fences, bounding mule deer, explosions of sage grouse, and folded foothills with a distant backdrop of tall, dark mountains. The view at the summit of the pass is worth savoring for a long while: pristine, largely bare mountain ridges rippling away as far as the eye can see. The **Sacajawea Historical Area** picnic and primitive camping site is nestled in an aromatic grove of tall conifers, just below the pass down a gravel road on the Montana side.

Before beginning the climb to Lemhi Pass, think about this: If you can't get enough wild country to suit your fancy, if you're riding a fat-tire bicycle, and if you're not in any great hurry to get from here to there, consider a side trip on the Great Divide Mountain Bike Route. About midway between Clark Canyon Reservoir and Grant on CR 324, you'll see a road going south that's known as the **Big Sheep Creek Back Country Byway** (Bureau of Land Management; 406–494–5059). The narrow dirt road penetrates one of the emptiest, most remote areas found along the entire length of the Great Divide, the longest off-pavement touring route in the United States. Part of it follows the Corinne-Bannack Road, which was established in 1862, the year of the original gold strike at Bannack, Montana. (Now a state park protecting the ghost-town remains of Bannack, this is another very worthwhile side trip. To get there, from just under a mile east of Grant, leave the route and ride 13 miles north.) The wagon road linked Montana with Corinne, Utah, a settlement that was created expressly to serve as the departure point for shipping goods north to the gold fields. During the 1870s Corinne came to be known as the "Gentile Capital of Utah," owing to the fact that none of its roughly 1,000 residents was Mormon—a situation that church leader Brigham Young despised, and one that he eventually crushed by building the narrow-gauge Utah Northern Railroad from Ogden, Utah, to Franklin, Idaho, bypassing Corinne altogether.

So primeval are your surroundings as you ride along Medicine Lodge Creek that you'll almost expect to see and hear a horse-drawn supply wagon come storming through. After about 60 miles you'll rejoin I-15 at Dell, where you can ride 20 miles north back to Clark Canyon Reservoir and the junction with CR 324. Or you may opt instead to continue following the Great Divide east. In another 75 miles you'll cross what truly is the "most distant fountain" of the Missouri River: Hellroaring Creek, flowing at the foot of the high and wild Centennial Range.

Mileage Log

0.0   At 0.2 mile, after turning onto Helena Street in Dillon, turn right onto North Atlantic Street/Business I-15.

1.0   Turn left onto East Chapman Street.

3.5   Railroad overpass.

4.0   Cross Beaverhead River.

8.0   Ride under I-15. Barretts. Ride onto I-15 South.

13.0   Leave I-15 at exit 51 (Dalys). At stop sign turn left and ride under I-15 onto Frontage Road.

14.5   Cross Beaverhead River on Pipe Organ Bridge. Ride under I-15 three times over next 5.5 miles.

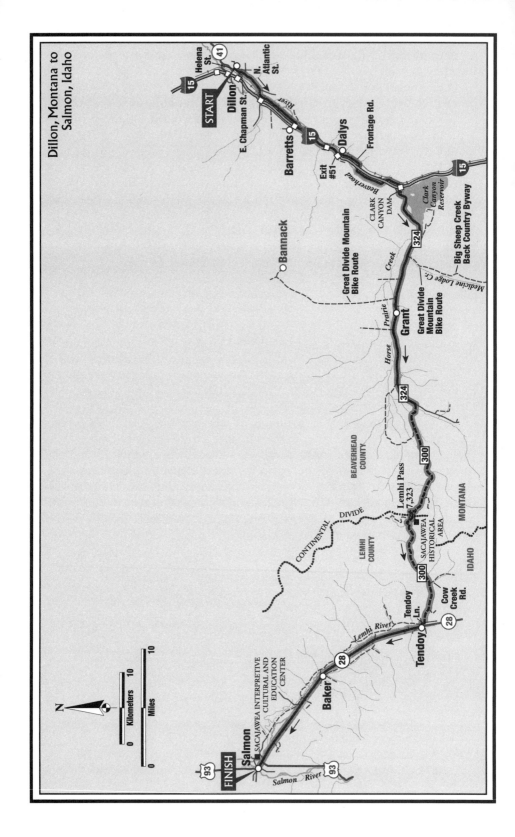

Dillon, Montana to Salmon, Idaho

21.0	Clark Canyon Dam and the Forty-fifth Parallel. Route becomes CR 324.
33.5	Grant.
43.5	At turnoff toward Lemhi Pass, go right onto unsigned Road 300. Road turns to gravel for 25 miles, with frequent cattleguards.
45.5	Bear left at Y.
56.0	Lemhi Pass and the Continental Divide. Enter Lemhi County, Idaho.
64.0	Cow Creek Road.
68.0	Pavement resumes. Turn right at T onto Tendoy Lane. At second T, 0.2 mile later, turn left.
68.5	Tendoy. Turn right onto State Road 28.
79.0	Baker.
88.5	SR 28 ends; ride straight onto U.S. Highway 93. Salmon.

30 Salmon, Idaho to Darby, Montana
77 miles (2,497.5 miles cumulative)

". . . we assembled the Chiefs & warriers and Spoke to them (with much dificuel[t]y as what we Said had to pass through Several languages before it got into theirs, which is a gugling kind of language Spoken much thro the throught . . ."
—CAPT. WILLIAM CLARK
Tuesday, September 5, 1805
On meeting with the Flatheads

You're sure to enjoy your overnight stay in Salmon, where the Lemhi River joins forces with the Salmon, the River of No Return. The fine little town of roughly 3,000 residents serves as a center of trade for the timber, agriculture, and recreation industries—the latter, predominantly fishing and river rafting. A mile south of Salmon—you passed it on the way into town—is the new **Sacajawea Interpretive Cultural and Education Center** (208–756–1188; www.sacajaweacenter.org), open daily 9:00 A.M. to 5:00 P.M. (beginning in June 2003). Exhibits focus on the culture of the Lemhi Shoshone, including fish weirs, tepee rings, and other exterior displays. You'll also find foot trails and fishing access on the Lemhi. The admission fee is $3.00.

The entire Lewis and Clark expedition didn't get over Lemhi Pass until August 26, 1805. In the meantime, Capt. Clark had set out on a scouting mission that took him far enough down the turbulent Salmon River—from today's Salmon to the approximate location of Shoup—for him to conclude that the steep-sided canyon was passable neither by water nor by land. He had also received discouraging news from the Shoshones about trying to travel south then west across the deserts of future Idaho. So, with autumn approaching, the expedition would be compelled to head north, aiming for the only remaining alternative: the Lolo Trail, a rugged route over the Bitterroot Range that was used by the Nez Percé to access the buffalo prairies to the east.

From North Fork an 18-mile off-route spur leads west to Shoup along the portion of the Salmon River that led Clark to deem its canyon impassable. His party's horses could make it only about half that distance before the terrain grew too troublesome, so he and four others—including a geography-savvy Shoshone the men called Old Toby—pushed farther upstream, judiciously traveling by foot along the steep riverside slopes.

Modern highways make travel *so* much easier, even for those traveling by foot, or by bicycle. Today the road heading toward Shoup is paved, gently graded, and beautiful for cycling; along it you can view the treacherous rapids and nearly vertical cliffs that turned Clark back, as well as such wildlife as Rocky Mountain elk and bighorn sheep. The latter is a species the expedition members spied after bushwhacking their way over Lost Trail Pass; however, the sheep were too far away to consider pursuing, and a few grouse were about all the hungry travelers could find to eat. To make matters worse, it was already early September and it was cold and snowing.

At Lost Trail Pass you'll skirt **Lost Trail Powder Mountain** (7674 Highway 93 South, Sula, MT 59871; 406–821–3508), one of a handful of ski areas in the United States that straddle the boundary between two states. Although you probably won't see it in its winter finery, the slopes in both Idaho and Montana are covered under some of the deepest and lightest powder found anywhere in either state. And the homey, inexpensive, family-friendly ambience is a throwback to the low-tech ski days of the 1940s and 1950s. If you're a downhill skier, you should by all means come back in the winter someday.

As you continue down Lost Trail Pass, you'll look out over some of the remains of the huge forest fires that raged through the upper Bitterroot Valley in summer 2000: vast acreages of charred timber, mud slides, and formerly well-protected houses and outbuildings now standing naked amidst forests of skeleton trees. At the location of today's Sula, at the mouth of a valley known historically as Ross' Hole, Lewis and Clark met with a group of approximately 400 Flathead Indians, from whom they purchased a few additional horses to augment those they had acquired from the Shoshones. Farther north, when the expedition finally reclaimed relatively level and open ground (below the confluence of the east and west forks of the Bitterroot River), their first glimpse of the high crags of the Bitterroot Range must have given them pause. As you ride beside the range, consider what it must have been like for Lewis and Clark to know that at some point they had to try to get to the other side of that immense barrier.

As you proceed northward downstream, you'll discover that the word "bitterroot" is ubiquitous—worn not only by the river and the mountains to the west but also by the surrounding national forest and countless area businesses. These all derive from the same source: Montana's lovely state flower, a pink beauty whose blossoms grow close to the ground.

The bitterroot's Latin name, *Lewisia rediviva*, celebrates the fact that it was Meriwether Lewis who brought the plant to the attention of western science. Lewis first encountered it in the form of dried roots, which, along with a couple of other species, George Droulliard had brought to him in a hide bag that he'd collected following an unfriendly encounter with some Shoshones. Lewis sampled the root boiled, which is how the Indians told him it should be prepared. He found it soft but extremely bitter. Yet his

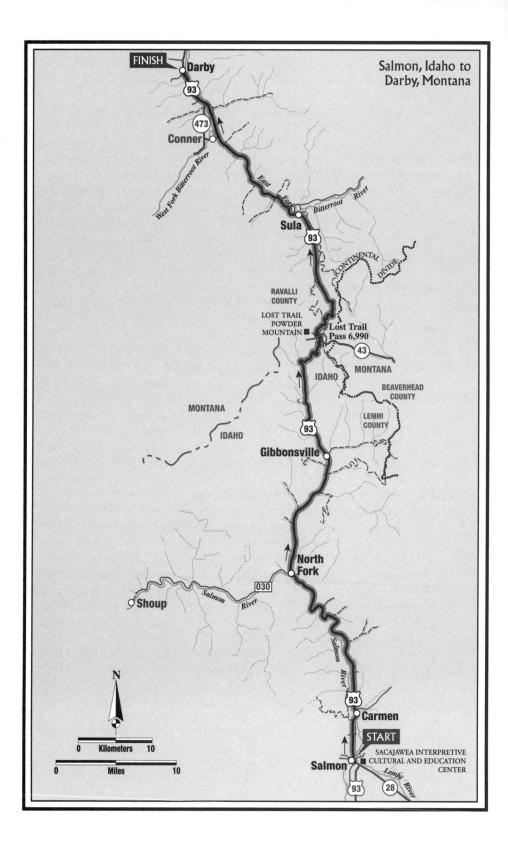

Indian acquaintances gobbled them right down; the root was, in fact, considered a delicacy by the natives. Lewis collected some entire plants of the species at Travelers' Rest during the return trip east in July 1806, and back in Philadelphia he transferred them to Frederick Pursh, a noted botanist of the day, who established *Lewisia* as a new genus in the purslane family. The species name *rediviva* is a refence to the hardiness of the plant, which can survive more than a year without water; it can even be revived after being dried, a feat that earned bitterroot its nickname, "resurrection flower." Montanans chose the bitterroot as the official state flower in a popular vote in the 1890s, giving it 3,621 votes, compared with just 787 for the evening primrose and 668 for the wild rose. The name bitterroot, incidentally, is a literal translation of *racime amere*, which is what French trappers called the plant.

Mileage Log

0.0   Ride west on U.S. Highway 93.
0.5   Salmon River. Turn right, following U.S. 93.
5.5   Carmen.
22.0 North Fork.
32.0 Gibbonsville.
46.5 Lost Trail Pass. Enter Ravalli County, Montana.
59.0 Sula.
69.0 Conner, 0.5 mile west off route.
77.0 Darby.

31 Darby to Missoula, Montana
70.5 miles (2,568 miles cumulative)

". . . as our guide inform me that we should leave the river at this place and the weather appearing settled and fair I determined to halt the next day rest our horses and take som scelestial Observations. we called this Creek Travellers rest."
—CAPT. MERIWETHER LEWIS
Monday, September 9, 1805
At today's Lolo, Montana

As you continue north between Darby and Hamilton, you'll know that you're getting into a more heavily settled region of Montana. That sense will only intensify as you travel between Hamilton and Lolo, despite that for much of the way you'll follow secondary roads rather than riding on bustling U.S. Highway 93. Yet even the endless rural subdivisions and ever-increasing traffic counts have not destroyed the beauty of the Bitterroot Valley—a broad, open basin of hay fields, truck farms, and ranchettes enclosed on the east by the low Sapphire Mountains and sheltered to the west by the lofty crags of the Bitterroot Range.

At Traveler's Rest—the town of Lolo—leave the route to take a side trip into Missoula. So heartily recommended is the trip, in fact, that it's not even considered a spur but officially an out-and-back part of the main route. Although the site of Missoula was not encountered by Lewis and Clark during the expedition's westbound travels, on the return trip east the nine-man contingent led by Capt. Lewis passed the location of the future city. There they camped in damp bottomlands along the north bank of the Clark Fork River, where the mosquitoes were so terrible that they had to stoke smudge fires to provide the men and horses some relief.

Missoula has been described as the Washington, D.C., of the Northern Rockies, owing to the abundance of federal agencies stationed there, as well as to the proliferation of national nonprofit organizations calling the city home. A number of these make great places to visit: Arguably, the top three are the **U.S. Forest Service Smokejumpers Visitor Center** (7 miles west of town on Broadway, adjacent to Johnson-Bell Airport; 406–329–4934); the Rocky Mountain Elk Foundation's **Wildlife Visitor Center** (2291 West Broadway, Missoula, MT 59807; 406–523–4545); and world headquarters of the **Adventure Cycling Association** (150 East Pine, Missoula, MT 59802; 406–721–1776).

At the Smokejumpers Center (tours start at 10:00 and 11:00 A.M. and 2:00, 3:00, and 4:00 P.M.), the largest active base of its kind in the country, you can take a tour (offered daily on the hour Memorial Day through Labor Day) to learn about the hows, whys, whens, and wheres of the Forest Service's elite corps of air-dropped firefighters. As if fighting wildfires weren't dangerous enough, these brave men and women further risk their lives by parachuting into the most remote of fires in Alaska and the lower forty-eight states. Not surprisingly, only the strongest and fittest of applicants make the grade, and here you can see for yourself just how rigorous the testing standards are.

The goal of the Missoula-based Rocky Mountain Elk Foundation is to protect, enhance, and increase high-quality elk habitat throughout the West and even in locations in the East, Midwest, and elsewhere. At the organization's Wildlife Visitor Center (open daily Memorial Day through Labor Day from 8:00 A.M. to 6:00 P.M.), displays interpret the ways of the magnificent wild wapiti. You'll also see high-quality wildlife art exhibited, along with animal mounts, including ones of mountain goats and the grizzly bears that so impressed and intimidated members of the Corps of Discovery—and continue to impress and intimidate backcountry travelers in Montana today.

A pilgrimage to the Adventure Cycling headquarters (open 8:00 A.M. to 5:00 P.M. weekdays) is made by hundreds of touring cyclists each year. Many adventure cyclists go so far as to tailor their trips specifically so that they'll be able to visit the headquarters and the city of Missoula, which, thanks largely to the presence of Adventure Cycling, has garnered a reputation as the bicycle-touring capital of North America. On display here are a collection of historic bicycles and a quarter century's worth of photos documenting many of the cyclists who have toured on the organization's routes.

As a university town and regional hub of culture, Missoula offers some of the sorts of things you may be missing on the trail—things that you haven't run across for many hundreds of miles (and some so unique that you won't ever run across them again, anywhere): farmers' markets; outstanding coffee shops, bakeries, breweries, and restaurants; well-equipped independent bookstores; outdoor summer concerts; alternative-film screenings; and **Rockin' Rudy's** (237 Blaine, Missoula, MT 59801; 406–542–0077), quite possibly the best record store between Minneapolis and Seattle.

 Mileage Log

0.0   Continue riding north from Darby on U.S. 93.

14.0   Skalkaho Road going right. Stay on U.S. 93.

17.0   Hamilton. Turn right onto Marcus Street/County Road 269 and cross railroad tracks. Route becomes Eastside Highway.

23.5   Corvallis.

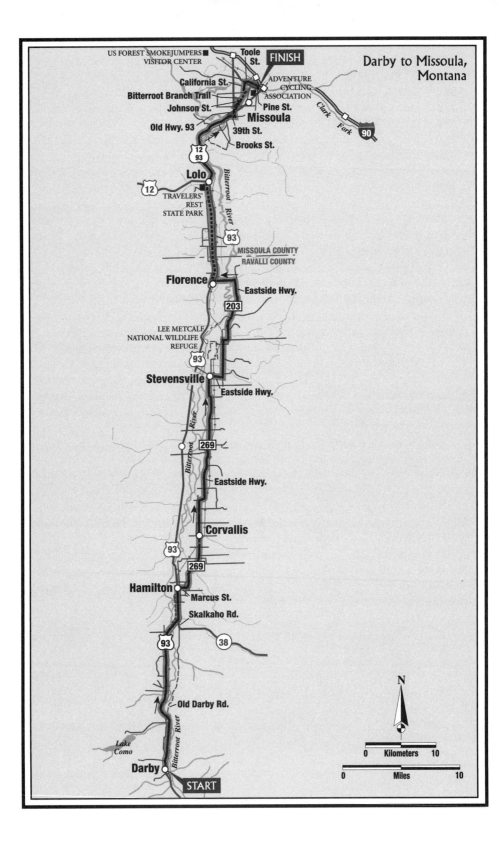

Darby to Missoula, Montana

US FOREST SMOKEJUMPERS
VISITOR CENTER
Toole St.
FINISH

California St.
ADVENTURE CYCLING ASSOCIATION
Bitterroot Branch Trail
Johnson St.
Pine St.
Old Hwy. 93
Missoula
39th St.
Brooks St.

Clark Fork
90

12 93

Lolo
12
Bitterroot River
TRAVELERS' REST STATE PARK

93

MISSOULA COUNTY
RAVALLI COUNTY

Florence
Eastside Hwy.
203

LEE METCALF NATIONAL WILDLIFE REFUGE
93

Stevensville
Eastside Hwy.

Bitterroot River
269

Eastside Hwy.

Corvallis
93
269

Hamilton
Marcus St.
Skalkaho Rd.
93
38

Old Darby Rd.

Lake Como
Bitterroot River

Darby
START

N

0   Kilometers   10
0   Miles   10

38.5 Stevensville. Turn right onto Eastside Highway/CR 203 and cross railroad tracks.

39.5 Bear left.

42.5 Bear right

43.0 Bear left to stay on Eastside Highway/CR 203.

48.0 Bear left.

49.5 Florence. At light, cross U.S. 93 and turn left into Conoco parking lot; at north end of lot, ride onto separated bike path.

58.0 Lolo. At light, cross highway and go north on U.S. 12/93.

66.0 Missoula. Turn right onto Thirty-ninth Street, then go left onto Reserve Street and ride across U.S. 12/93. Turn right onto Old Highway 93, then left onto the Bitterroot Branch Trail.

67.0 Turn left onto Livingston Avenue, then immediately right onto Kemp Street. In 1 block turn right onto South Avenue. One block later, turn left onto Johnson Street.

67.5 Turn right onto North Avenue. After 2 blocks, turn left onto the Bitterroot Branch Trail.

69.0 Trail bends left/west for 3 blocks. Turn right onto California Street.

69.5 Cross the Bitterroot River on pedestrian bridge, then turn right onto Toole Street.

70.0 Curve right to stay on south side of railroad tracks.

70.5 Turn right onto Higgins Avenue; 2 blocks later, turn left onto Pine Street. Go 1 block and you'll see Adventure Cycling headquarters on your left.

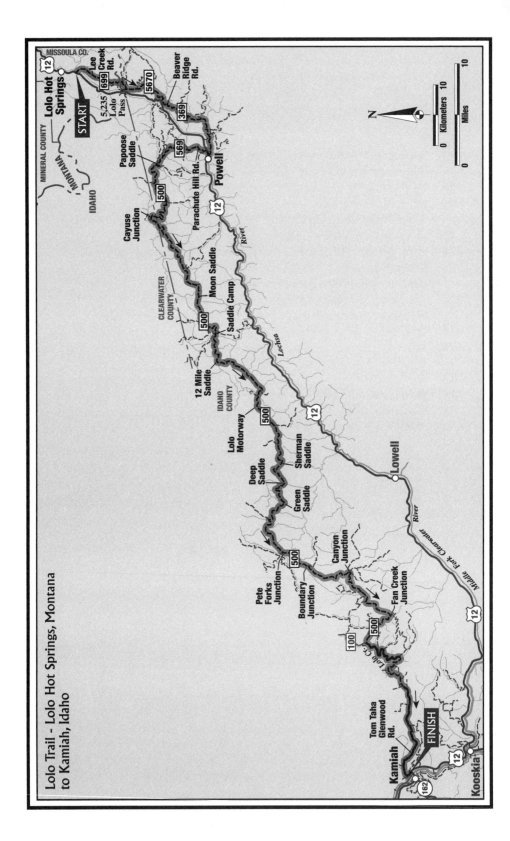

Lolo Trail - Lolo Hot Springs, Montana
to Kamiah, Idaho

CHAPTER 6

Missoula, Montana to Clarkston, Washington (242.5 miles)

Lewis and Clark departed Traveler's Rest on September 11, 1805. As they made their way into and over the Bitterroot Mountains, the expedition encountered the most gruelling test of their entire journey. Despite that for the most part they followed a well-defined Nez Percé trail, the terrain was exceedingly rugged and littered with deadfall. Game was scarce, too, and the men came closer to starving here than at any other place. Compounding matters was the miserable weather, which culminated in 4 inches of new snow on September 16, piling up on top of several inches already blanketing the ground.

To supplement the few wild animals the expedition's hunters managed to take during the mountain crossing, the men killed three of their own colts to eat and partially ward off hunger. Seven days into the odyssey, it was decided that Capt. Clark, accompanied by six others, should travel ahead into better hunting country and bring back meat to the others. Three days later, near present Weippe *(WE-eyep)*, Idaho, Clark and company encountered a pair of Nez Percé encampments, whose residents provided them with food. But the men's empty stomachs, coupled with the radical change of diet—they gorged themselves on the Nez Percé staples of dried salmon, berries, and camas roots—caused them to become violently ill, some of them for days. Ultimately, though, the food sustained them—as it did Lewis and the rest of the party (after likewise sickening them), who regrouped with the others in the open country here on September 22.

As you follow paved U.S. Highway 12 southwest from Lolo to Powell, you'll be roughly tracing the actual route of Lewis and Clark. To approximate the route from Powell to Weippe, however, you would have to climb high up on the ridges to the north and access the rough roller coaster of a dirt road known as the Lolo Motorway. Some riders on mountain bikes no doubt will want to explore this unique and scenic pathway. If you'd like to be one of them, be aware that the Forest Service, anticipating heavy demand, is limiting travel on the motorway during the three years of the Lewis and Clark Bicentennial by way of a permitting system. For details call (208) 476–4541, or visit www.fs.fed.us/r1/clearwater/LewisClark/LewisClark.htm. In addition to the map included in this chapter, the Adventure Cycling Association's Lewis & Clark Bicycle Trail maps detail the optional trail with a mileage log.

U.S. 12, the main route, continues on its twisting way from Powell through the corridor of the Lochsa Wild and Scenic River. There are no services between Powell and Lowell, a distance of 65 miles. So, stock up—or consider fasting to gain an inkling of what the Corps of Discovery suffered through while traveling in this wilderness stronghold!

The Lochsa joins forces with the Selway River at Lowell, where the two transform into the Middle Fork of the Clearwater. Thirty miles from Lowell, at Kamiah *(KAM-ee-eye)*, the recommended route leaves the Clearwater River and U.S. 12. Alternatively, if you were to continue along U.S. 12 and follow the Clearwater into Lewiston, you would be staying true to Lewis and Clark's actual route, but you would have to contend with a great deal of traffic to do it. The road is narrow, winding, and largely lacking in shoulders, to boot. The main route, in contrast, hides a wonderful surprise of low-traffic byways rolling past the forests and through the farmlands of the southern reaches of the Nez Percé Indian Reservation. In fact, many cyclists feel that this is one of the most enjoyable portions of the entire Lewis & Clark Bicycle Trail. The route does traverse some of the same country traipsed through by Sgt. John Ordway and a couple of companions, who, during the Corps of Discovery's return trip east in 1806, were sent back west from Kamiah to Lewis's River (the Snake) to obtain salmon.

32

Missoula, Montana to Powell, Idaho
59 miles (2,627 miles cumulative)

*"At 2 miles passed Several Springs which I observed the Deer Elk
&c. had made roads to, and below one of the Indians had made a
whole to bathe, I tasted this water and found it hot & not bad
tasted in further examonation I found this water nearly boiling hot
at the places it Spouted from the rocks . . ."*
—CAPT. WILLIAM CLARK
Friday, September 13, 1805
At Lolo Hot Springs

After finding your way from Missoula back to Lolo, swing in to have a look
at **Traveler's Rest State Park** (P.O. Box 995, Lolo, MT 59847; 406–
273–4253; www.travelersrest.org), open weekdays 11:00 A.M. to 4:00 P.M. and
weekends 8:00 A.M. to 5:00 P.M. Newly opened in summer 2002, the park is
situated immediately south of the main junction in Lolo, west off U.S.
Highway 93, a short distance up Mormon Creek Road. Developed under a
partnership between the Traveler's Rest Preservation and Heritage Association and the Montana Department of Fish, Wildlife & Parks, the park preserves the Traveler's Rest campsite, or a place very near it. This is where the
Corps of Discovery stayed the nights of September 9 and 10, 1805, resting
up before their arduous trip through the Bitterroots. They laid over here
again for a couple of days in early summer 1806, before splitting into two
groups to explore different routes back to the Missouri-Yellowstone confluence. Today the park is enveloped by development, making its fifteen acres
a particularly important harbor of history. Interpretive programs are given
by docents during the official hours; you can also visit at other times by calling in advance for an appointment or simply coming in if the gate at the
road is open.

As you head west up U.S. 12, sparkling Lolo Creek dances along below
the road. A curious mix of human habitations line the roadway, ranging
from vehicle- and junk-strewn menageries to picturesque ranchettes with
green lawns sprawling beneath robust ponderosa pine trees. The mountain
slopes above are under the mixed ownership of the U.S. Forest Service and
private timber companies, so you'll see everything from thick, diseased
forests, to healthy-looking stands, to ghastly clearcuts.

There's no shortage of Lewis and Clark historical signs to stop and read
as you continue up the road. About 25 miles from Lolo, you'll come to **Lolo**

A runner jogs downstream along the Clark Fork River, with downtown Missoula and the Rattlesnake Range in the background.

Hot Springs (38500 West Highway 12, Lolo, MT 59847; 406–273–2290; www.lolohotsprings.com; pool open in summer 10:00 A.M. to 10:00 P.M.). Members of the Lewis and Clark expedition were the first white men to soak at the springs, which they did during their homeward-bound travels on June 29, 1806; but Native Americans no doubt beat them to the baths by centuries. By 1885 the springs had evolved into a popular spot for hunters and vacationing families. Today, come the snowy Bitterroot Range winters, it's a major staging area for the snowmobiling crowd. In the snowless months at the resort you can dine, sleep in a tepee, and even play Lewis and Clark bumper boats (like bumper cars in a pond)—or simply enjoy a soak in the indoor/outdoor pools and continue up the road a short way to the far more peaceful **Lee Creek Campground** (USFS; Missoula Ranger District, Fort Missoula Bldg. 24-A, Missoula, MT 59804; 406–329–3750).

Beginning at Lee Creek Campground, you can hike what is believed to be a stretch of the original Lolo Trail, now designated as Wagon Mountain Trail #300. It climbs for 5 miles to Packer Meadows, where—like today's hikers and cross-country skiers—the expedition broke out of forest into a broad wetland area. In many summers the sea of blue camas filling the meadow is a most extraordinary sight.

Back on the highway, a climb of 5 to 6 miles from the Lee Creek Campground delivers you to Lolo Pass, where displays in the new **Lolo Pass**

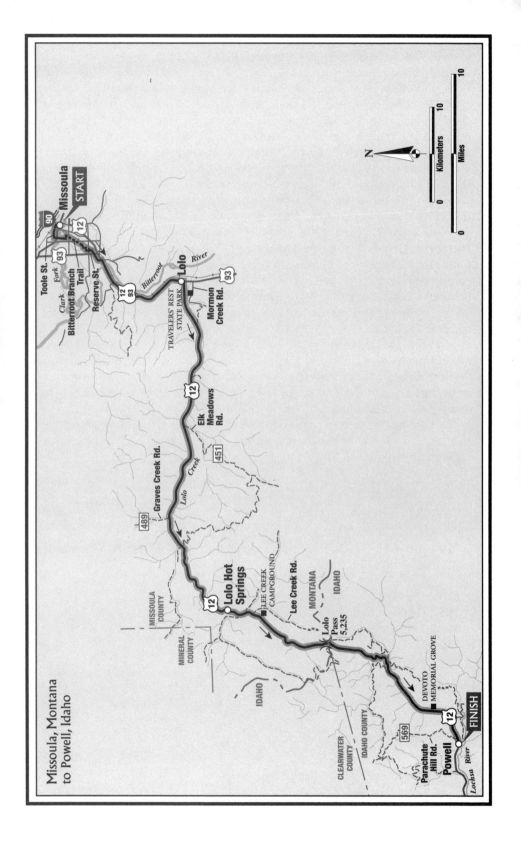

Missoula, Montana
to Powell, Idaho

Visitor Center (208–926–4274; open weekdays 8:30 A.M. to 4:00 P.M. May 15 through September 30) detail the Corps of Discovery's travels in the area. From Lolo Pass, Lewis and Clark had intended to follow the ridges to the north. But Old Toby, their Shoshone guide, made a wrong turn that led them down to the upper Lochsa River valley and the vicinity of Powell. They did not repeat the mistake on their return trip in 1806.

As you zip down the road into Idaho (entering the Pacific time zone), you'll begin to understand why the men had such a tough time traveling through this country, much of which probably looks a lot like it did 200 years ago. Pedaling the road along the Lochsa quickly becomes a tunnel-like, timbered-in experience. About 3 miles before Powell, be sure to pull over and enjoy strolling in the shade of the ancient cedar trees at **DeVoto Memorial Grove.** The grove is dedicated to Bernard DeVoto, a conservationist and western historian who is perhaps best remembered for his work editing the journals of Lewis and Clark. DeVoto also was an authority on Samuel Clemens, writing *Mark Twain's America* in 1932 and additional books on Clemens in later years. DeVoto's trilogy on America's westward expansion included 1947's *Across the Wide Missouri*, winner of both the Pulitzer and the Bancroft Prizes. Born in Utah in 1897, DeVoto was schooled at the University of Utah and Harvard and went on to teach English literature for several years at Northwestern and then at Harvard. Following his death in 1955, his ashes were scattered in this peaceful cedar grove, where today paved trails feature interpretive signs.

Just downstream from the DeVoto Memorial Grove, look high above the river and check out the osprey nest sitting on a tall snag to see if there's any big-bird activity under way.

Mileage Log

0.0 Adventure Cycling headquarters. Return to Lolo by the same route you took into town.

13.0 Lolo. Turn right to follow U.S. 12.

23.0 Elk Meadows Road on left.

28.5 Graves Creek Road on right.

38.5 Lolo Hot Springs.

46.0 Lolo Pass. Enter Idaho.

59.0 Powell.

33

Powell to Kamiah, Idaho

96 miles (2,723 miles cumulative)

". . . here we were compelled to kill a Colt for our men &
Selves to eat for the want of meat & we named the South
fork Colt Killed Creek . . ."

—CAPT. WILLIAM CLARK
Saturday, September 14, 1805
At White Sand Creek,
near present-day Powell

After finding their way from the Lochsa River bottoms to the lofty ridges to the north, Lewis and Clark continued along the Lolo Trail, a rugged travel way that had been used for decades by the Nez Percé. The expedition re-traced the Lolo Trail during their eastward passage through the Bitterroots in 1806. After that, it reverted to a pathway traveled only by Indians and perhaps the occasional mountain man.

In the 1850s, nearly a half century after Lewis and Clark's journeys, government geologist Dr. John Evans investigated the route followed by the trail to judge its potential as a road. He found it "by far the most difficult and un-inviting country I have ever examined in all my tours through the Rocky Mountains," and the idea was abandoned—for the time being. A few years later, in 1865, Congress appropriated $50,000 to improve the trail and turn it into a wagon road. The amount fell far short of the funds needed for the job, so after the work was finished it was still a trail, not a wagon road. But it was a vastly improved trail, a fact that was a blessing for Chief Joseph and his band of Nez Percé, who followed the trail eastward in 1877 in their ulti-mately unsuccessful quest for freedom (see text on the Nez Percé National Historic Trail in Chapter 4, Section 24). After another half century had passed, portions of the trail were incorporated into the Lolo Motorway, a narrow dirt road running high above the Lochsa River, constructed by the Civilian Conservation Corps as part of President Franklin Roosevelt's New Deal.

As mentioned in the introduction to this chapter, those riding fat-tire bikes may opt to ride the Lolo Motorway, which runs the high ridges form-ing the watershed divide between the Lochsa River and the North Fork of the Clearwater. To get to it, immediately east of Powell turn north onto For-est Road 569/Parachute Hill Road and climb for about 7 miles.

Back on the main highway, some 10 miles west of Powell you'll pass the Warm Springs Pack Bridge on the left. By walking across it and continuing

for about a mile, you can find your way to the noncommercial Jerry Johnson Hot Springs. A few miles farther down the road, this time on the right,
near Milepost 142, is a trail leading to Weir Hot Springs, another undeveloped site. In the interest of not facilitating overcrowding, we won't divulge
any more information about these two very special places. Just let it be said
that they're well worth the off-route travel necessary to reach them.

Lewis and Clark were compelled to deal with many hardships, no doubt
about it. One thing they *didn't* have to contend with was the RVs and loaded
log and grain trucks that will aggravate you as you continue down the madly
twisting U.S. Highway 12. Yet your surroundings in this wilderness corridor
are spectacular: a medley of bright-green grasses and ferns, subdued forests
of mixed conifers, sunlight dancing off the bubbling river, boulders making
"Vs" in the current, and, perhaps, puffy white clouds hanging in the deep-
blue sky. If it's later in the summer, you'll see huge logs that were deposited
on midriver rocks and islands when the water was much higher. Avalanche
chutes stripe the steep slopes above, and white-sand beaches attempt to
beckon you to the far side of the river. As you lose altitude and approach
Lowell, you'll note a growing number of small slopeside prairies; west of Syringa the terrain turns even drier, with folded scree slopes and an abundance
of knobby outcrops. One fascinating man-made feature you'll notice are the
roadside gondolas that take folks across the river on stout cables to their private residences.

Between Powell and Lowell you'll pass the **Lochsa Historical Ranger
Station** (Lochsa Ranger District, Kooskia, ID 83539; 208–926–4274), open
daily 9:00 A.M. to 5:00 P.M. Memorial Day through Labor Day. The beautifully
renovated station, where most of the buildings date from 1926 to 1931,
keeps alive the days and fire-management ways prior to 1952, when the outpost was finally accessible by road. As you walk through the peaceful and
open yet well-shaded grounds, you'll hear the breeze whispering through
trees to the accompaniment of the Lochsa River hissing in the distance.

A keen eye for things botanical was among the many attributes possessed
by Meriwether Lewis that led Thomas Jefferson to choose him as leader of
the president's cross-country expedition. As in most if not all other matters,
Lewis didn't let Jefferson down: All told, he identified more than 175 plant
species new to western science. (Capt. Clark, by comparison, recorded only
one.) Even in the Bitterroot Range, where the going was so terrible, Lewis
somehow found the time and energy to continue discovering and recording
new plant and tree species. Among the larger of these were the lodgepole
pine *(Pinus contorta)*, ponderosa pine *(Pinus ponderosa)*, and western larch
(Larix occidentalis).

One of the most beautiful and unusual of conifers, the western larch is
the largest of several Pacific Northwest tamarack species. It boasts a rich,
reddish-brown trunk that grows impossibly straight and up to 200 feet high.
One of a rare breed of deciduous conifers, the larch sheds its needles every
autumn, leaving them looking dark and dead in winter. But in the spring,
fresh needle growth lends the somber forests wonderfully bright accents of

Steep, deeply creased mountain slopes surround you as you make your way down the Middle Fork of the Clearwater River.

Powell to Kamiah,
Idaho

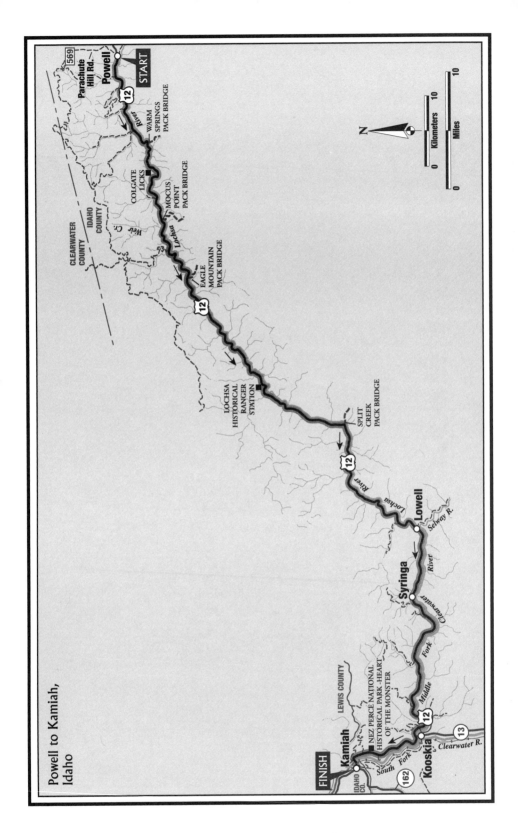

light green. Yet larches are at their most beautiful in the fall: After turning absolutely golden, the needles typically stay on the tree for two or three weeks before finally being blown off to blanket the forest floor in rich autumn color. The relatively dense wood and straight grain of the larch—it's *so* easy to split—make it a favorite of firewood gatherers in the region. Native Americans made a tea from its bark that reportedly was used as a treatment for tuberculosis and other maladies, and they chewed its pitch like a gum. They also used larch wood for making bowls and smoking buckskins.

Of more material interest to the Lewis and Clark expedition than the western larch was the ponderosa pine. On crossing the Weippe Prairie and reaching the Clearwater River, the expedition spent nearly two weeks at "Canoe Camp," located about 5 miles west of present-day Orofino. Here they felled big ponderosas and burned and hollowed them out to fashion five large dugout canoes. Once again, and for the first time since Camp Fortunate, they would be traveling by water. After arranging to leave their more than three dozen remaining horses—all of them branded with U.S. CAPT. M. LEWIS—under the care of the Nez Percé for the winter, Lewis, Clark, and the rest were headed at last downstream toward the Columbia River and the Pacific Ocean.

You may opt to stay at the **Lewis and Clark Resort** (Route 1, Box 17–X, Highway 12, Kamiah, ID 83536; 208–935–2556; www.lewisclarkresort.com), a couple of miles before reaching Kamiah. One of the largest private campgrounds in Idaho, it's conveniently—and, you might say, ironically—situated immediately across the road from the Heart of the Monster, which you can read about in the next section.

Mileage Log

0.0 Ride west out of Powell on U.S. 12.
10.0 Warm Springs Pack Bridge on left.
14.0 Colgate Licks.
18.0 Mocus Point Pack Bridge.
26.0 Eagle Mountain Pack Bridge.
40.0 Lochsa Historical Ranger Station.
50.5 Split Creek Pack Bridge.
65.5 Lowell.
72.5 Syringa.
88.5 Kooskia *(KOO-ski)*.
95.5 Cross Clearwater River and Enter Lewis County.
96.0 Kamiah. Turn left onto State Road 162.

34

Kamiah, Idaho to Clarkston, Washington
87.5 miles (2,810.5 miles cumulative)

*". . . Sixty miles below the forks arived at a large southerly
fork which is the one we were on with the Snake or So-So-
nee nation . . ."*
> —CAPT. WILLIAM CLARK
> Thursday, October 10, 1805
> At the confluence of the Clearwater and Snake
> Rivers, now the site of Lewiston and Clarkston

The **Heart of the Monster** is one of more than three dozen components of **Nez Percé National Historical Park** (39063 U.S. Highway 95, Spalding, ID 83540; 208–843–2261; www.nps.gov/nepe). Heart of the Monster is an isolated rock outcrop that is the focus of an important Nez Percé legend: It was here that their people were created from drops of blood squeezed from the monster's heart. From the small parking area, a short paved trail leads to the rock, where a play-on-demand audio tape relates the story of the Coyote and the Monster. It's a peaceful spot, with a small wetlands pond in sight below that is largely responsible for its double role as an official Idaho state watchable wildlife site.

You'll climb out of Kamiah on State Road 162, a narrow ribbon of bitumen that wraps into steep, golden hills holding flat-faced volcanic rocks and timber-filled troughs. When you finally break out in the open on top, you'll be surrounded by hay and wheat fields. Particularly if it's the harvest season, you'll see numerous raptors on the hunt for combine-flushed field mice and other rodents. After cresting a low divide, you'll be treated to splendid views of the Camas Prairie to the southwest. For centuries the Nez Percé and other tribes traveled here annually to harvest the starchy camas *(Camassia quamash)* bulb, which made up an important part of their diet. The bulb was typically steamed but could also be eaten raw. The flower of the camas, which appears from April into July, is light blue in color, and low-lying fields of the plant often appear from a distance like small lakes.

Death camas *(Zygadenus venenosus)*, a close relative of the camas, should never be sampled. Very much like the edible camas in its leaf and bulb structure, the death camas can be identified by a yellow to greenish-white flower. During the time of flowering, the Nez Percé and other Native Americans would delineate areas where the true camas grew by marking them with strips of bark. When they returned to dig bulbs, the edible plants would be more easily recognizable.

Tepee frame, Nez Percé National Historical Park

Where you turn onto U.S. Highway 95 it's a four-laner, but it soon narrows to two lanes with a wide asphalt shoulder. You'll pass several trestles of the Camas Prairie Railroad, a legacy of the railroad wars at the turn of the twentieth century, when the Hills and the Harrimans battled for rail control of the inland Pacific Northwest. The Camas Prairie Railroad's nickname, the "railroad on stilts," reflects the fact that it boasts the largest concentration of tall trestles of any rail line in the country. None of the trestles you'll encounter is more impressive than the one spanning Lawyer's Canyon. It was built in 1908, roughly midway between now and the Lewis and Clark expedition: Things such as this make you realize how young the West really is in terms of white settlement.

Today the historic but still active railroad is one of a handful of lines that permit private motorcars and rail cars on its tracks. Early in the line's history, railroad workers often employed rail bikes for such tasks as checking the tracks and getting to worksites. Rail bikes appeared very early on, and more than two dozen models had been patented by 1900. Now certain areas of north Idaho are hotbeds of a resurging interest in the activity, which is pursued by cycling enthusiasts who would prefer that the rails of abandoned railroads be left in place rather than removed for rail-trail construction.

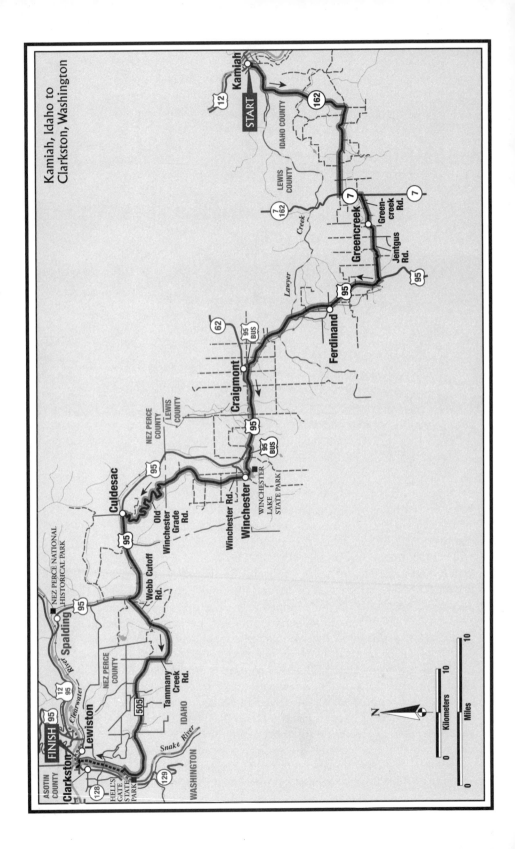

Kamiah, Idaho to
Clarkston, Washington

Winchester Lake State Park (P.O. Box 186, Winchester, ID 83555; 208–924–7563; www.idahoparks.org/parks), located roughly halfway between Kamiah and Clarkston, makes a great spot for an overnight. (One of the best places to camp in the Clarkston area is Chief Timothy State Park, 8 miles west of town. See Chapter 7, Ride 35, for more information.) Here you can camp under the stars, in your tent or in a furnished rental yurt (call 208–799–5015 for reservations). The park's namesake 103-acre lake, surrounded by stands of beefy Douglas fir and ponderosa pine, sits at nearly 4,000 feet, making for good sleeping temperatures in summer. You'll pass the campground about a quarter mile before reaching the town of Winchester, whose greeting banner, depicting the .30–.30 lever-action rifle that won the West, you will find most unusual.

Leaving Winchester you'll follow the Old Winchester Road, which begins modestly enough as a patched-up, one-and-a-half laner. Soon, though, it serves up one of the wildest and most unforgettable descents you'll ever experience as the road dips and dives hundreds of feet into the river basin below.

Mileage Log

0.0	Leave Kamiah on SR 162.
2.5	Enter Idaho County.
15.5	Turn left onto SR 7.
17.0	Turn right onto Greencreek Road.
19.0	Greencreek.
20.0	Go straight onto Jentgus Road.
23.5	Turn right onto U.S. Highway 95.
27.5	Ferdinand.
35.0	Craigmont.
41.0	Turn left onto Business U.S. 95.
43.5	Winchester. In 0.2 mile, continue straight onto Winchester Road.
50.5	Enter Nez Percé County and continue down the steep and winding Old Winchester Grade Road.
58.5	Turn left onto U.S. 95.
65.0	Turn left onto Webb Cutoff Road.
71.5	Turn right onto Tammany Creek Road/County Road 505.
82.5	Lewiston. At HELL'S GATE STATE PARK sign, turn left. Ride north onto bike path.
86.5	Ride under the Snake River bridge and turn right onto pedestrian bridge that takes you into a park. At the end of the park, jog left onto D Street, then right onto First Street. Bear right onto Main Street/U.S. 12 and ride over Snake River bridge.
87.5	At west end of bridge, bear right onto Confluence Way, which takes you into a park in Clarkston and the end of this section.

CHAPTER 7

Clarkston, Washington to Astoria, Oregon (443.5 miles)

On October 10, 1805, the Corps of Discovery arrived at the mouth of the Clearwater River, a location today surrounded by the twin cities of Lewiston, Idaho, and Clarkston, Washington. Natural geographer that he was, Capt. William Clark knew intuitively that the river flowing in from the south, the Snake, was at least in part formed by the Salmon—the same river he'd investigated for its navigability shortly after the expedition surmounted Lemhi Pass. As the party continued down the Snake River, the battle of the rapids they had begun on the Clearwater continued raging, as it did after they hit the Columbia on October 16 near the present-day cities of Pasco and Kennewick. There they were met by a greeting party of Yakamas and Wanapams, whose main mode of travel was the canoe. Before leaving these Indians two days later, the men traded manufactured goods such as thimbles and knitting needles for forty dogs, which would serve as sustenance as they continued downstream.

Progressing downriver through a remarkably dry, barren landscape, the Corps encountered numerous makeshift villages, representing various Indian nations, that had been established along the river for the fall salmon runs. Occasionally the men noted a piece of clothing or a manufactured item—a sailor's jacket here, a British musket there—that revealed the Indians had traded with whites along the coast, or at least had traded with other Indians who had done so. It was one sign of many that they were nearing the Pacific Ocean.

It didn't take Lewis and Clark long to realize that when it came to negotiating rapids and big waves, their cumbersome dugout canoes were far inferior to the local natives' lightweight dugouts, which rode high in the water. The captains were carrying copies of maps published by the British explorer George Vancouver, who had traveled upstream on the Columbia as far as

Beacon Rock, and they knew they were getting close to there. Once below the Cascades of the Columbia (now inundated by the waters of the Bonneville Dam), they arrived at Beacon Rock, where, for the first time, they noted the river rising and falling with the tide. They were also in the midst of harbor seals and other sea-going wildlife. The ocean was close!

Yet the expedition was still above present-day Portland, and the ebbing and flowing tide and battering November weather would present new challenges that would keep them from reaching the Pacific for another two weeks. After undertaking explorations in various directions on both sides of the Columbia, they decided to locate winter camp somewhere to the south, close to the ocean, rather than at a site upriver or to the north. The decision was reached by popular vote, and in a harbinger of an America of the future, both York, the black slave, and Sacagawea, the Shoshone woman, voted right along with the others. They settled on a site located about 3 miles up the Netul River (now the Lewis and Clark) from Youngs Bay, at present-day Astoria.

Where the Snake River bends northwest about 9 miles west of Clarkston, you'll leave Lewis and Clark's westbound route and not join it again until you hit the Columbia River west of Walla Walla. Much of the bicycle route between these two cities, however, does follow the approximate overland route taken east by the Corps in early May 1806. Your windy—and potentially very hot—ride through the Columbia River Gorge and on to the coast will be a study in contrasts: from stretches of traffic-clogged Interstate 94 to a couple of closed-to-cars sections of the Historic Columbia River Highway, now a beautiful state trail; and from the bustle of metropolitan Portland to small, serene communities that barely earn dots on the map. U.S. Highway 30, unfortunately, is a busy way to end the trip, but there's a good reason all of those motorists are heading west—to get out to that beautiful coastline.

When they established winter camp at Fort Clatsop in early December 1805, the Corps of Discovery still had more than nine months of camping and traveling in the wilds before they would be back in St. Louis. Yet they had reached their ultimate goal—and you will have, too, by the time you're finished pedaling this section of the Lewis & Clark Bicycle Trail.

35 Clarkston to Walla Walla, Washington
94.5 miles (2,905 miles cumulative)

". . . I think Lewis's [Snake] River is about 250 yards wide, the Koos koos ke River about 150 yards wide and the river below the forks about 300 yards wide . . ."

—CAPT. WILLIAM CLARK
Thursday, October 10, 1805
At the confluence of the
Clearwater and Snake Rivers

As you ride west from Lewiston along the wide shoulder of U.S. Highway 12, you'll probably spot numerous barges floating against the opposite bank of the broad Snake River, taking on loads of Inland Empire logs and grain that will soon be bound for the Pacific and points beyond. About 8 miles from town, below to the right, you'll see the groves of trees marking **Chief Timothy State Park** (13766 Highway 12, Clarkston, WA 99403; 509–758–9580; www.parks.wa.gov/parks). The park makes a fine place to camp, with more than 2 miles of riverfront and tall trees providing ample shade—a highly prized commodity in these hot, deserty parts. For privacy for the nonmotorized, the camping includes a couple of primitive sites. The 282-acre park occupies an island composed of glacial tills that were deposited by some of the torrents of water released when the ice dam holding back Glacial Lake Missoula failed. When the floodwaters reached the narrow passageway known as Wallula Gap, they backed up eastward, dropping their load of rocks and sediments here and at other locations. (See more on this subject in Section 36.) The park's **Alpowai Interpretive Center** (open Memorial Day through Labor Day, 1:00 to 5:00 P.M. Wednesday through Sunday) recalls the ancient Nez Percé village that stood at the location where, on October 11, 1805, Lewis and Clark purchased dogs and salmon for food and hired a trio of Indians to help see them through the Snake River rapids they knew were not far ahead.

It's worth your time to prowl the backstreets of picturesque Dayton, where the Jolly Green Giant stands tall on a hillside above town. Dayton boasts a bevy of century-old-plus beauties—homes and other structures, that is—in the Italianate, Gothic, Craftsman, and Queen Anne styles. You can also have a gander at Washington's oldest active county courthouse (1887) and oldest train depot (1881), both of which have been extensively renovated.

The Snake River west of Clarkston, Washington

The most influential of Dayton's town fathers was German emigrant Jacob Weinhard, who in 1880 came to town via Portland, where he'd worked in the beermaking establishment of his uncle, Henry Weinhard (whose name was destined to become better known than his nephew's). Jacob recognized that the fertile land surrounding Dayton would be ideal for growing barley, and by the early twentieth century the entrepreneur had built a small empire that included his own Weinhard Brewery, a malt house with a German beer garden outside, the Weinhard Saloon ("perhaps the finest in the State of Washington, and we doubt if there is anything of the kind to surpass it on the Pacific Coast," wrote one newspaper), the Weinhard Theater opera house, and part ownership of the Local Citizens National Bank. Today you can bed down at the **Weinhard Hotel** (235 East Main Street, Dayton, WA 99328; 509–382–4032; www.weinhard.com), which occupies the 1890 Weinhard Saloon and Lodge building and incorporates many original architectural elements of the Weinhard Lodge. The inn features fifteen Victorian-appointed rooms embellished with the expected modern amenities.

Four miles west of town—or 60 miles from Chief Timothy State Park, perhaps your previous camping location—is **Lewis and Clark Trail State Park** (36149 Highway 12, Dayton, WA 99328; 509–337–6457; www.parks.wa. gov/parks). (This park is not to be confused with Washington's Lewis and Clark State Park, which lies south of Centralia in the Interstate 5 corridor.) The thirty-seven-acre park fronting the Touchet River is a diamond in the

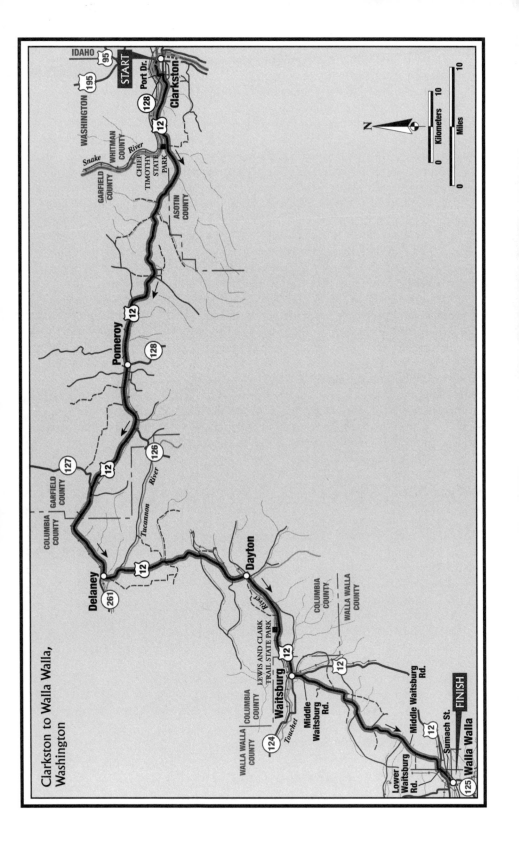

Clarkston to Walla Walla, Washington

rough, with its wetlands, floodplain cottonwood forests, and old-growth stands of ponderosa pine, all sitting smack in the middle of thousands of acres of arid grasslands. Responsible for this lush microclimate are the periodic flooding of the Touchet, along with the very nature of the narrow valley itself, which restricts air movement and traps moisture. Reenactments of Lewis and Clark's 1806 doings in the area take place at the park every Saturday evening between Memorial Day and Labor Day. Even if you don't plan to camp here, at least swing in and visit the park's facilities, which offer something unique: Men will find a silhouette of Lewis and Clark painted in black on the wall of their rest room, while women can admire one of Sacagawea and baby Pomp in theirs.

The 2-mile climb out of Waitsburg on a narrow back road wending through a golden moonscape is one to remember—particularly if the mercury is topping 100 degrees. On the far side of the hill, you'll descend toward Walla Walla, a welcome oasis of civilization—and that's doubly true if you're an oenophile: The Walla Walla Valley has evolved into one of the most important wine-producing regions of the Pacific Northwest, and some three dozen wineries operate in the area. The valley is equally renowned for its sweet onions. Try, for instance, the lip-smacking, deep-fried Walla Walla Sweets concoction cooked up at **Jacob's Cafe** (416 North Second Avenue, Walla Walla, WA 99362; 509–525–2677), where you can dine in air-conditioned comfort in a classic railroad dining car. In the morning grab a latte and check your e-mail at **Coffee Connection Cafe** (226 East Main Street, Walla Walla, WA 99362; 509–529–9999), where the caffeinated brews are head-spinningly strong and the Internet connections lightning fast.

Mileage Log

0.0 Leave the park in Clarkston, riding west on the bike path. Turn right onto Port Way, then curve left and turn right onto Port Drive.
1.0 Turn right onto SR 128, then right onto U.S. Highway 12.
12.0 Enter Garfield County.
29.0 Pomeroy.
44.0 Enter Columbia County.
50.5 Delaney. Bear left to continue on U.S. 12.
65.5 Dayton.
73.0 Enter Walla Walla County.
75.0 Waitsburg. Bear left to continue on U.S. 12.
76.0 Turn right onto Middle Waitsburg Road.
93.0 Turn left onto Lower Waitsburg Road, and continue straight across U.S. 12.
93.5 Turn right onto Sumach Street.
94.5 Downtown Walla Walla.

36

Walla Walla, Washington to Umatilla, Oregon

55.5 miles (2,960.5 miles cumulative)

". . . saw a mountain bearing S. West conocal form
Covered with Snow . . ."
> —CAPT. WILLIAM CLARK
> Friday, October 18, 1805
> Glimpsing Mount Hood from near
> the mouth of the Walla Walla River

On departing Walla Walla you'll pedal along a stretch of U.S. Highway 12 that can be quite busy, but it offers a wide shoulder at first. After about 7 miles you'll pass the road heading south into the **Whitman Mission National Historic Site** (Route 2, Box 247, Walla Walla, WA 98362; 509–522–6357; www.nps.gov/whmi). The monument protects the site of a mission that was established among the Cayuse Indians in 1836 by Marcus and Narcissa Whitman. It contains the foundations of original mission buildings, along with other artifacts, such as the mission's millpond and a short stretch of the Oregon Trail. Native grasses have been planted to provide a glimpse of how the grounds may have appeared in the 1840s.

Until Narcissa Whitman and Eliza Spalding, accompanying their husbands, arrived at the Columbia River after setting out from St. Louis, no white woman had completed an overland crossing of the continent. Their successful journey helped persuade other families to follow in their tracks, readying the way for the thousands who would travel the Oregon Trail. The Reverend Henry and Eliza Spalding moved on to establish a mission among the Nez Percé at Lapwai, Idaho; the Whitmans opened their mission here at Waiilatpu, "place of the people of the rye grass." Marcus Whitman worked diligently to persuade the Cayuse to forget their nomadic hunter-gatherer lifestyle and settle down to become farmers, but for the most part the Indians showed little interest in the spiritual and material matters considered important by the white Protestants. In fact, the Cayuse feared that their very way of life was being threatened—a fear that culminated in a tragic massacre on November 29, 1847, when a group of Cayuse attacked and killed Marcus, Narcissa, and about a dozen others.

From the visitor center you can walk to the grave where the victims of the attack were buried, then on up the steep, paved trail to the Memorial Monument. Erected on the fiftieth anniversary of the Whitmans' death, it resides high on the hill where Narcissa would climb to watch for her husband returning home from his duties afield.

Memorial monument at Whitman Mission National Historic Site, outside Walla Walla, Washington

A few miles farther west, high on the ridges to the south, you'll encounter a long parade of turbines, their propellers spinning in the ever-present Columbia Basin winds. They are part of the Stateline Wind Project, which comprises some 400 turbines distributed in several strings on the ridges here and north of Pendleton, Oregon. Each turbine is capable of generating 660 kilowatts, for a grand total of approximately 265 megawatts. About a third of this power, 90 megawatts, is being purchased by the Bonneville Power Administration—enough to power approximately 18,000 homes in the Pacific Northwest. It's the agency's largest wind-energy acquisition to date.

Soon you'll turn southeast off U.S. 12 to ride along U.S. 730, initially on a good shoulder. However, it soon narrows a bit, then *really* narrows once you enter Oregon. Where you first hit U.S. 730, you're in the vicinity of Wallula Gap, where the Columbia River cuts through the Horse Heaven Hills. This is at the southern end of eastern Washington's "Channeled Scablands," a deeply scarred landscape largely void of vegetation that resulted from the Spokane Flood, the greatest known flood in earth history. Evidence of the flood remains all the way from western Montana to the Pacific Ocean, but it is here in the Channeled Scablands of eastern Washington that the evidence is most impressive. The flood, which occurred between 18,000 and 20,000 years ago, was the culmination of a unique meeting of geological and meteorological phenomena: A series of widespread lava flows, then a regional down-tilting of the landscape, followed by the deposition of a thick layer of loess, or wind-blown silt.

Around 100,000 years ago, massive ice fields to the north in Canada began extending their frozen fingers into major valleys in the Northwest. One of these was the valley of the Clark Fork River, in the vicinity of where the river enters Lake Pend Oreille. The ice dam on the Clark Fork backed up Glacial Lake Missoula, the biggest of the Pacific Northwest's Ice Age lakes. At its maximum, Glacial Lake Missoula covered approximately 3,000 square miles and contained a volume of water equal to approximately half of what Lake Michigan holds today. The lake was an estimated 2,000 feet deep at the ice dam and about half that deep at present Missoula. Eventually, summer rains and melting snow filled the basin, and the water attempted to rise higher than the top of the ice dam. Overflow began, and the water started melting and cutting down through the ice dam, eventually causing its complete failure. The water poured forth, letting gravity tell it where to go. Where these floodwaters of unprecedented volume ran into the barrier of the Horse Heaven Hills, they had to squeeze through Wallula Gap, a process that took perhaps a month to complete.

A few miles into Oregon you'll pass **Hat Rock State Park** (call 800–452–5687 to reserve picnic facilities) on the right. A day-use park only, it's a fine place to enjoy lunch on a riverside lawn spreading beneath the shade of beefy cottonwood and black locust trees. The park's namesake, one of several volcanic plugs that resisted erosion during the Spokane Flood, was noted by Capt. William Clark.

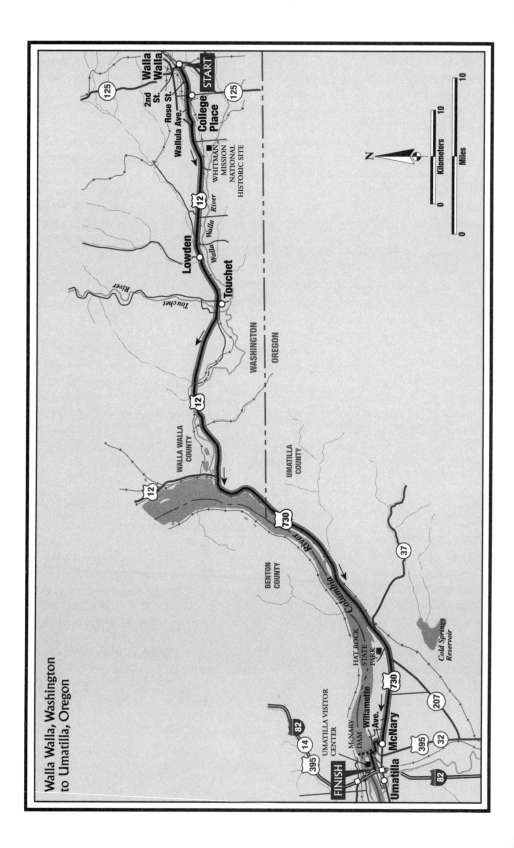

Walla Walla, Washington
to Umatilla, Oregon

At Mile 54 below, swing in to visit the **McNary Dam Interpretive Center** (P.O. Box 1230, Umatilla, OR 97882; 541–922–3211; call for hours), where you can learn about this, one of a quartet of dams creating lakes along the Oregon-Washington border. The Pacific Salmon Visitor Information Center explains some of the complex issues surrounding management of salmon in the presence of these large dams. You can learn how the salmon—or some of them, at least—get around these immense barriers to reach their upriver spawning grounds.

Mileage Log

0.0   In downtown Walla Walla, turn south onto Second Street, then, in 0.1 mile go right onto Rose Street.

2.5   College Place. Bear right onto Wallula Avenue.

5.5   Turn left onto U.S. 12.

12.5   Lowden.

17.5   Touchet.

29.5   Turn left onto U.S. 730.

35.5   Enter Oregon.

53.0   Turn right onto Willamette Avenue.

54.0   Curve right, then left, then right. Near the McNary Dam, turn left onto Third Street.

55.5   Turn right onto bike path paralleling Interstate 82 (camping and Umatilla Visitor Center straight ahead).

37 Umatilla to Biggs, Oregon
85 miles (3,045.5 miles cumulative)

". . . the sight of This Indian woman, wife to one of our interprs.
confirmed those people of our friendly intentions, as no woman
ever accompanies a war party of Indians in this quarter . . ."
—CAPT. WILLIAM CLARK
Saturday, October 19, 1805
Among the Wallula, or Walla Walla, Indians

Although this section's beginning and ending points are both in Oregon, almost all the riding takes place on the Washington side of the Columbia River. Most of the route is along State Road 14, which is open, exposed to the sun, and somewhat humdrum and where traffic can range from substantial to quite light. The most interesting attractions are clustered toward the western end of the section. Assuming that you spent the previous night in Umatilla, you'll want to plan on either a short day to Crow Butte State Park (pleasant, but can suffer from winds) or a long one to Maryhill State Park.

After climbing the big hill near the Jonn Day Dam, you'll top out to be greeted with a stunning view of what, considering your desert and possibly overheated surroundings, you may initially believe to be a mirage: distant, snow-clad Mount Hood. But there it is—provided, of course, that the day is clear.

Before reaching the U.S. Highway 97 junction, pull down to the left to view a most unexpected sight: **Maryhill's Stonehenge,** America's own full-scale replica of the ancient and mysterious monument of stones that stands above the Salisbury Plain of Wiltshire, England. Occupying an isolated bluff above the Columbia, the monument was conceived and constructed by road builder Samuel Hill as a memorial to Klickitat County soldiers who died in World War I. Hill, a Quaker, had erroneously believed that the original Stonehenge was built to serve as a place of human sacrifice, so he built his personal version as a reminder that "humanity is still being sacrificed to the god of war." Dedicated in 1918, it was finished not long before Hill passed away in 1931. The name "Maryhill" is easily explainable: Hill's mother, wife, and daughter were all named Mary, and their last names were Hill (and the place is definitely hilly!). Now also at the site are memorials to Klickitat County victims of World War II and the Korean and Viet Nam Wars.

Another monument of sorts—a reminder of Hill's planned but unsuccessful utopian settlement, to which he had hoped to attract hordes of fellow Quakers—wends through the Klickitat Hills from just north of Maryhill's Stonehenge. The 3.6-mile **Historic Loops Road,** built by Hill in 1913, was reportedly the first paved road in the Pacific Northwest. Several experimental methods were used to build different sections of the road, including one that incorporates natural asphalt shipped from the La Brea Tar Pits in Los Angeles. It's your favorite kind of road, too—open daily from 7:00 A.M. until dark to pedestrians and cyclists only.

A large array of items relating to Hill's road-building endeavors are on display at the **Maryhill Museum of Art** (35 Maryhill Museum Drive, Goldendale, WA 98620; 509-773-3733; www.maryhillmuseum.org), open 9:00 A.M. to 5:00 P.M. daily March 15 through November 15; $7.00 general admission. But these barely scratch the surface of the incredible collection housed at the museum, located about 4 miles west of Maryhill's Stonehenge, off the route west of the U.S. 97 junction. Opening on May 13, 1940, the facility occupies the mansion that Hill built as a home beginning in 1914, utilizing poured concrete and steel beams (no wood was used as structural components, which you might expect in a highway builder's home). Considering its outback location, the museum is home to a remarkable and surprisingly cosmopolitan assortment of art, largely the result of worldwide contacts the entrepreneur made during his business dealings and travels. Among the permanent displays are an acclaimed collection of watercolors and sculptures by the French master Auguste Rodin; a royal collection that belonged to Queen Marie of Romania, comprising a coronation gown, crown, and other sparkling items; one of the world's foremost collections of historical chess sets; and a large selection of European paintings from Holland, England, and other countries. Of particular interest to American history buffs are the exhibits of Native American prehistoric rock art and artifacts, including ones similar to those collected by Lewis and Clark from natives in the Columbia Gorge and elsewhere. Outside the museum you'll find a series of panels interpreting the Corps of Discovery's travels through this very area in April 1806.

Whether you get there by following U.S. 97 or by sneaking in the back way via the narrow road plummeting down to river level from Maryhill's Stonehenge, **Maryhill State Park** (50 Highway 97, Goldendale, WA 98620; 509-773-5007; www.parks.wa.gov/parks) makes a good destination for a lunch stop or an overnight. The park boasts nearly a mile of Columbia River frontage and ample quantities of that most coveted of eastern Washington assets: shade. Just east up the road from the park you'll find a couple of open-air fruit stands, where you can procure delicious fresh Washington fruit—depending on the season, cherries, peaches, or apricots, among others—to augment your next few meals.

Umatilla to Biggs,
Oregon

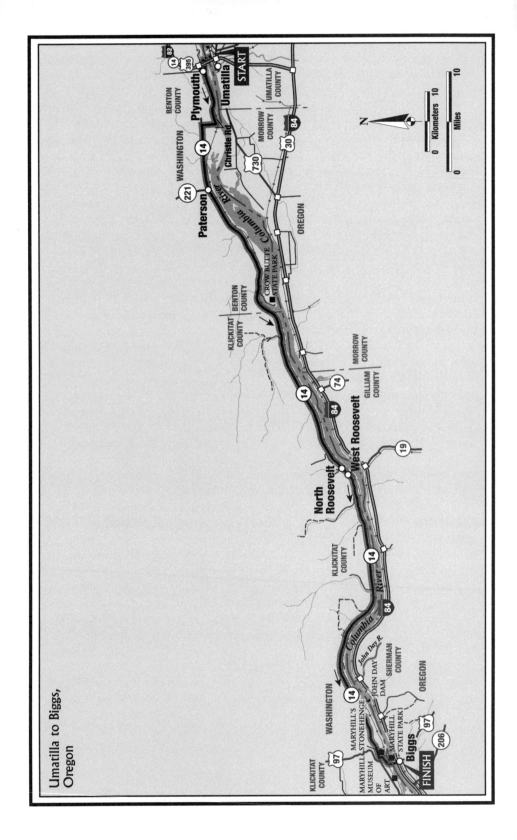

Mileage Log

0.0 Cross Columbia River on bike path, entering Washington.

1.5 Drop down to the right, then ride under Interstate 82. Ride through gate and onto Christie Road. Plymouth.

9.5 At T, turn left onto SR 14.

16.0 Paterson.

28.5 Crow Butte State Park entrance.

31.5 Enter Klickitat County.

49.0 North Roosevelt.

50.0 West Roosevelt.

82.0 Turn left onto U.S. 97.

83.5 Maryhill State Park entrance.

84.5 Cross Columbia River into Oregon.

85.0 Biggs.

38 Biggs to Hood River, Oregon
45 miles (3,090.5 miles cumulative)

". . . The whole of the Current of this great river must at all Stages pass thro' this narrow chanel of 45 yards wide."
—CAPT. WILLIAM CLARK
Thursday, October 24, 1805
At The Dalles

Now that you're back on the Oregon side of the river, not far west of Biggs you'll come across the **Deschutes River State Recreation Area** (89600 Biggs-Rufus Highway, Wasco OR 97065; 541–739–2322; www.oregon stateparks.org), a well-treed park surrounding the mouth of the swift and storied Deschutes River. The campground, which includes twenty-five primitive sites, makes for an excellent overnight—one that is particularly well positioned if your previous night was spent at Crow Butte State Park. In addition to the tent camping, cabins, yurts, tepees, and camp wagons are all available for rent. Another highlight (if it can be called that after you've been bicycling day in and day out) is the dirt- and gravel-surfaced rail-trail heading upstream along the Deschutes for some 17 miles.

A not-to-be-missed attraction located just off-route northwest of The Dalles is the splendid **Columbia Gorge Discovery Center** (5000 Discovery Drive, The Dalles, OR 97058; 541–296–8600; www.gorgediscovery.org), open daily 10:00 A.M. to 6:00 P.M., general admission $6.50. Incorporated into the same complex are the **Wasco County Historical Museum** and, outside, the **Living History Park,** where you can meet members of the Lewis and Clark expedition, Oregon Trail travelers, and other modern-day old-timers. Exhibits inside illuminate the complex geological past of the gorge; others interpret its much more recent human history and prehistory. Archaeological excavations at Five Mile Rapids, a natural fishing site east of The Dalles, have turned up evidence of people in the area as long ago as Paleoindian times, some 10,000 years ago. Later, natives ancestral to the Yakamas, Umatillas, Nez Percé, and other nations lived at least part-time in the vicinity, where they would obtain salmon, an integral part of their diets.

If you think about such things at all, you can't help but wonder why the Columbia River cuts *through* the Cascade Range. Most rivers, after all, form their headwaters high in mountain basins and begin as trickles moving down the range, either on one side or the other. The answer is that the Columbia is a very old river. Its course was altered numerous times during the past several million years, coerced this way or that in response to massive

West of Rowena you'll wind up the twisting roadway, then spin down through a blur of black rock and brown slopes.

lava flows that emanated from ancestral Cascade Range volcanoes. Between six and two million years ago, basalt flows finally filled the Bridal Veil Channel, which the Columbia had occupied for approximately ten million years until then. This forced the river northward to its present course, where the modern Cascade Range uplifted around it. In other words, the river cut down through the mountains as they slowly rose upward. Later, in very recent geologic times, the floodwaters of Glacial Lake Missoula scoured the gorge into essentially what we see today, minus the man-made alterations and intrusions.

Arguably, the number-one highlight of the Lewis & Clark Bicycle Trail in Oregon—or maybe number two, next to reaching the ocean!—is the ride along the Historic Columbia River Highway through the Columbia River Gorge. You'll begin riding the historic roadway in this section and continue doing so intermittently all the way to just east of Portland.

After its completion, and while it was still intact, the Historic Columbia River Highway extended along the south side of the river for around 75 miles, from The Dalles to Troutdale. Construction on this, the first modern highway built in the Pacific Northwest, commenced in 1913. The goal of its engineers was not the same as the objective of those who build today's highways—that is, to get from point A to point B in the shortest and flattest way practicable. Rather, their goal was to provide a scenic roadway for the enjoyment of pioneer motorists. Initially, prosperous Portland families would take drives along the spectacularly situated roadway, pulling over to view the multitude of high waterfalls and to picnic at one of the rest areas distributed along the way. It wasn't long, however, before other individuals in addition to the affluent owned cars. Progressively, the road was used more and more by people traveling in cars and trucks to get somewhere, often for work or other utilitarian reasons.

Sadly, the original highway was destroyed in many places during construction of the river-grade road that would evolve into Interstate 84. A large share of the most spectacular sections of the roadway were bulldozed or dynamited, and tunnels were destroyed or filled with rubble. The isolated sections that do remain retain many of their original features, such as bridges and masonry walls. Several of these surviving segments are for nonmotorized use only, and they provide some of the most enjoyable riding on the entire Lewis & Clark Bicycle Trail.

West of Rowena you'll wind yourself up the twisting roadway, then spin down like a top through a blur of black rock, baked-brown slopes, green trees, and, quite possibly, intense heat. The dizzying ride in this section finally ends at Hood River, the windsurfing capital of America, where big winds billow sails and build huge waves. If you've never tried the sport but would like to, a number of businesses in the area offer lessons. Among them is **Hood River Waterplay** (Port Marina Park, P.O. Box 1524, Hood River, OR 97031; 541-386-9463; www.hoodriverwaterplay.com), with two locations in town.

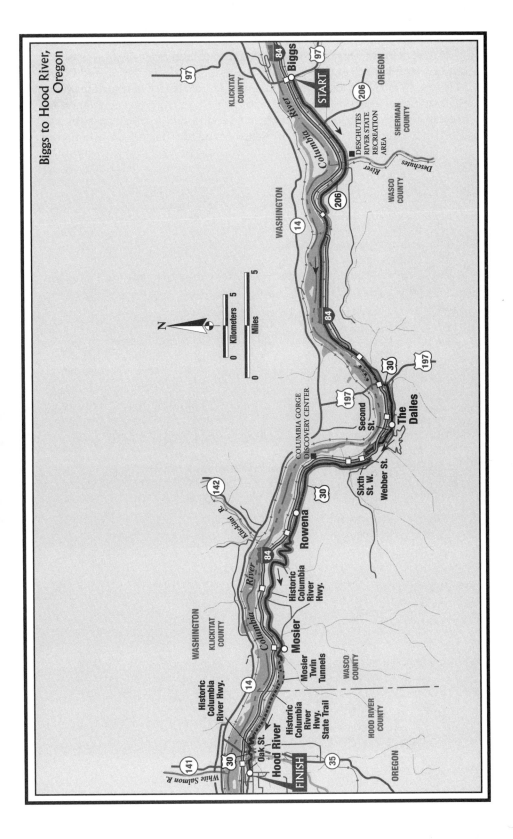

Biggs to Hood River, Oregon

If time permits, consider also taking a four-hour round-trip ride on the **Mount Hood Railroad** (110 Railroad Avenue, Hood River, OR 97031; 541–386–3556; www.mthoodrr.com), whose line is a designated National Historic Site. Departing from the depot in Hood River, the excursion takes in a cross-section of Oregon's very best river-and-mountain scenery. Finally, don't miss exploring Hood River's attractive and bustling downtown district.

0.0	At Biggs, turn right onto unsigned frontage road.
3.0	Continue straight where SR 206 joins route.
4.5	Enter Wasco County.
8.5	Turn right and ride under I–84. In 0.1 mile turn left to ride up and onto I–84.
18.0	Exit I–84. Turn left onto U.S. Highway 30/U.S. 197.
18.5	Turn right to continue on U.S. 30.
20.0	The Dalles. Continue straight on U.S. 30/Second Street.
21.0	Turn left onto Webber Street, go beneath the interstate, and turn right onto U.S. 30/Sixth Street West.
28.5	Rowena.
38.5	Mosier. Continue straight on Historic Columbia River Highway; U.S. 30 leaves route.
39.0	Turn right onto Historic Columbia River Highway State Trail.
40.0	Mosier Twin Tunnels.
43.5	Continue straight on Historic Columbia River Highway.
44.5	Ride straight across State Road 35 onto U.S. 30. Hood River.
45.0	Curve right to continue on U.S. 30/Oak Street.

39

Hood River to Portland, Oregon
66.5 miles (3,157 miles cumulative)

". . . here the mountains leave the river on each Side, which from the great Shute to this place is high and rugid; thickly covered with timber principalley of the Pine Species . . ."
—CAPT. WILLIAM CLARK
Saturday, November 2, 1805
At the exit of the Columbia Gorge

As anyone who has driven over the Cascades would know, the contrast between the east and west slopes is startling. Traveling ocean-bound, you go from arid, nearly treeless terrain to virtual rain forest in a matter of miles. When you're cutting *through* the Cascades in the Columbia Gorge, however, the changes seem more gradual. You know that you enter the gorge in desert and exit it in Pacific Northwest forest, but it's not so clear where one ends and other begins. Keep your eyes open, though, and you'll detect subtle changes in the nature of the timber and plant cover. And probably the least subtle sign that you've gone from the dry of eastern Oregon to the soggy Pacific Northwest are the copious waterfalls that begin pouring in from the south.

This section's stretches along Interstate 84 (13 miles-plus total) are by no means the most serene segments of the Lewis & Clark Bicycle Trail. They're worth suffering through, though, because they enable you to ride additional portions of the fabulous Historic Columbia River Highway. Care is needed on that roadway, too, owing to its exceedingly winding and narrow character. Once you get to Troutdale, you'll be in the environs of metropolitan Portland for the next 20 miles or so, where camping becomes a bit problematic. Unless you expressly want to stay in the city, a good strategy is to make a short day of it out of Hood River—taking your time to enjoy the many waterfalls and hiking trails found in this part of the gorge—and stay the night at the outstanding Ainsworth State Park (30 miles from Hood River). Then, after making your way through Portland, you can camp the next evening at the pleasant county campground located a couple of miles north of Scappoose (60 miles from Ainsworth). This will leave a little less than 75 miles to Astoria and trail's end.

Cascade Locks was the site of a troublesome portage for the Corps of Discovery, as well as for early Oregon Trail emigrants who came this way forty years later, prior to the building of the Barlow Road, an overland route between The Dalles and Oregon City that opened in 1846. The navigational canal and locks were completed in 1896, changing the look and the nature of the river forever—maybe. These set the stage for the era of the stern-wheelers, which traveled the waters between Portland and The Dalles. You can still sample this romantic mode of travel by taking a cruise aboard the Stern-wheeler *Columbia Gorge* (P.O. Box 307, Cascade Locks, OR 97014; 541-374-8427; www.sternwheeler.com), boarding at Marine Park at Cascade Locks. The triple-deck paddle wheeler is owned and operated by the Port of Cascade Locks. The cruises, generally two hours in duration, are offered at various times of the day and week and include the captain's commentary on Lewis and Clark, the Oregon Trail, and other topics.

The Spokane Flood wasn't the only deluge to rip through this part of the gorge. Geologists tell us that sometime before Europeans arrived here, but probably not more than 400 years ago, a mountain on the north side of the Columbia opposite present-day Cascade Locks let loose and slid into the river. The rubble blocked the river's flow and backed up an immense lake. When the dam finally failed, the impounded waters rushed through, tearing away at earth and stone and flooding the site of present-day Portland on its way to the sea. More than likely, Native Americans were killed by the flooding, and the Klickitats and other tribes tell legends about the earth dam, which they called Bridge of the Gods. After the floodwaters subsided, a great deal of debris remained that was too massive for the rushing water to remove, and this created the Cascade Rapids. Like the great falls of the Missouri and so many other falls and rapids the Corps of Discovery had to contend with, they are now submerged (in waters backed up by the Bonneville Dam). The man-made Bridge of the Gods was added in 1926, built by the Wauna Toll Bridge Company. Twelve years later, with the completion of the Bonneville Dam and the resultant rising water levels, the bridge had to be raised 44 feet, to its present height of 135 feet above the water. Its north end rests upon debris from the original landslide.

Continue riding through the Columbia Gorge National Scenic Area, where, remarkably, state and federal agencies apparently have agreed on uniform signage. **Ainsworth State Park** (P.O. Box 100, Corbett, OR 97019; 503-695-2301; www.oregonstateparks.org) comes highly recommended as an overnight, particularly if you like hiking trails and waterfalls. The lushly canopied campground includes four peaceful walk-in sites.

Be sure to stop and survey your surroundings from the beautiful and aptly named **Vista House,** a 1917 creation that recently underwent extensive renovation. It proffers one of the best views in the entire Columbia Gorge. After making your winding way through Corbett and Springdale, you'll come to Troutdale, beyond which begins metropolitan Portland. One of the most notable aspects of your ride into the city on, or parallel to, Marine Drive are the numerous houseboats you'll see sitting in placid Columbia River waters. You'll also pass what is, according to many, Portland's best seafood restaurant: **Salty's** (3839 Northeast Marine Drive, Portland, OR 97211; 503-288-4444). If you're interested in staying downtown, you might

Hood River to Portland, Oregon

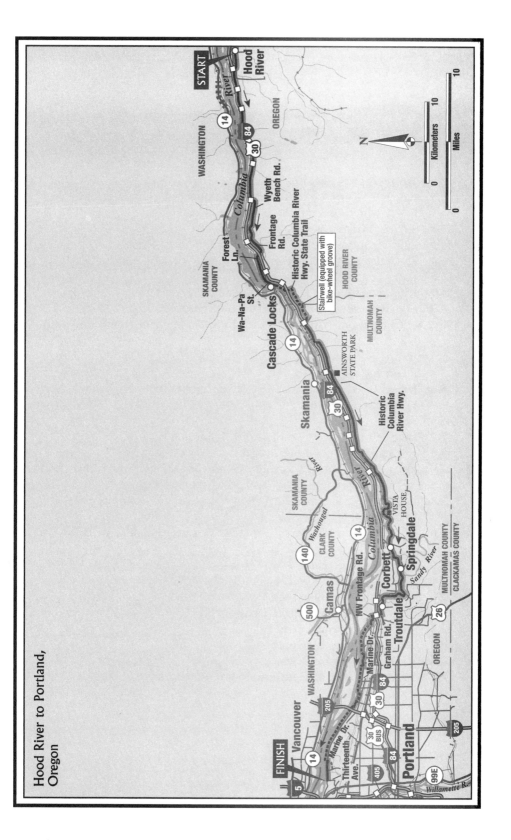

even succeed in arranging a ride there and back via the restaurant's shuttle service.

Mileage Log

0.0   Hood River.
2.5   Turn left and ride onto I–84.
13.5 Exit I–84. Turn left and, in 0.1 mile turn right onto Herman Creek Road, which becomes Wyeth Bench Road.
17.5 Turn left onto unsigned frontage road.
18.5 Turn right onto Forest Lane. In 0.1 mile bear left.
20.0 At T, turn right onto Wa-Na-Pa Street.
20.5 Cascade Locks.
21.0 Ride straight onto Historic Columbia River Highway State Trail.
24.0 Stairwell, equipped with bike-wheel groove.
25.0 Turn right onto unsigned road. In 0.1 mile turn left and ride onto I–84/U.S. Highway 30.
27.5 Exit I–84. Turn left and then right onto Historic Columbia River Highway.
30.0 Bear left to continue on Historic Columbia River Highway; in 0.2 mile bear left again.
44.5 Corbett.
46.0 Bear left to continue on Historic Columbia River Highway.
47.5 Springdale.
52.0 Turn left over bridge to continue on Historic Columbia River Highway.
52.5 Troutdale. In 0.3 mile turn right onto Graham Road and ride under I–84.
53.0 Turn left onto Northwest Frontage Road toward Marine Drive.
53.5 Bear right onto Marine Drive.
54.0 Ride onto bike path.
56.0 Ride onto Marine Drive.
57.5 Bear right onto bike path.
59.5 Bike path crosses Marine Drive.
60.5 Ride onto Marine Drive.
61.0 Bear right onto bike path.
64.5 Ride onto Marine Drive.
66.5 Junction with Thirteenth Avenue in Portland.

40 Portland to Astoria, Oregon
97 miles (3,254 miles cumulative)

*"Rained all the after part of last night, rain continues this morning,
I [s]lept but verry little last night for the noise Kept [up] dureing
the whole of the night by the Swans, Geese, white & Grey Brant
Duck &c. on a Small Sand Island . . . they were emensely noumer-
ous, and their noise horid."*

—CAPT. WILLIAM CLARK
Tuesday, November 5, 1805
Near Sauvie Island

Approximately 10 miles northwest of Portland you'll pass the easterly turn
toward the bridge connecting the mainland with Sauvie Island. The buccolic
24,000-acre island squeezed between the Columbia River and the Mult-
nomah Channel harbors a state-run waterfowl sanctuary, dairy farms, you-
pick-'em flower gardens, seasonal farmers' markets, and at least a couple of
bed-and-breakfasts, including **River's Edge B&B** (22502 Northwest Gilli-
han Road, Portland, OR 97231; 503–621–9856; www.riversedge-bb.com).
The setting is remarkable for its quiet, considering the island's proximity to
the city.

Continuing along U.S. Highway 30 and through several small towns,
you'll pass signs pointing to things that will attempt to beckon you off the
route—a lavender farm here, a Coast Range hiking trail there—but really,
what you'll want the most at this point is to get to the salt water! When at
last you arrive in the bustle of cars and humanity that is Astoria, you'll come
to the official end of the route at the **Columbia River Maritime Museum**
(1792 Marine Drive, Astoria, OR 97103; 503–325–2323; www.crmm.org),
open daily 9:30 A.M. to 5:00 P.M., $8.00 general admission. Definitely swing
in and spend at least a couple of hours at this top-notch museum, which
houses one of the most complete nautical collections in the country. You'll
learn about the Astoria area's long and fascinating seafaring history: ship-
wrecks, lighthouses, the fishing industry, and much more. Inside the archi-
tecturally stunning facility, whose roofline echoes the form of a Pacific
Ocean wave, you can even pilot a destroyer, help out with a Coast Guard res-
cue, or learn the basics of rope-making, a skill possessed by any sailor worth
his salt.

When many people think about the Lewis and Clark expedition, they en-
vision a group of men—and one woman, once Sacagawea joined up—as a

unit, always traveling together in one another's company. The more initiated student of the expedition, like you, knows that the group often split up, with smaller contingents exploring various spurs and routes and rivers and streams. Such was the case as they approached the mouth of the Columbia River and the Pacific Ocean, in preparation of completing the fourth and final of President Jefferson's wishes: to establish an overland route all the way to the Pacific. So it's no surprise that there are plenty of Lewis and Clark–related sites to visit in the area. Among them, on the Washington side of the Columbia: **Cape Disappointment** and its **Fort Canby State Park,** which includes a Lewis and Clark Interpretive Center, and the **Ilwaco Heritage Museum** in Ilwaco. In Oregon they include the **Salt Camp** in Seaside and, in Cannon Beach, **Les Shirley Park** and **Ecola State Park.** One of the guidebooks mentioned in the Introduction will tell you more about these sites and others—and the Adventure Cycling maps detail routes leading to them.

If you visit only one additional site, make it **Fort Clatsop National Memorial** (92343 Fort Clatsop Road, Astoria, OR 97103; 503–861–2471; www.nps.gov/focl), open daily 8:00 A.M. to 6:00 P.M. Even if you were to ignore its important Lewis and Clark heritage, the park would be worth visiting just to stroll in the humid shade of ancient spruces, hemlocks, and other giant trees. The park centerpiece is a 1955 replica of the 50-foot-square log stockade where the Corps of Discovery was headquartered from December 7, 1805, through March 23, 1806. They called their quarters Fort Clatsop in honor of a tribe of friendly local Indians, just as they had done at Fort Mandan, where they'd spent the previous winter. Throughout the winter on the coast, both captains concentrated on revising their journals, and Clark also worked on maps, while the men hunted deer and elk, distilled salt from seawater on the beach at present-day Seaside—and tried to stay dry. That was no mean feat: Out of the 106 days they spent here, only 12 were rain-free. Also within the memorial park are a good visitor center with two theaters and an exhibit hall and the canoe landing thought to be the point where Lewis and Clark docked on December 7, 1805. Living history demonstrations are offered in the summer.

As for you, to stay dry (even if it's not raining!) consider proceeding down the back road from Fort Clatsop to Seaside, where you'll finally view the whitecapped waves of the open sea and feel the ocean's sticky humidity. You might treat yourself to an overnight on the beach, where you can ceremonially dip your wheel in the water and study a West Coast sunset. As good a place as any to do these things is at **Gearhart by the Sea** (Tenth and Marion Streets, Gearhart, OR 97138; 503–738–8331; www.gearhartresort.com), a resort situated a mile or two north of Seaside that offers reasonably priced condominiums. Nearby you'll find an excellent bakery and a small but well-stocked market, where you can pick up some fresh seafood and, perhaps, a bottle of wine to toast your final day on the Lewis & Clark Bicycle Trail.

"End of the Trail" memorial, Seaside, Oregon

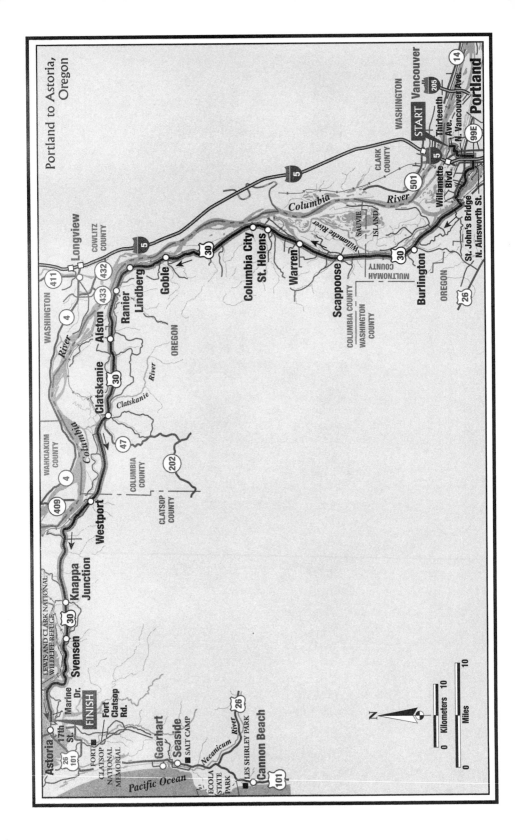

Portland to Astoria, Oregon

Mileage Log

0.0 Turn left off Marine Drive onto Thirteenth Avenue.

0.5 Turn right onto Gertz Road.

1.0 Turn left onto North Third Avenue. Curve right, then cross Martin Luther King Boulevard. Route becomes North Schmeer Road.

2.0 Turn left onto North Vancouver Avenue.

3.0 Turn right onto North Ainsworth Street.

4.5 Turn right onto Willamette Avenue, then left in 0.2 mile to remain on Willamette Avenue.

7.5 Turn right onto North Baltimore Avenue. In 2 blocks turn right onto North Ivanhoe Street, then, 1 block later, right onto Business U.S. 30.

8.0 Cross St. John's Bridge.

8.5 Turn right onto U.S. 30.

9.0 Turn left to continue on U.S. 30.

14.5 Burlington.

20.0 Enter Columbia County.

22.0 Scappoose.

26.5 Warren.

30.0 St. Helens.

32.5 Columbia City.

42.0 Goble.

46.5 Lindberg.

49.0 Ranier.

54.0 Alston.

62.0 Clatskanie.

70.5 Enter Clatsop County.

71.0 Westport.

82.0 Knappa Junction.

86.0 Svensen.

97.0 Astoria. Main route ends at Columbia River Maritime Museum.

EPILOGUE

Further Adventures

The main route of the Lewis & Clark Bicycle Trail, stretching 3,254 miles from Hartford, Illinois, to Astoria, Oregon, will provide all the riding needed by most cyclists wanting to "do Lewis and Clark." Certain adventurous, energetic, and/or history-addicted individuals, however, will want to do even more. The opportunities to continue bicycling on routes related to the journeys of the Corps of Discovery fall into two main categories: (1) the travels of Meriwether Lewis before the expedition and (2) the Corps of Discovery's travels back East in 1806, after their winter spent at Fort Clatsop near the Pacific Ocean.

1806 Eastbound

First, the latter: In the midst of their homeward travels in 1806, Lewis and Clark split up at Traveler's Rest (Lolo, Montana) to lead contingents over new routes. Capt. Lewis and nine men returned to the great falls of the Missouri via the Blackfoot and Sun Rivers, crossing the Continental Divide at what would later be called Lewis and Clark Pass. After a meandering journey through the Marias River country, Lewis's contingent proceeded from Fort Benton back down the Missouri to its confluence with the Yellowstone River.

Capt. Clark and the rest of the expedition returned to Camp Fortunate (Clark Canyon Reservoir) and then to the Missouri headwaters. From there Sacagawea led them up the Gallatin River, over Bozeman Pass, and to the site of today's Livingston, Montana. From here they followed the Yellowstone River downstream through the home territory of the Crow Indians, at first traveling overland and then by water to the Missouri confluence.

If you wish to emulate these 1806 travels, it is recommended that you obtain map sections 5, 6, and 8 of Adventure Cycling's Lewis & Clark Bicycle Trail. Together, they depict road routes that approximate both Lewis's and Clark's eastbound travels.

William Clark's etched signature can still be seen at Pompeys Pillar National Historic Landmark in the Yellowstone River Valley of eastern Montana.

1803 Travels Before the Expedition

Meriwether Lewis began preparing for the journey more than a year before his men would set out from Camp Dubois. President Jefferson sent him to Lancaster and Philadelphia, Pennsylvania, to receive training in such subjects as celestial navigation, botany, and medicine from some of the young nation's foremost scientists. In Philadelphia he began procuring medicine, tools, cargo boxes, and other supplies, which were transported to Harpers Ferry, West Virginia (although then it was in Virginia; West Virginia didn't secede until the Civil War). During that spring he also spent time at the federal arsenal in Harpers Ferry, obtaining arms and having an iron boat frame designed and built. The 176-pound frame ultimately proved useless when at last he broke it out—and had it covered with the hides of four bison and more than two dozen elk—above the portage around the great falls of the Missouri.

After Harpers Ferry, and following a short visit with the president, Lewis arrived in the shipbuilding center of Pittsburgh in July, where he ordered a keelboat capable of navigating the Ohio, Mississippi, and Missouri Rivers. It was finally finished in late August, by which time his wagonloads of goods from Harpers Ferry had arrived in Pittsburgh as well. Sometime during this period he also bought his dog, Seaman, a Newfoundland, a breed developed for ocean rescues. When Lewis, Seaman, and several soldiers headed downstream toward the Mississippi on the Ohio, they found that the river was running low, so Lewis added two pirogues to the fleet to help lighten the keelboat's load. On arriving in Clarksville, Indiana, in October, he picked up his co-leader, William Clark, and some men that Clark had recruited. (It was called Clarksville because Clark's older brother, Revolutionary War hero George Rogers Clark, had donated the land for the town—land given to Clark for his important role in taking the Illinois Territory for the United States.) Proceeding downstream and taking on additional recruits as they went, the men and their three boats made the Mississippi River in mid-November, where they turned upstream, reaching the mouth of the Wood River on December 12.

You might, then, choose to make a symbolic beginning at Thomas Jefferson's Monticello and bicycle something akin to Lewis's pre-expedition route. From Washington, D.C., you would ride to Pittsburgh then down the Ohio River to the Mississippi, turn right, and travel north along the Mississippi on either the Illinois or the Missouri side to the St. Louis area. There is no designated bike route for these pre-expedition travels; however, the list of contacts below can help you plan your own trip—or at least lead you to the best information sources for doing so.

Trip-planning Resources

General

Allegheny Trail Alliance, 419 College Avenue, Greensburg, PA 15601; (724) 853–2453; www.atatrail.org. This alliance of organizations is working toward completing the Great Allegheny Passage, a 152-mile bicycle and pedestrian trail linking Cumberland, Maryland, and Pittsburgh. At Cumberland the trail links up with the C&O Canal Towpath, which leads to Washington, D.C. When completed (2004 is the projected date), this will mean continuous pathways running all the way from Washington to Pittsburgh.

Virginia

Virginia State Bicycle Coordinator, Department of Transportation, 1401 East Broad Street, Richmond, VA 23219; (804) 786–2985; www.virginiadot.org.

Bike Virginia, P.O. Box 203, Williamsburg, VA 23187; (757) 229–0507; www.bikevirginia.org.

Virginia Bicycle Federation, P.O. Box 5621, Arlington, VA 22205; www.vabike.org.

Maryland

Bicycle/Pedestrian Coordinator, State Highway Administration, 707 North Calvert Street, Mailstop C-502, Baltimore, MD 21202; (410) 209–5025; www.sha.state.md.us/oppe/bicyclists.htm.

West Virginia

Bicycle & Pedestrian Coordinator, Department of Highways, Building 5, Room A-817, 1900 Kanawha Boulevard East, Charleston, WV 25305; (304) 558–3115; www.wvdot.com.

Bicycle West Virginia; www.bicyclewv.com.

Pennsylvania

Pedestrian and Bicycling Program, Bureau of Highway Safety & Traffic Engineering, Pennsylvania DOT, P.O. Box 2047, Harrisburg, PA 17105; (717) 783–8444; www.dot.state.pa.us.

Ohio

Bicycle & Pedestrian Program Manager, Ohio Department of Transportation, 1980 West Broad Street, Columbus, OH 43223; (614) 644–7095; www.dot.state.oh.us/bike.

Ohio Bicycle Federation, P.O. Box 253, Xenia, OH 45385; www.ohiobike.org; chuck@ohiobike.org.

Indiana

Bicycle Division of Outdoor Recreation, Map Sales, 402 West Washington, Room W160, Indianapolis, IN 46204; (317) 232–4180; www.state.in.us/dnr/outdoor/bikeinfo.htm.

Indiana Bicycle Coalition, P.O. Box 20243, Indianapolis, IN 46220; (317) 466–9701; www.bicycleindiana.org.

Kentucky

Kentucky State Bicycle/Pedestrian Coordinator, Transportation Cabinet, Division of Multimodal Programs, 125 Holmes Street, Third Floor, Frankfort, KY 40622; (502) 564–7686; www.kytc.state.ky.us.

Illinois

State Bicycle Program Manager, Illinois Department of Transportation, 2300 South Dirksen Parkway, Room 330, Springfield, IL 62764; (217) 785–2148; www.dot.state.il.us.

Missouri

State Bicycle/Pedestrian Coordinator, Missouri Department of Transportation, P.O. Box 270, Jefferson City, MO 65102; (573) 751–2551; www.modot.state.mo.us/info/bikeped.

Bi-State Bicycle Tours, HIAYH Gateway Council, 7187 Manchester, St. Louis, MO 63143; (314) 644–4660; www.gatewayhiayh.org.

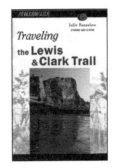

OCT 8 - 2003